AGON Institute of Sports Ministry Series, vol. 5

SENT:
Missiology for the
Sports Outreach Community

Dr. Greg Linville

Overwhelming Victory Press
Canton, Ohio

Copyright © 2021, Overwhelming Victory Press

ISBN: 978-1-7345001-2-7

All Rights Reserved. No part of this book may be reproduced or transmitted in any form or by any means, electronic or mechanical, including photocopying, recording, or by any information storage and retrieval system without written permission from the author, except for the inclusion of brief quotations in a review.

For any reproduction rights, including federal copying, computer reproduction, etc., contact:

Dr. Greg Linville, CSRM International
P. O. Box 9110
Canton, OH 44711

Email: sportsminresources@gmail.com

This book is dedicated to
my mother and father.

My father was my first coach.
My mother pitched me more batting practice than anyone.
Together they raised six sons to love God, family and sport...in that order.
They were college sweethearts and celebrated 69 years of marriage.
They both entered into their heavenly reward this year...
passing within four weeks of each other.
I miss them dearly and dedicate this book to their memory
as they helped me know and understand the mission for my life.

Other books in the Institute of Sports Outreach Series:

- Volume 1: Christmanship: A Theology of Competition and Sport
- Volume 2: Sports Outreach Fundamentals
- Volume 3: Putting the Church Back in the Game: The Ecclesiology of Sports Outreach
- Volume 4: The Saving of Sports Ministry: The Soteriology of Sports Outreach
- Volume 8: The Life of the Shoe: Sports Outreach for the World

TABLE OF CONTENTS

- III Dedication
- IV Other Books in the Institute of Sports Outreach Series
- V Table of Contents
- VII Foreword
- IX Endorsements
- XIII Vision for This Book
- XV Prologue

SECTION # 1 – OVERVIEW AND REVIEW
- 1 Chapter 1: Review of Previous Books in the Institute of Sports Outreach Series
- 9 Chapter 2: Preview of *Sent: Missiology for the Sports Outreach Community*

SECTION #2 – THEOLOGICAL, PHILOSOPHICAL, HISTORICAL & BIBLICAL FOUNDATIONS OF MISSIOLOGY
- 15 Chapter 3: The Theological & Philosophical Relevance & Importance of Missiology in Relationship to SR&F Outreach Ministry
- 29 Chapter 4: History of Missiology in Relationship to SR&F Outreach Ministry
- 39 Chapter 5: Biblical Foundations of Missiology for SR&F Outreach Ministry
- 59 Chapter 6: Missiological Foundations for SR&F Outreach Ministry

SECTION #3 – MISSIOLOGICAL APPLICATIONS FOR SR&F OUTREACH MISSIONS
- 79 Chapter 7: Missiological Applications for Local Church SR&F Outreach Ministry
- 101 Chapter 8: Missiological Applications for Sport-Related, Para-Ministries & Sports Chaplaincy
- 117 Chapter 9: Missiological Applications for Sports Outreach in a Multi-Faith World

SECTION #4– RELEVANCE OF MISSIOLOGY FOR THE BROADER SR&F COMMUNITY
- 135 Chapter 10: Summary of Missiology in Relationship to SR&F Outreach & Final Proposals

APPENDIX
- 145 Addendum 1: Glossary
- 163 Addendum 2: Explanatory Notes for Institute of Sports Outreach Book Series
- 173 Addendum 3: Explanatory Notes for This Book
- 179 Addendum 4: Acknowledgements
- 183 Addendum 5: Proposals for Local Church & Para-ministry Integration
- 187 Addendum 6: Sports Challenge Event
- 189 Addendum 7: Conversation
- 193 Addendum 8: Laborers-List
- 195 Addendum 9: Financing SR&F Ministry
- 197 Addendum 10: Sources used for this book
- 203 Addendum 11: Sources used for this book series
- 217 Addendum 12: Epilogue

FOREWORD

Dr Greg Linville has faithfully served the sports ministry community for over 40 years. Greg has been a keen sportsman all of his life; has modelled servanthood as a sports and recreation minister in a local church for over a decade, has served as an academic in a university as both a professor and department chair for over 35 years; has gained both an honorary and an earned doctorate; and he has designed several sports ministry qualifications at the master's degree level. As the executive director of Church Sports and Recreation Ministers (CSRM), Greg led a movement that has positively influenced tens of thousands of people through sport, and his books have educated two generations of sports ministers on a global scale. His ministry and influence continues in his role as the Director of Resource Development for CSRM, where he serves as the General Editor for CSRM's publishing house Overwhelming Victory Press and the Executive Producer of Overwhelming Victory Flix. It is fair to say that Greg is a modern father of sports ministry.

I first connected with my friend when I was a 30-year old, ex-pro, soccer player. After I had become a Christian and was serving as a pro coach and sports minister, I reconnected with Greg to learn how to reach people through sport. I was full of enthusiasm and ideas but short on skills, resources and wisdom. Greg was there to help me then, and has continued to be there ever since. My roles and tasks have changed somewhat over the years, including having served as a missionary in Wales for over two decades but the one thing that has never changed is I know my friend prays for me and my family every single day. I'm confident that he also does this for many others.

As to Greg's books…they ooze wisdom because he has studied and practiced both the Bible and sports ministry for many years. Besides creating new paradigms and concepts for us all to learn and use, he gives sports ministers the gift of 'words'* to describe what sports ministers are trying to personally accomplish and perhaps more importantly, has given them a sports outreach language so they can 'produce, reproducing, reproducers'* (equip and teach others). This is very precious and rare.

In this book, in a thorough and robust way, Greg calls the sports ministry community to move from merely creating gatherings of unchurched people to hear the gospel preached, to a model that encourages proclamation of the gospel in and through incarnational, one-on-one, relationships: in other words, to true mission. He explains that when a good and trusted person first lives out (incarnates) the gospel, and then verbally shares (proclaims) the gospel with their unbelieving friends, the message is better able to be nuanced and made personal

FOREWORD

and relevant. An incarnational gospel messenger is more attuned to a gospel receiver's situation and mindset, and thus, they are able to deliver the message in more personal and less offensive ways.

Well organised* sports events to gather people are of course essential, but if we think that a short testimony or message at an event, even if it is from a well-known sports personality, makes disciples, we are gravely mistaken. It is just the beginning. Disciple making happens when we strategically identify those people who show a God-inspired interest in Christ and we spend the extra time needed to sincerely befriend them, invest time in them, model the Christian life to them, build their confidence to witness and send them into their world to do the same with someone God leads to them. This is truly disciple making and it is the primary thing all Christians (not just sports ministers), are called (even commanded), to do by Jesus Himself.

I think you'll enjoy this book immensely. Greg fully answers the 'niggles'* and the 'yes, buts'* we may come up with. As always, he comprehensively explains himself in a deeply researched and practical, yet winsome way. He takes a stance as cheerleader rather than the all-knowing franchise owner. He cheers us on from within…that's what we love about him.

Time to read another great book from Dr. Greg Linville!

Rob Burns Bio. After a brief pro soccer playing career and 11 years of coaching professionally in Houston and Dallas, Burns returned to the U. K. when he moved to Wales in 2000. During his time in America, Rob founded and led several Christian organisations* beginning in1989. Burns currently serves in a number of roles.
- Founding director of Missional Links Wales (www.missionallinkswales.org.uk)
- Missional leadership consultant with Evangelical Alliance, Wales
- Teacher
- Preacher (regularly in churches across the whole of Wales)

Rob holds a Masters degree in theology and has worked long-term in the ecclesiastical, academic and training arenas. Burns also held an 'A' football licence* for many years, working as a professional youth coach in the USA.

Burns is passionate about leadership training, coaching and mentoring people who are looking for direction, encouragement and purpose. He is married to Jenny and they have three adult lads, everyone both taller and far more handsome than their father.

*All spelling and grammar follow the British style and rules.

ENDORSEMENTS

Dr. Greg Linville continues to be a prominent voice and effective advocate for local church sports, recreation, and fitness ministries worldwide. I have spent the last 20 years using sports, recreation, and fitness as tools to break down barriers and build relationships in order to advance the gospel. Yet, I continue to learn from Greg Linville. His passion, his commitment, and his heart for Jesus never cease to inspire! Dr. Greg's books are built on solid theological, philosophical, and methodological foundations, effectively equipping the reader for *Evangelistic-Disciplemaking* impact. His latest book, ***SENT: Missiology for the Sports Outreach Community,*** **may very well be his most important because it provides a timely reminder of why we engage in sports ministry in the first place**—to "go and make disciples for Jesus."

— **John Longworth**
Recreation Pastor, Germantown Baptist Church
Former Chair, CSRM Board of Trustees

It is my joy and honor to recommend Greg Linville to you as a writer and most importantly as a person. He embodies the principles he preaches in this book. **Dr. Greg's heart for the Word of God as the transformational agent in our missional endeavors will challenge and encourage all.** Thank you Greg for always pointing us to the Living Word and His Gospel.

— **Jay Martin**
Sr. Director Camp and Sports Outreach
A Ministry of Perimeter Church

ENDORSEMENTS

If…
- You or your church are thinking of starting up a Church Sport, Recreation & Outreach Program
- Your current church outreach could use a shot in the arm
- Your SR&F outreach ministry needs help getting refocused and headed back in the right direction…

You can't go wrong by spending time with Greg Linville and the other CSRM experts in person or by book as they know of which they speak and **Dr. Greg's latest book continues in a great tradition.**

— **Mike Molony**
Retired Local Church Sports Minister, Sandia Presbyterian Church
Former CSRM Board Member

The Christian with a heart for missional outreach is instructed by the Lord to "stand at the crossroads and look…ask where the good way is, and walk in it" (Jeremiah 6:16).

Dr. Greg Linville, with his unique sports ministry experience and expertise, hammers in yet another significant signpost to illuminate the path for the sports ministers and church recreators to tread. He hoists the sail for sports mission and provides both the means for rudder adjustment and a vision for fresh courses. The gentle breeze of the Holy Spirit will then do the rest. Enjoy the equipping that this inspired *"Ology"* brings to you, its readers.

— **Bryan Mason**
Founder of Higher Sports; CSRM Staff Emeritus
Worchester, England

ENDORSEMENTS

In this, his most recent book Dr. Greg Linville slays some of sports ministry sacred cows that have been grazing while protected for many years under the banner of "but we've always done it this way." The Church can't afford to wait for the reins of sports, rec & fitness ministries to be pried from the "cold dead hands," of the Boomer generation who have led for the past 40 years. Millennial and Gen Z leaders will receive a mega-dose of theological ammunition that will guide the needed change to re-envision missions. Dr. Greg's practical suggestions found in this book's "Scoreboards" should be discussed by established sports ministries everywhere." **Linville's at his best when he calls local congregations of The Church to engage in missions that are laser focused on going to: "Make Disciples, baptizing them and teaching them to obey all that I (Jesus) have commanded you."** Dr. Greg's decades of knowledge and involvement in local church sports ministry will enable all readers to make sense of the American Christian/Church theological/missional journey from the 1980's to the 2020's and from there know how to engage in truly *Strategically-Relevant & Efficiently-Effective* mission in the present and future.

— **Dr. Timothy Conrad**
Founder *Uncharted Waters/UW Sports Ministry*
South Carolina

The *Mission of Sports Ministry* adds yet another piece to this thoughtful, and thought-provoking, Institutes of Sports Outreach book series. In it Dr. Greg expands and deepens the importance of basing all sports and recreation ministry on a solid theology. In this specific installment, he focuses on of the mission of The Church and its local congregations, and produces a powerful and seminal mandate for SR&F mission through the local church. Yet, this is not solely a "high brow" work of an academic but rather an insightful integration of solid Christo-centric theology and gospel-centric philosophy from which incarnational outreach ministry can emerge. **As a life-long, local church sports and rec minister, I am grateful to CSRM and Dr. Greg for their commitment to calling us all to, local as well as international, missions. I wish I would have had this book and book series when I started in ministry decades ago.**

— **Barb Wagenfuhr**
Retired Director of Recreational Ministries
1st Presbyterian Church, Colorado Springs
Founding Board Member & Past Board President – CSRM

VISION FOR THIS BOOK: A Future or a Past?

The current "*Sports Outreach Movement*"[1] has had a great past but, its future is uncertain!

This was the opening sentence in the previous book in this Institutes of Sports Outreach book series. It was true when that book was written and it remains a pivotal ongoing question. Yes, there are local congregations that are initiating or expanding their SR&F outreach ministries but the fact remains: the *Sports Outreach Community* is at a crossroads.

Will we (*The Sports Outreach Community*) continue to organize and administer the same old sports and fitness programs or will we choose to embrace a radical re-envisioning of missional sports outreach? Will we continue to be satisfied to have a people "raise their hands" at a season ending *Mega-Event* where a *Platform-Proclamation* of the gospel invites all to make a *Day's-Decision;* or will we boldly decide to engage in a catalytic re-inventing of our *Repetitive-Redemptive-Relational* sports outreach ministry in our pursuit to make life-long, *Dedicated-Disciples*? Are we content with large numbers of participants in our fitness ministry who improve their physical health; or will we commit to gospel-centric, *Evangelistic-Disciplemaking* that will enable not only physical fitness but more so, enable those far from Jesus to embrace Him as Savior… and inspire all believers to make Jesus the Lord in every aspect of their life? Are you content to *Count-Conversions* not knowing if any of those who "raise their hand" will ultimately follow Jesus; or do you desire to *Convince-Converts* on an ongoing daily basis to grow in their faith? Are you satisfied by sports buildings that are filled with activity; or do you long for Holy Spirit empowered missional outreach. Are you directing a morning-to-evening sports activity ministry or mobilizing missional sports ministry for eternity?

I believe the overwhelming majority of SR&F outreach ministers deeply desire to "go and make disciples" and this book is written for each one of them. It is written for all who want to transform their sports activities and fitness programs into a dynamic missional sports outreach.

This book is designed to provide *The Sports Outreach Community* a solid theological foundation for determining an effective, pragmatic missional approach upon which to build a future that mobilizes congregations to reach those far from Jesus and His Church. It builds on the foundation of previous

---

[1] The italicized words and phrases used here and throughout this book and book series have been coined, defined, repurposed and/or defined throughout CSRM's Institute of Sports Outreach book series. For specific definitions the reader is referred to the Glossary of this book and all of the books in the series which explain in detail the growing language of the *Sports Outreach Community* as represented by the italicized words and phrases. The rationale behind italicizing these words is to repeatedly bring them to the attention of readers and emphasize their unique usage. They are quickly becoming the standard language for sports, recreation and fitness ministries and have, more importantly, helped to unify the meanings and definitions of commonly used language.

VISION FOR THIS BOOK

Institute of Sports Outreach books but also furthers and deepens that foundation for future books in this series to build upon.

Another significant part of the vision of this book has to do with affirming and reassuring all SR&F outreach ministers and missionaries that what they do is anchored in solid theological truths of evangelism and rooted in historical missional models. While this will not replace knowing how to operate effective leagues, events and classes, it will be a great aid when talking to pastors, elders and finance committees.

In summary, it is my opinion that the future of the so called *Sports Outreach Movement* depends upon a "sail-adjusted," refocusing on mission that can only occur if we truly comprehend missiology (the theology of missional outreach) and know how to apply its principles to envision how to organize and structure SR&F outreach ministry that is truly a *Strategically-Relevant* and *Efficiently-Effective* mission.

My prayer is that each and every reader will embrace the vision for this book and choose to become missional in all they do.

> **Lord come to me . . . I am Yours.**
> **I abandon myself for You. Fill me with Yourself. . .**
> **Lord let me help those who are wretched**
> **because they do not know You. . .**
> **Send me where You want me to go**
> **and to the people You have me to meet.**
>
> Robert Falconer [2]

---

[2] George MacDonald and Michael R. Phillips. *The Musician's Quest*. Minneapolis: Bethany House Publishers, 1984. ISBN 0-87123-444-0). It was originally published in 1868 under the title Robert Falconer by Hurst and Blackett, London.

PROLOGUE

Harold, a well-intentioned young Christian and exceptional athlete, accepted an invitation by "unchurched" friends to join a baseball team. Besides thoroughly enjoying the game and being an above average player, Harold was hopeful the experience would not only be enjoyable but also provide him opportunities to share his faith in Christ with his teammates and others players. When told half of the games were scheduled to be played on Sunday mornings all second thoughts were quickly set aside by spiritual mentors who encouraged him to "go for it;" citing a theology of missiology that encourages the "going" mandate of the Great Commission's "Go and make disciples." …And so, empowered and encouraged by their sage advice, Harold enthusiastically proceeded on his athletic and evangelistic quest.

Things started out well. He was accepted into the core of the team and was greatly appreciated for his excellent defense, daring base-running and all around hustle. He felt he was making a real difference on the field and his "no alcohol" post-game conviction became so respected that his teammates took to including a pitcher of Coke for him in their weekly beverage order. The post-game stops at the pub (which happened to be the team's sponsor) even afforded Harold a few chances to initiate spiritual conversations that were generally well received by a number of his teammates.

By the end of the summer however, Harold realized his own spiritual fervor was waning. It had been months since he had attended a worship service or heard a good sermon. The ongoing weekly Bible study was helpful when he could make it and he faithfully continued for many weeks to start and end his day with his "morning and evening watch" personal quiet time devotions; but even that had become "spotty." Realizing his overall spirituality was waning, Harold made a pledge to start attending church the Sunday after the season ended, and rejoiced as the old feelings returned and his spiritual fervor was revived.

After the service of his first week back at church Harold was welcomed by one of his mentors who asked about a couple of Harold's teammates they had been praying for. He replied, that yes, a couple of them seemed interested in Jesus but sadly, none were willing to accompany him to church.

Harold was genuinely blessed by his return to regularly attending church and Bible study… and definitely felt his faith growing again. He tried to keep up some of the relationships with guys from the team but after a couple of nights hanging out with them at the pub, he realized how vapid that life really was. By January, he had stopped going to the pub and he honestly felt much more fulfilled hanging out with the young adult group from church. Harold was also excited about going out with one particular young woman from the church.

The following Spring, the team was getting back together and they

PROLOGUE

contacted Harold to once again join the team. Initially Harold was much less enamored with the whole experience but with the support of his mentors and encouragement from both his fellowship group and new girlfriend, he agreed to play again…even on Sundays. He renewed his commitment to be even more verbally bold about his faith that summer as he sincerely desired to reach his teammates for Jesus. He was excited to find that July 4th fell on a Sunday and thus the games scheduled for that Sunday were cancelled…affording a perfect chance to invite his teammates to join him at church.

As April practices led to early May scrimmages and subsequently to June games, Harold began occasionally to mention to some of his teammates about the July 4th opportunity to go to church. All gave him a "yeah sure" response, but by the last week in June he realizes the best he could hope for is to have Jim and DeShawn join him. He confirmed the time and place with them at the post-game pub time.

To his surprise, Jim and DeShawn did join him…but he "died a thousand deaths" during the service as he watched them squirm and sweat through off-key singing and a sermon on church eldership preached from second Timothy. At one point Jim leaned over to ask who the first Timothy was!

Both Jim and DeShawn, politely thanked Harold for inviting them… saying it was informative and the people seemed nice; "especially that guy Paul" (Harold's spiritual mentor and prayer partner), but it was clear they couldn't wait to get away.

If anything, Jim and DeShawn's visit to Harold's church seemed to create a polite distance between them. Harold was treated with respect and cordially interacted with but the warmth in their relationship had chilled. Harold endured the rest of that summer and remaining baseball season, feeling like a bit of an outsider. He even now had to pay for his own soft drinks.

SECTION 1: Overview and Review

Chapter 1

Review of Previous Books in the Institutes of Sports Outreach Book Series

I. Introduction – Where are we? Where are we going? - 2
   A. The Current View - 2

II. Review of the Books of the Series - 5
   A. Review of Book #1 (*Christmanship: A Theology of Competition & Sport*) - 5
   B. Review of Book #2 (*Sports Outreach Fundamentals - The Transferable Concepts of SR&F Outreach Ministry*) - 5
   C. Review of Book #3 (*Putting The Church Back In The Game: The Ecclesiology of Sports Outreach*) - 6
   D. Review of Book #4 (*The Saving of Sports Ministry: The Soteriology of Sports Outreach*) - 6
   E. Review of Book #8 (*The Life of the Shoe: Sports Ministry for the World*) - 7

III. Summary of the Review - 7

TIMEOUT

He Needed a New Inspiration

In 1895 a young British man, Peter Cameron Scott, needed a fresh source of inspiration. He found it when he visited a tomb in Westminster Abby that held the earthly remains of a man who had inspired so many others to missionary service in Africa: David Livingston.

The Holy Spirit, through the example of Livingston, inspired Scott as he knelt in reverence and read the inscription on his tombstone: "I have other sheep, which are not of this fold; I must bring them also." (John 10.16) Scott felt the Holy Spirit stirring his heart, and accepted the call to service in Africa and subsequently, the Africa Inland Mission was born. *

* https://eu.aimint.org/why-are-we-focused-on-reaching-the-unreached/

> "I have other sheep, which are not of this fold;
> I must bring them also." **

** *The inscription on David Livingstone's tombstone.*

I. Introduction - Where are We? Where are We Going?

This is the sixth book released from the Institutes of Sports Outreach book series.[1] The entire series is envisioned from, organized by, and follows, a structure based in a theological, philosophical and methodological trilogy.[2] It establishes and outlines the third of many theological concepts that serve as the foundation for the entire book series.[3] Portions of this first chapter also appear in the first chapter of most of the books in this series and act as a rudder and guide for the entire series. The following retrospective look at previous books is primarily for the purpose of bringing new readers of this series up to date; although it is also hoped readers of the previous books will benefit from a brief review of the former material.

The even more significant purpose of this chapter is the ever-so-short look forward as to the overall purpose for why this specific book is necessary... the woeful state of The Church's current understanding of missiology as it relates to gospel-centric, missions.[4]

A. The Current View

A sad reality is occurring in many North American congregations. Local congregational leaders are struggling with significant questions about being connected and relevant. They ask the following questions:

- As the chasm between the secular world and the church world continues to widen, how are we supposed to connect with people with whom we have so little in common?
- How can our congregation effectively reach those who are so far away from Jesus and His Church?
- How should we readjust our mission?

Is your congregation asking the same or similar questions? Are you also struggling with how you can break out of the rut that only runs youth sports activities that only attract church kids? Are you eager to initiate a new missional model that can also reach non-churched kids with the gospel? Do you earnestly desire to connect with the adult men or women who currently play in the highly competitive open leagues in your area? Have you clearly understood and defined the mission of your SR&F outreach? Can you clearly define and differentiate between your vision and mission? You're not alone. Most congregations struggle

---

1   It is positioned as the fifth book in the series but a number of the books are being written simultaneously and thus while it falls as number five in the series, it actually is the sixth book in the series to be released.

2   See the Glossary for the definition and description of what is called the *The 3-Tier Paradigm*.

3   What are called *The Sports Outreach Ologies* which is also described and defined in the Glossary.

4   Such Great Commission efforts are summarized throughout the Institutes of Sports Outreach books by the phrase: *Evangelistic-Disciplemaking* efforts.

CHAPTER 1: Review of Previous Books in this Series

with having a clearly defined vision (the ultimate goal) that leads them to determine their mission (how to accomplish the vision/goal). No wonder recent research indicates congregations are declining when they can't differentiate between their goal (vision) and how to accomplish that goal (mission).

Yes, it's true that the Bible assures us that God is consistently and constantly at work in fulfilling what Jesus said was His goal: "I came to seek and save the lost."[5] However, The Church finds itself at a pivotal and cataclysmic time in terms of defining a strategic mission with what is currently transpiring in the early 21st century. Despite the occasional encouraging report of a specific congregation that is experiencing revival and/or growth, it is troubling to know most local churches in the West are in decline. Furthermore, the worldwide Church now exists in an increasingly hostile and secular time, including many regions around the world where The Church is being persecuted into oblivion; even where it had long flourished. All of this makes it ever more difficult to conceptualize a strategic, missiological plan and bring that plan to fruition.[6] Into this current situation this book builds on previous books in this series and opens the doors to the pragmatic concepts in books that follow.

This book pushes further into the question of defining success in ministry as introduced in the previous book *The Saving of Sports Ministry: The Soteriology of Sports Outreach*. It furthers the question as to what is being counted and assessed and expands what the previous book revealed concerning a congregation's effectiveness.[7] It strengthens the call for The Church's efforts to be based on the making of life-long followers of Jesus,[8] rather than on attempting to get someone to pray "the sinner's prayer."[9]

Making disciples often entails years (not minutes)[10] of concerted efforts to help new believers form a true Christian world view and ethic.[11] Rather than being satisfied with someone raising a hand one day at an evangelistic service, it is imperative to complete the Great Commission by "teaching them all" Jesus commanded.[12]

In the previous book *The Saving of Sports Ministry*, it was determined the main reasons for the disconnect between the reports of the vast numbers of

---

5 Luke 19.10.
6 A plan that fulfills the *4-Fold Evaluative Rubric* of being: *Strategically-Relevant* and *Efficiently-Effective*.
7 What is referred to in this book series as: *Success-Statistics*.
8 What is referred to in this book series as: *Dedicated-Disciples*.
9 What is referred to in this book series as: settling for what is called a *Day's-Decision*.
10 What is referred to in this book series as: *Laboring-Long*.
11 What is referred to in this book series as: *Convincing-Converts*.
12 Matthew 28.20. What is referred to in this book series as: settling for *Counting-Conversions*. It is interesting to reflect on 1 Thessalonians chapter 4 where Paul instructs the Thessalonians about ethical (Christ-like) living and he states that what he is writing is the same as what he had already instructed them. The poignancy of this is the fact he only spent three weeks with them and yet in that brief time, Paul was diligent to teach them all Jesus had commanded! For Paul, coming to faith in Jesus was immediately followed by discipleship!

TIMEOUT

Day's Decision or Dedicated Disciple

A conversation with a friend who was a state director for a prominent sports-related, para-ministry confirmed the importance of rooting coaches and athletes in a Bible-based congregation.

My friend heard me talking about the need to get athletes and coaches intimately involved in a local church and he challenged me! He said it wasn't good enough to get players to become part of just any church because in his experience, unless Christian athletes became involved with a solid Bible-teaching and Christ-honoring congregation that takes "making disciples" seriously, the faith of the players in question was doomed to become ship-wrecked.

How's your sports-related, para-ministry doing in this regard? Is your local church SR&F outreach ministry really connecting those who participate in your outreach activities with the discipling activities of your church?

"salvations" and the shrinking of congregational attendance and membership numbers came down to what is meant by the word salvation. In essence the incongruence and disparity lies in what is being counted. When "salvation" is used to describe the number of people who raised a hand or prayed the "sinner's prayer" at a particular outreach; rather than the number who became disciples of Jesus, it becomes clear that the chasm between evangelism and discipleship is in great need of being linked and that when ministries, missions and churches report "salvations" they mean something much different than reporting the numbers of disciples that were "made."[13]

So it is highly recommended for The Church[14] in general, and local congregations specifically, to adapt their missiological approach. It is recommended this new approach be built upon a solid soteriology (theology of salvation). Congregations can now envision, plan for, administrate and expedite endeavors that are truly effective.[15]

Is envisioning a new catalytic missiology important to *The Sports Outreach*

---

13 What is referred to in this book series as *Success-Statistics* (the need to adjust what is assessed and counted); moving away from *Counting-Converts* (*Days-Decisions*); and moving to *Convincing-Converts* to become lifelong *Dedicated-Disciples*.

14 Whenever the universal Church is referenced both words are capitalized (The and Church). Conversely, when a local church is referenced both words appear in lower case (the and church). In addition, other terms such as congregation, assembly or body of Christ are used instead of the words local church.

15 These would thus meet the *4-Fold Evaluative Rubric: Strategically-Relevant & Efficiently-Effective*.

CHAPTER 1: Review of Previous Books in this Series

Community? I thought so. In fact there may not be a more important *Level #1 Theological-Truth,* sports-outreach *Ology* than missiology…and that's why I wrote this book!

II. Review of the Books in the Series

As a previous book in this series stated:

"GPS has made maps a thing of the past. Call me old school, but no matter how sweet the digital voice sounds, I find a map to be much more helpful. Why? At a glance, maps not only tell you when and where to turn, they also show where you are, how you got there, and provide all kinds of options for where you could go—and whether you want to take the circuitous scenic route or the lickety-split super highway. This chapter serves as a kind of a map, in that it recaps where we've been and how we got there. Where we can go is the topic for the next chapter. However, before we proceed, the following needs to be reviewed."[16]

A. Review of Book #1 – *Christmanship: A Theology of Competition and Sport*

Christmanship was a seminal work that explored the theology and philosophy of the integration of faith and sport. It was designed to provide a foundation for biblical sport and a Christ-honoring ethic for participation in sport. It included the following.

1. Philosophical and theological foundations for competition and sport
2. Principles for determining biblical, Christ-honoring sport
3. Historic models of biblical sport
4. A Christian ethic of competition
5. Frequently asked questions about sport including sport & the Lord's Day

B. Review of Book #2: *Sports Outreach Fundamentals: The Transferable Concepts of SR&F Outreach Ministry*

The second book in the AGON Institutes of Sports Outreach book series is an explanation of the major *Level #2 Philosophical-Principles* of SR&F outreach ministry. These transferable concepts interconnect and build on one another. Collectively, they make up the organizational structure for *The Sports Outreach Community* that truly fulfills the Great Commission of going and making disciples. What follows is the title of each of the transferable concepts of the second book. They are transferable because they can be transferred to any culture, country, geographic area, denomination or climate. They are concepts because they are overarching philosophical themes rather than specific outreach activities. Even though this book was published prior to the following three *Ology* books,

---

16 This paragraph is a direct quote and much of the next few pages are taken from the first chapters of previous books in this series. Greg Linville, *Putting The Church Back In The Game: The Ecclesiology of Sports Outreach* (Canton, OH: Overwhelming Victory Press, 2019). P.2.

the substance, and much of the writing of those three books, pre-dated *Sports Outreach Fundamentals*. The contents of the book include:

1. The *Evangelistic-Disciplemaking Mandate*
2. The *2-Dysconnects of SR&F Outreach Ministry*
3. The *3-Tier Paradigm*
4. The *4-Fold Evaluative Rubric*
5. The *5-B's of SR&F Outreach Ministry*
6. The *7- Sports Outreach Continuums*

C. Review of Book #3 – *Putting The Church Back In The Game: The Ecclesiology of Sports Outreach*

The content of book #3 was designed to connect sports outreach leaders with historic ecclesiology for the purpose of engaging them in thinking how they might apply these *Level #1 Theological-Truths* to enhance and expand their SR&F outreach ministry. The outline of the book included:

1. The theology of The Church
2. Ecclesiastical SR&F sub-topics
3. Relevance of ecclesiology for the *SR&F Community*

D. Review of Book #4 – *The Saving of Sports Ministry: The Soteriology of Sports Outreach*

Book #4 concentrated on helping sports outreach leaders wrestle with what successful gospel-centric, *Evangelistic-Disciplemaking* entailed. It encouraged sports ministers to re-evaluate what they assessed[17] and made the case that gospel-centric, ministry strives to go and make disciples.[18] It included:

1. The theological, philosophical and biblical foundations of sports outreach soteriology
2. The application of soteriology for SR&F outreach ministry
3. The relevance of soteriology for a) the local church; b) sports-related, para-ministries; and c) sports chaplaincy
4. The difficulty and peril of engaging in SR&F outreach ministry in a world that is hostile to Christianity

---

17   What is referred to in this book series as: *Success-Statistics*.
18   What is referred to in this book series as striving to make *Dedicated-Disciples (Convincing-Converts)* rather than settling for *Day's-Decisions (Counting-Conversions)*.

E. Review of Book #8 – *The Ministry of the Shoe: Sports Outreach for the World* [19]

The Life of the Shoe: Sports Outreach for the World is the first practical sports outreach ministry book written specifically for the *International Sports Outreach Community* and emerges out of the life experiences of both the author and other indigenous leaders from around the globe. It articulates solid Christo-centric, *Theological-Truths*; biblically-based, *Philosophical-Principles*; and *Strategically-Relevant* and *Efficiently-Effective Methodological-Models* (*The Three Tier Paradigm*). When fully understood and applied, the transferable concepts found in this book can catalytically empower local churches to accomplish their worldwide, Great Commission goals. Envisioned as the 8th book in the Institutes of Sports Outreach Series, it is based in, builds upon, explains and expands the theological, philosophical and methodological foundations of the book series' for application in the international arena.

Authored by the modern day Apostle Paul of sports outreach, this book provides both the pragmatic "how-to's" for all sports ministers as well as the academic theologies and theories for seminary and university courses. Additionally through many anecdotal stories from around the world, the reader will find practical application and inspiration to trust God more fully and grow in their calling, vision and ministry.

III. Summary of the Review

So far in this AGON Institutes of Sports Outreach Book Series we have established: a) a basic theological and pragmatic apologetic and foundation for competition; b) a biblical defense for both sport in general, as well as for most individual sports; c) an ethical model for Christian engagement in and with competition and sport (*Christmanship*);[20] d) six transferable concepts for how to structure and organize SR&F outreach ministries according to biblically-based, principles[21] and e) the ecclesiology and soteriology of SR&F outreach ministry.[22]

This book now takes on the missiology of The Church.[23] Missiology is a most important foundation for everything that makes up this series. The next chapter will provide the specific route we will take as our journey continues.

---

19 While this book was designed as #8, chronologically it was the 5th book published in the Institutes of Sports Ministry book series.
20 Sub-points "a-c" are considered foundational *Level #1 Theological-Truths*.
21 Sub-point "d" is considered a *Level #2 Philosophical-Principle*.
22 Sub-point "e" lists what are considered the first two sports outreach *Ologies*.
23 What is referred to in this book series as the third *Level #1 Sports Outreach Ology*.

SECTION 1: Overview and Review

Chapter 2

Preview of *SENT: Missiology for the Sports Outreach Community*

I. Introduction – What this Book and Chapter are about and Where They are Headed - 10

II. Vision for This Book - 12

III. Mission for This Book - 13

IV. Section by Section Overview - 13

TIMEOUT

Surrounded by Witnesses
Why Did It Take Your People So Long?

The famous missionary David Livingston was once asked a most poignant question by an African Tribal Chief who had converted to Christianity. After the Chief's conversion, Livingston shared that all who died outside of a personal faith in Christ were doomed to eternity in hell. This realization deeply grieved Chief Sechele as the full weight of knowing all of his ancestors were at that very moment experiencing eternal damnation. Knowing Jesus had been crucified, dead, buried and resurrected over 1800 years prior to Livingston bringing Christianity to Africa…he simply stated: "This is wonderful, but my forefathers were living, at the same time yours were. How is it they never heard of the love of God and of Jesus the Saviour? Why did they all pass away into deep darkness?" His question was basically: Why did your people wait almost 2,000 years before coming to tell my people about Jesus? This is a question that indicts all modern day Christians who are not actively engaged in missions.*

*David Livingstone: The Pathfinder of Africa. From Giants of the Missionary Trial by Eugene Myers Harrison found at: Wholesome words .org
* Global Frontier Missions: www.globalfrontiermissions.org

"God had an only son and He made Him a missionary"

David Livingstone

I. Introduction – What this Book and Chapter are about and Where They are Headed

Have you ever been frustrated by the fact your sports ministry isn't reaching the elite athletes in your community? You may even play on an "open league" team but you've been unsuccessful at getting the people you play with and against in that league to sign up for your church league, let alone ever visit your church or consider a personal relationship with Jesus.

Are you increasingly concerned that the numbers of participants in your youth leagues are dwindling year after year because more and more families are registering their kids in the burgeoning "travel team" world?

Perhaps you find yourself completely at a loss for how to move the ladies in your Pilates class to a Sunday School class or successfully move the men from only playing on your softball field to also attending worship in the sanctuary of your church?

Are you a church elder and baffled that your congregation hasn't grown in years…even though your SR&F Outreach Ministry reports dozens, scores and perhaps even hundreds of "conversions" each year?

Your **vision** is clear: "First Church exists to reach those far from Jesus and His Church."

The problem isn't your **vision**! The real issue has to do with your **mission**. It's one thing to know where you're headed (reach those far from Jesus) or what your

SCOREBOARD

Reflections of an Elder

"At first, our congregation rejoiced when we heard about a dozen high school basketball league participants who 'accepted Jesus.'

We were further encouraged when we received the report that 50 summer soccer campers raised their hand to 'get saved.'

We praised God for the end of the year report that indicated that more than a hundred people who were involved in our church's SR&F outreach activities prayed a 'salvation prayer.'

However, when we assessed the attendance of our Lord's Day morning services, we realized our numbers had plateaued over the last few years. In fact it appeared they had even gone retrograde. So, we began to ask ourselves the question: 'How can our weekly worship attendance and congregational membership be on a downward trend after having hundreds, if not thousands, of decisions for Christ occur in our sports ministry?'"

CHAPTER 2: Preview of The Mission of The Sports Outreach Community: Missiology

goal is (make disciples who make disciples). It's quite another to know how to accomplish your **vision**.

This book is intended to help sports outreach ministers and ministries understand the difference between **vision** and **mission**....and more importantly how to envision, plan for, organize, administrate and implement a gospel-centric, **mission** that effectively accomplishes your **vision**.

This book is written for all SR&F outreach ministers who have ever struggled with why conversations about Jesus (and even conversions to Jesus), that occur in your sports outreach ministry rarely result in the making of disciples?

If this is even close to your situation, it may well be, that your ministry is not fully aligned with core theological foundations and sound biblical philosophical principles.[1] More to the point, it may well be your ministry is not based in and on a missiology that is positioned to reach those far from Jesus and His Church![2]

Sadly, the ineffectiveness of your ministry may well lead church leaders to doubt the effectiveness of SR&F outreach ministry and when combined with the need to tighten up budgets, the hard decision will be made to curtail or eliminate the congregation's SR&F outreach missions.

This "knee-jerk" reaction is certainly understandable and can only be combatted by a reset of an effective missiology. It is hoped this book will shed light on this and provide insight on how to re-envision outreach efforts through a re-evaluation of missiology for the ultimate purpose of aiding congregations in their efforts to reach those far from Jesus and His Church.

The missiology discussed in this book is an essential and core foundation for any successful SR&F outreach ministry and along with soteriology (the topic of the previous book in this series) is one of the most overlooked and misunderstood foundational "*Ologies*" of *The Sports Outreach Community*. It remains one of the most important! So then, what follows in this book seeks to provide pragmatic answers for truly effective SR&F outreach ministry.

This chapter will lay the foundation for understanding how and why a proper understanding of missiology can empower and enable SR&F outreach missionaries to reposition, enhance and expand their efforts to reach those far from Jesus and His Church.

This book defines, describes and explains how and why missiology is relevant and important to *The Sports Outreach Community*. It was preceded or is followed by other *Ologies* such as ecclesiology, soteriology and Christology, and when taken as a complete whole, the books in this series focusing on the theological underpinnings of sports outreach provide the basis from which to build an

---

1   What are referred to in this book series as Christo-centric, *Level #1 Theological-Truths*, and a biblically-based, *Level #2 Philosophical-Principles* organizational-structure.

2   What is referred to in this book series as the *4-Fold Evaluative Rubric* that consists of being *Strategically-Relevant & Efficiently-Effective*.

effective and successful gospel-centric, SR&F outreach mission.

Individually, this book is another *Level #1 Theological-Truth* of the *3-Tier Paradigm*.[3] It deals specifically with how *The Sports Outreach Community* views, engages with, and envisions its collective mission to reach those far from Jesus and his Church. Possibly the most important part of this book includes a novel proposal to see local churches envision and understand how to engage in local mission through their SR&F outreaches.

Collectively, the *Sports Outreach Ologies* provide foundational *Level #1 Theological-Truths* that undergird answers to such pragmatic questions as: Sunday sport; worship and sport; Church/congregational life and sport; sports outreach leadership criteria in relationship to gender and human sexuality issues; effective gospel-centric, *Evangelistic-Disciplemaking* strategies; the purpose, role and mission of sports-related, para-ministries and other "sticky wicket" issues experienced by SR&F outreach missionaries.

II. Vision for this Book

The **vision** for this book is similar to other books in this series: to see congregations around the world successfully fulfilling their Great Commission Mandate of "going" and "making disciples." It is assumed that the **vision** of local church SR&F outreach ministry is to bring all within their influence into a saving relationship with the Savior Jesus Christ. However, the question must be asked: what does a SR&F outreach ministry need to do (what is its **mission**) in order to accomplish its **vision** (bring people to faith in Christ)?

The shared belief that getting someone "saved" fulfills the **vision** of a local church remains fairly consistent throughout Christendom. However, the question concerning how congregations actually go about accomplishing that goal is not as universally agreed upon.[4] How the *Sports Outreach Community* answers the soteriology (theology of salvation) and missiology (theology of missions) questions, will directly impact how they envision, plan for and engage in their Great Commission endeavors. How they answer these questions, will greatly determine how they envision and plan their organizational structure from which their missional models emerge.[5]

Therefore, this chapter is designed to help all SR&F outreach ministers know why and how understanding the theology of missions (missiology) can empower

---

3   *The 3-Tier Paradigm* was introduced in the third chapter of a previous book in this AGON Institutes of Sports Outreach Book Series: *Sports Outreach Fundamentals*.

4   For a more in depth understanding of what is meant by getting someone "saved" see the previous book in this series *The Saving of Sport Ministry: The Soteriology of Sports Outreach*. It discusses "salvation" in relationship to such things as church attendance, tithing, witnessing and other "required" spiritual disciplines. It also takes on the question about the relationship between evangelism and discipleship.

5   Referred to in this book series as basing the vision in *Level #1 Theological-Truths*, which inform *Level #2 Philosophical-Principles* that serve as the organizational structure for *Level #3 Methodological-Models*.

their efforts to mobilize their congregation for outreach to people who are far from Jesus and His Church. It is also hoped the broader *Sports Outreach Community* will benefit from what follows so as to enhance and expand their effectiveness in reaching those far from Jesus and His Church.

III. Mission for this Book

The **mission** of this book is to provide the concepts and comprehensions[6] to *The Sports Outreach Community* about the key theological issues concerning the missional "going to make disciples" and then to provide both the training[7] and the motivation[8] for how to plan for, organize and carry out their outreaches.

This **mission** is accomplished in this book by both defining missiology and exploring how to relate it to both the local church SR&F outreach ministry and the broader *Sports Outreach Community*. It is hoped this broader community as expressed in sports-focused, para-ministries, camps and chaplaincies will be able to re-evaluate the very theological foundations their outreaches are based in and operate from.

Yet, perhaps the most relevant chapter in this book has to do with how to conceptualize contemporary SR&F outreach ministry in light of a multi-faith world and the ever increasing secularization of many former Judeo-Christian cultures. Whether it has to do with dealing with the reality that at times Muslims pretend to convert to Christianity only so as to cover their evil intent of spying on a congregation; or a sports-focused, para-ministry is denied access to a college or high school campus unless they adhere to prevailing social mores; *The Sports Outreach Community* is sailing in uncharted waters. It is hoped this book will help *The Sports Outreach Community* better accomplish its Great Commission goals by this study of, and application of, missiology.

For all of these and other reasons, this book is written. It is offered not so much as "end-all" theological statement, but more so as a beginning treatise upon which other and deeper conversations can start. Again, the **mission** of this book on missiology is to catalytically bring into reality its **vision** to see congregations around the world successfully fulfilling their Great Commission Mandate of "going" and "making disciples." May God add His blessings to this endeavor.

IV. Section by Section Overview

A. Section #2 – The Theological, Philosophical, Historical and Biblical Basis of Missiology

This section will focus on three main areas. The first chapter in this section (Chapter #3) will explore the theological and philosophical relevance of

---

6   What is referred to in this book series as the first "I" of SR&F outreach ministry: *Informing*.

7   What is referred to in this book series as the second "I" of SR&F outreach ministry: *Instructing*.

8   What is referred to in this book series as the third "I" of SR&F outreach ministry: *Inspiring*.

missiology and why it is vital to SR&F outreach ministry. The next chapter (Chapter #4) will explore the historical account of when, where and how missiology came to be and its relevance to SR&F outreach ministry. The third chapter of section #2 (Chapter #5) will provide the biblical basis for establishing a theology of missions in relationship to SR&F outreach ministry. The fourth chapter in section #2 (Chapter 6) outlines missiological foundations for SR&F outreach missions.

B. Section #3 – Missiological Proposals for SR&F Outreach Ministry

The third section of this book begins the process of applying the theology of mission[9] to the organizational structure of SR&F outreach ministry[10] by outlining how to envision, plan for, organize and administrate a *Strategically-Relevant* and *Efficiently-Effective*[11] mission to those far from Jesus and His Church.

Chapters #7 and #8 propose missiological applications for congregations, sports-related, para-ministries; camps; and sports-related, chaplaincy-based, ministries. Then, perhaps the most relevant chapter in this section is Chapter #9 in that it provides an introspective look at how comprehending missiology will greatly enable and empower *The Sports Outreach Community* to understand, engage with and reach, those living in a multi-faith world. Missiology has never been more important to reaching a world so far from Jesus and His Church; especially a world that is increasingly antagonistic to Christianity.

C. Section #4 – Relevancy of Missiology for *The Sports Outreach Community*

Section four will work to synthesize the first three sections, attempting to "connect all the dots" and offer a few concluding points. In addition it will introduce content of the next book in the Institute of Sports Outreach Book Series—Christology.

---

9   The theology of mission is referred to in this book series as a key *Level #1 Theological-Truth.*
10 The organizational structure is referred to in this book series as *Level #2 Philosophical-Principles.*
11 These words are referred to in this book series as the *4-Fold Evaluative Rubric.*

SECTION 2: The Theological, Philosophical, Historical and Biblical Foundations of Missiology

Chapter 3

The Theological and Philosophical Relevance and Importance of Missiology in Relationship to SR&F Outreach Ministry

I. Rationale for Reflecting on Missiology in SR&F Outreach Ministry - 16
   A. Practical Relevance of the Theology of Missiology in Relationship to Local Church Sports Outreach - 17
   B. All to Go and Go to All – Mandate of the Great Commission - 19
II. Definition of Missiology - 20
III. Why Missiology Matters Revisited—Effective SR&F Outreach - 22
IV. Theological Foundation for Missiology: The Great Commission Mandate - 24
   A. The Very Words and Command of Jesus - 24
V. The Missiological Bottom Line – Missions or Bust - 27

"I would recommend a gymnasium, classes, medical lectures, social receptions, music and all unobjectionable agencies."
D. L. Moody*
(Moody...speaking of methods to be used to reach those far from Jesus and His Church).

---

* Higgs, Robert, *God in the Stadium: Sports and Religion in America*, Lexington, KY: University Press of Kentucky, 1995, p. 248. Moody's missiology was that he believed there were many ways to reach boys & men.

I. Rationale for Reflecting on Missiology in SR&F Outreach Ministry

The task of reaching the world for Christ is far from complete and thus it could be said there has never been a more important time for gospel-centric, Christian missionary endeavors to occur.

At the time of this chapter's composition, conservative assessments estimated more than 5 billion people were not yet *Dedicated-Disciples* of Jesus, and depending on the source, there were anywhere from one to seven thousand unreached people groups! (See Research Reflections – Unreached People Groups on page 17; Unengaged and Unreached People Groups on page 19 and How many missionaries are sent on page 21)[1] Yet, in the face of this daunting reality, inexplicably, The Church is consumed with debating such topics as gender-related issues, modes of baptism and the politics of things such as global warming/climate change, communism, socialism and capitalism… all taking pre-immanence over how to be effectively engaged in missions to reach the world for Christ!

Don't get me wrong, each of these theological debates are important, have their place and need to be appropriately dealt with, but not ahead of, or at the expense of, concentrated efforts on: a) reaching and converting: both genders, every communist, socialist or capitalist, and all who either believe in or dismiss climate change; b) baptizing new converts (be it through immersion, sprinkling, pouring or being "dry cleaned" - in the old Quaker fashion of waterless baptism); and especially c) teaching them all that Jesus taught about morality, justice and racism! The importance of conversions, subsequent baptisms/confirmations and total life transformation would seem to be even more poignant and pressing in light of the doomsday predictions of climate change and potential nuclear war! So, there is no more pressing, relevant or important theological consideration than that of missiology (the strategic and relevant work of effectively sharing Jesus with the world) and soteriology (what does becoming a disciple of Christ entail and mean).

Thus, this chapter is written to aid Church and congregational leaders in their attempts to envision and establish a solid theology of mission for SR&F

---

1 In this day and age of "instant information" via the internet research engines, these statistics change on an almost daily basis. Believing that a book has a long shelf life, OVP doesn't want outdated data to unduly influence readers. Thus, even though this section of the book is greatly based on research at the time this was written, it may well be far out of date by the time it is read. Therefore, the reader is recommended do a search at the time of reading to see if current statistics verify and affirm the propositions made hear. Even if the situation has greatly improved when this is read, and there remains only 1 billion people who haven't yet accepted Jesus as their personal Lord and Savior, it is believed there would still be an urgency to understand missiology and be engaged in missionary endeavors to reach that 1 billion people; saving them from eternal separation from Jesus. The reader is also encouraged to read Chapter 10 of the eighth book in this Institutes of Sports Outreach book series: *The Life of the Shoe* by P. F. Myers which provides additional and complementary information about the unreached people groups and the 10-40 window.

Research Reflections

Unreached People Groups

- 7.67 billion people alive in the world
- 3.19 billion people live in "unreached" people groups

Unreached is defined as having little or no access to the gospel of Jesus Christ. Usually this means the gospel will only come from someone who lives outside the people group. When combined with a startling statistic as stated by Global Frontier Missions that most missiologists consider 2% of the population becoming Christ followers as the "tipping point" at which the group is generally considered "reached" with the gospel, the stark reality of how many are truly unreached is staggering.*

* Global Frontier Missions: www.globalfrontiermissions.org

— Dr. Vickie Byler
Professor & Department Chair of Physical Education,
Health & Sport Management
Lancaster Bible College

outreach…for the ultimate purpose of reaching those far from Jesus and His Church.[2]

A. Practical Relevance of the Theology of Missiology in Relationship to Local Church Sports Outreach

The rationale for this series of books is to further equip, empower and enable local church SR&F outreach ministers, sports-related, para-ministers and other Church leaders to envision, plan for, organize, administrate and expedite *Strategically-Relevant* and *Efficiently-Effective* missional activities that reach and redeem those far from Jesus and His Church; and through those redeemed lives, work to redeem communities, the world and culture. What follows are practical suggestions and insights for SR&F outreach ministers to consider as they pertain to missiological *Level #1 Theological Truths*.

---

[2] This is best done by establishing a Christocentric *Level #1 Theological Truth* of missiology which will inform a set of Biblically-Based, *Level #2 Philosophical Principles*, out of which *Strategically-Relevant* and *Efficiently-Effective Level #3 Methodological Models* can emerge.

TIMEOUT

Muscular Christianity Models*

D. L. Moody is best known today as a Crusade Evangelist and for founding the Moody Bible Institute, and yet one of his most significant contributions to the growth of the world-wide church was his leadership in the Student Volunteer Movement of the late 1800's.

Beginning with a couple of weeks and a hundred college-aged men, Moody's Northfield Conferences expanded to a full summer schedule that lasted for decades and was attended by thousands of enthusiastic missionaries who committed themselves to the two watchwords that defined a generation of missionary endeavors

- All to Go & Go to All
- Win the world for Christ in our generation

Northfield attendees were inspired by leading Christian preachers, theologians and missiologists such as: C. K. Ober; Luther Wishard; Kynaston Studd; Henry Drummond and of course Moody himself.

Using the Muscular Christianity philosophy of virile action, sport and strength, this youthful missionary movement took the world by storm.

---

* Many of the Side Bars in this book are entitled: Muscular Christianity Models and highlight lessons gleaned from historical forerunners of faith/sport integration. They are excerpts from the unpublished and forthcoming book by Dr. Greg Linville: *Sports Ministry Pioneers: 19th Century Models for 21st Century Sports Outreach*. This one is from the Chapter entitled - D. L. Moody: From Pocket Candy and Powerful Crusades to Personal Calls.

Research Reflections

Unengaged, Unreached People Groups

In addition to the Unreached People Groups categorized by The Joshua Project, another people group has been identified by Global Frontier Missions called the Unengaged Unreached. **"An Unengaged Unreached People Group is defined as a group of people that** no church, missionary or mission agency has yet taken responsibility to reach with the gospel of Jesus Christ. Thus, there are 269 remaining Unengaged, Unreached people groups numbering over 5.7 million souls that are still beyond the reach of the Gospel!*

* *The Joshua Project: www.joshuaproject.net/global/progress*
Global Frontier Missions: www.globalfrontiermissions.org
Finishing the Task: www.finishingthetask.com

— Dr. Vickie Byler
Professor & Department Chair of Physical Education,
Health & Sport Management
Lancaster Bible College

B. All to Go and Go to All – Mandate of the Great Commission

"All to go and go to all" was the watch-word of the Student Volunteer Movement (SVM) of the late 19th and early 20th Century.[3] This movement grew out of the early Muscular Christianity Era…the forerunner of The Sports Outreach Movement. Through the vision and efforts of D. L. Moody (See Time Out on p18) and others, the SVM captured the hearts of thousands of young collegiate-aged disciples of Christ that resulted in a special move of God that saw world missions work go into hyper-drive.[4]

---

3   John R. Mott, "*The Beginnings of the Student Volunteer Movement*" in The Student Volunteer Movement After Twenty-Five Years. Robert P. Wilder, *The Great Commission: The Missionary Response in North American and Europe*, London: Oliphants Ltd., 1936. Clarence P. Shedd, *Two Centuries of Student Christian Movements*, New York: Association Press, 1934.

4   There are some who would probably be surprised to see people like Moody, the Studd brothers and Drummond designated as Muscular Christians because in England, Muscular Christianity was associated with a liberal high church. My response is twofold: a) the Muscular Christian community in America was much more aligned with conservative evangelicalism; and b) other people who were contemporaries of Moody and others described them as being Muscular Christians. Nonetheless I understand they themselves may not have wanted to be associated with a liberal church or the associated title of Muscular Christian.

A second watch-word of the SVM was: "In our generation." This communicated the passion of the SVM. The urgency of this passion was driven by an expectation that the return of Jesus was imminent, and from a desire to be good stewards of the resources of time, energy and resources God had blessed that generation with. They wanted to make their lives count for all of eternity and indeed, they made a significant and lasting impact on the world.

It is recommended that all SR&F outreach missionaries research the SVM. If they do, they will be inspired and encouraged by the passion of a former generation and the hope would be this would rekindle a passion to reach people for Jesus.[5] The main lesson to be learned would be to go to the entire world for the purpose of *Evangelistic-Disciplemaking*.

The first question for all SR&F outreach ministers remains: "Are all committed to go and committed to go to all?" The second is: "Why are you a SR&F outreach minister?" If the answer is to run sports leagues, then perhaps working for a parks and rec department would pay a higher salary. If the answer is to improve the health of people or lead fitness classes, then most often working for a spa or other health facility would provide better facilities and equipment.

Where's your passion? Has it waned?

II. Definition of Missiology

Missiology is the specific area of Christian theology that considers the theological, philosophical, historical and methodological foundations for going "into all the world" for the purpose of "making disciples."

Missiology includes examining the teaching of the entire Bible as well as applying the results of reliable research that mandate and reveal best practices of gospel-centric, *Evangelistic-Disciplemaking*.

The word missiology is derived from the Latin word *missio* that means to send. Just as the word missive means a letter is sent, *missio* also has to do with a sending. Thus missiology is the study of sending. This, in and of itself, helps to set the framework for missions: it is more about the sending, than it is about the going! The question all SR&F outreach ministers should ask is: "Am I sent?" Of course being willing to go is imperative as is being called, but these are both to be affirmed by being sent by a church or denomination. Missiology understands both the going and the sending to be essential for any ongoing effective missionary endeavors.

Missiology begins with the life and work of God (Jesus), Who was sent to "seek and save those who were lost."[6] His being sent resulted in His incarnation and strongly suggests (if it doesn't definitively indicate) The Church is sent on

---

5   See the Time Outs throughout this book.
6   Luke 19.10.

CHAPTER 3: The Theological and Philosophical Relevance and Importance of Missiology in Relationship to SR&F Outreach Ministry

Research Reflections

How many missionaries are sent each year?

- 3,105   Groups engaged by 5,101 teams
- 29,553   Fully Focused vocational workers sent by 414 engaging ministries
- 86.639   Bi-vocational and part time workers
- 142,317   Churches planted
- 3,369,127   Reported believers
- 22   People Groups
- 6,014,568   Total People*

Sources:
* *Finishing the Task: www.finishingthetask.com*

The Finishing the Task Network reported in March 2020 the following updates since the November 2005 report. According to research posted on the traveling team.org the following statistics on Missionaries is reported.

www.thetravelingteam.org/missionaries-and-workers

— Dr. Vickie Byler
Professor & Department Chair of Physical Education,
Health & Sport Management
Lancaster Bible College

mission and that mission is to be based in a personal, relational outreach that is indwelt and empowered by the Holy Spirit.

The major distinction of Christian missiology from other world religions has to do with the fact that it is based on what God has done for humankind, not what humankind does to earn God's love and forgiveness. The very bedrock of Christian missiology is based on being sent and being sent is dependent on there being someone who is willing "to go into all the world."

So, what has any of this to do with SR&F outreach ministry; why does missiology matter? Read on...

III. Why Missiology Matters Revisited—Effective SR&F Outreach

Once again, I envision my friends and fellow sports outreach ministers shaking their heads and saying: "It's unbelievable how many books Linville can write based on yet another *Ology* and a bunch of Greek and Latin words!"

For those of you who don't know me or have recently joined our *Sports Outreach Community* and have somehow stumbled upon this book, you may not fully understand the good natured "ribbing" that occurs amongst our members. Many of the conversations between me, local church sports ministers and university professors go something like this:

Me: "Missiology is one of the most important theological issues SR&F outreach ministry faces today."

My local-church-practitioner partner: "Okay Doc, I'm sure there's something here I need to know and understand but please put it in English words that I can understand."

My university associate: "What research is all of this based on?"

So, let me attempt to communicate to both wings of our community. Clear and simple, it's about successfully navigating the turbulent waters of bringing people into a personal relationship with Jesus with the end goal of "making disciples!"

Perhaps said more obtusely—this book is about gospel-centric, *Evangelistic-Disciplemaking*. It's about communicating why SR&F outreach missionaries; other congregational leaders; sports-related camps, sports chaplains and sports-oriented, para-ministries; need to not only have a solid soteriology (theology of salvation) but also a robust missiology (theology of mission). This book is designed so SR&F outreach missionaries can envision, plan for, organize, administrate and implement a SR&F outreach ministry that effectively sends missionaries to reach those far from Jesus and His Church with the end goal of "making disciples."

Once understood, missiology joins the other *Sports Outreach Ologies* in becoming relevant and profound. For example: If a congregation or

International Insights

Sports equipment destroyed a church's witness

Some years ago I was a part of a sports mission baseball team that travelled to the Dominican Republic to supposedly partner with local pastors and churches. The purpose was to organize clinics and games with community teams to verbally share the gospel and also to cast a vision for how sports ministry could be used to reach their communities. As a tangible blessing to those we came to serve, our team brought thousands of pounds of sports equipment to leave behind. What was intended to be a blessing became a real problem.

One of our coaches decided to start passing out equipment randomly to players after the first game. At first things remained calm, but as more and more players realized what was happening, a riot erupted. Players began pushing, shoving, shouting, and grabbing for the equipment in desperation. Most had never owned a new pair of cleats or baseball glove, so they fought and struggled for the equipment without regard for anyone else. Fights broke out before peace could be restored, and of course there was no opportunity to verbally share the gospel!

Needless to say the whole situation left a bad taste in everyone's mouth. The pastors were offended because there was a lack of understanding and sensitivity to the culture and situation, which led to poor planning and execution of any relevant mission. Perhaps the most important factor that was missed was the impromptu distribution of equipment denied the local congregations of the opportunity to build relationships with those who would receive the equipment.

Had the right channels been followed, the players would have received the equipment, the gospel would have been heard and local congregations would have been connected to the baseball players of their community. Instead, people left frustrated, angry, and upset and the relationship between the community, the church, and the mission team was severely damaged. Needless to say this poor witness and testimony did little to further the gospel mission in this community.

— P. F. Myers
CSRM International Director

ministry is based in a theology that believes anything supersedes *Evangelistic-Disciplemaking* their organizational philosophy of ministry will focus on serving the needs of those who have already come to Jesus and His Church. All methodologies based on this view can be described as *Feeding-the-Flock* rather than *Locating-the-Lost*. Such methodologies that are focused on *Maintaining-Members* rather than *Winning-Waywards* will typically be designed around styling ever new worship venues and experiences; engaging in an ever more entertaining preaching series; and investing in ever expanding building programs; rather than envisioning *Strategically-Relevant* mission to those far from Jesus and His Church.

Conversely, if a ministry is based on a theology that believes The Church's purpose is "to go into all the world and make disciples" their organizational philosophy will include sending missionaries to conduct missional activities that will reach the unchurched and lead new believers into full spiritual maturity.

So like soteriology, missiology is about taking seriously the Great Commission's mandate to "go and make Disciples;" which is more than *Feeding-the-Flock and Maintaining-Members*. The vital importance of missiology for SR&F outreach ministries has both theological and pragmatic rationales.[7]

IV. Theological Foundation for Missiology – The Great Commission Mandate

The simplicity of the Great Commission mandate is often the very reason why it is so overlooked, underappreciated and thus unfulfilled. In addition, it is so often referenced that its poignancy slips by us and is often lost.

A. The Very Words and Command of Jesus

The very last words of Jesus and His very last command were: "to go and make disciples." Should this not get our attention?

Reflect on the very last things you say to loved ones when you are leaving … especially when you don't anticipate seeing them for a very long time? Last words carry extra weight because they represent the highest values and priorities of the speaker. This is no different for Jesus. He was leaving His Disciples for the last time and He impressed them with what was the most important thing to do. He was sending them to "go and make disciples." This was missiology in action. Jesus was **sending** His Disciples into all the world. He wasn't asking them to erect buildings; He was **sending** and commissioning them to *Locate-the-Lost*. He wasn't asking them to *Feed-the-Flock;* He was **sending** them to *Win-the-Wayward*.

With this in mind, are we content to plan-programs, build buildings, lead leagues and conduct classes as mere activities? Unless any of these *Methodological-Models* are envisioned, planned for, organized, administrated

---

[7] I am not proposing pastors and other congregational leaders neglect their "flock," but rather care for them in such a way that would include mobilizing and empowering them to be disciplemakers.

CHAPTER 3: The Theological and Philosophical Relevance and Importance of Missiology in Relationship to SR&F Outreach Ministry

International Insights - Scoreboard

When doing international missions it is imperative to:

✓ **Work through** local congregations

✓ **Work with** indigenous, reputable church leaders who understand the culture and dynamics of a community better than any foreigner and can get resources to those who need them most

✓ **Any material gifts** provided by a mission team should be distributed through local congregations as it gives them the platform to establish relationships with unchurched people

✓ **Lack of sensitivity to the culture** and lacking an understanding about community, neighborhood and cultural dynamics can create division and push people away from Jesus instead of towards him, so the goal should be to support local churches in their *Evangelistic-Disciplemaking* efforts in every way possible

✓ **Relationships are key, not dependency.** There needs to be honest and open communication between mission teams and indigenous leaders and both sides must: interact with humility; respect, and honor one another; be willing to learn from one another; and appreciate the ingenuity and giftedness the other brings to the mission

✓ **It is important to make sure that the "gospel of goods" is not being promoted over the gospel of Christ.** This is a counterfeit gospel which confuses people about what it means to be a true disciple of Jesus by offering material wealth and possessions along with the true gospel, and of course ... Jesus warned against this after the feeding of the 5,000 (John 6.26 & 66)

— *P. F. Myers*
CSRM International Director

Research Reflections

How many missionaries are sent each year?

Christian Missionaries:
- The Entire World Total Missionaries (Catholic, Protestant, Orthodox): 400,000 foreign missionaries [1]
- Reached World Missionaries: 309,315 foreign missionaries (77.3%) [2]
- Unevangelized People Missionaries: 77,610 foreign missionaries (19.4%) [2]
- Unreached People Groups Missionaries: 13,315 foreign missionaries (3.3%) [2]

Christian Workers:
- Full time Christian Workers in the World : 5.5 million workers
- Christian workers to Reached People: 4.19 million local workers (75.9%)
- Christian workers to the Unevangelized People Groups: 1.3 million local workers (23.7%)
- Christian workers to the Unreached People Groups: 20,500 local workers (0.37%)

[1] World Christian Database, 2015,*Barrett and Johnson. 2001. World Christian Trends, pg. 656, and

[2] Atlas of Global Christianity 2009.   Also see: Deployment of Missionaries

[3] International Journal of Frontier Mission, Clarifying the Remaining Frontier Mission Task, by R. W. Lewis, issue 35:4 Winter 2018, p164

Global status 2018
www.thetravelingteam.org/missionaries-and-workers

— Dr. Vickie Byler
Professor & Department Chair of Physical Education,
Health & Sport Management
Lancaster Bible College

and implemented for the purpose of sending trained and empowered missionaries to fulfill the Great Commission, they are at best wholesome activities. They are certainly not missional. They may even be appreciated by people who participate in them, but they are not obeying the very command of Jesus' last words: "go and make disciples!"

V. The Missiological Bottom Line – Missions or Bust

So, the real bottom line for both SR&F outreach ministers and local church leaders comes down to one thing: missiological effectiveness. If the SR&F outreach ministry is built upon a weak and under-developed theology of mission, it most likely will not effectively "go and make disciples." Therefore, no matter how strategic, relevant or efficient a sport, recreation or fitness activity

THE PRACTIONER'S PERSPECTIVE

Mission has its root in sending and calling.

Therefore, a local church SR&F outreach ministry can only be considered truly missional if it sends out missionaries who are called by God.

So the questions for each of us who lead SR&F outreach ministries are:

First...am I "calling" those in my congregation to become sports, recreation and fitness missionaries to our local community

Second...am I resourcing, training, equipping and mentoring those who are called for effective missionary endeavors

Third...am I "sending" these local missionaries into our community to reach those who are far from Jesus and our church

— Greg English
Sport & Rec Minister - Cool Springs
Adjunct Professor – Chowan University

may be, it will not reach its potential to enhance and expand The Church. In essence the inability to comprehend and apply a strong missiology results in *The Sports Outreach Community* signing its own death warrant!

Beyond being committed to mobilize missional SR&F outreach ministry, knowing and understanding the history of missiology is important and is the topic of the next chapter.

SECTION 2: The Theological, Philosophical, Historical and Biblical Foundations of Missiology

Chapter 4

The History of Missiology in Relationship to SR&F Outreach Ministry

I. Introduction to the History of Missiology - 30
   A. Alexander Duff: Father of Missiology - 30
   B. Missiology Today - 30

II. Missiology History and The SR&F Outreach Community - 32

III. Summary - 35

SCOREBOARD

Is Your SR&F Outreach Ministry Strategically-Relevant

Strategic – having to do with a strategy to obtain a goal, aim or purpose

Relevant – having to do with what relates to making a connection

Strategically-Relevant – having to do with envisioning both what might be relevant to the perceived needs of people who are far from Jesus and His Church, and then to envision a strategy to reach such people based upon what is relevant

Strategic-Relevance for Local Church Sport Outreach - The most strategic activity for Church missiological endeavors remains the same in all cultures: sport, recreation & fitness outreach. However, the most relevant specific sport or leisure pursuit for each culture changes. For example, basketball is the most relevant sport for the state of Indiana, whereas Cricket is the most relevant sport for the country of India.

Missiology seeks to enlighten and empower *Strategically-Relevant Mission*.

> "Lord, what am I that I should be so highly honoured as to be the instrument of conveying such truths...
> which are made to flow to those streams that enrich and fertilize the neighbouring lands." *
>
> *Alexander Duff*

* George Smith, *Twelve Pioneer Missionaries* (London: Thomas Nelson and Sons, 1900). P. 29.

I. Introduction to the History of Missiology

Christian theology as a whole has developed over two millennia. Surprisingly however, missiology as a unique theological discipline developed much later, first appearing in the mid-19th century in a country known for its missionary zeal.

A. Alexander Duff – The Father of Missiology[1]

Growing up as a boy in a God-fearing home in the middle of Scotland, Alexander Duff's parents never imagined their "wee bairn" would grow up to be a missionary and world influencer. Nonetheless they did prepare the soil, plant the seed and cultivate the growth of their son's heart and mind for world missions. Those pious parents' accounts of the triumph of the gospel throughout the world, and stories about the millions living without God and dying without Jesus stirred up a strong fire within their son. Pictures of false gods infused feelings of horror toward idolatry, while scenes of all who in their blindness worshipped at the heathen altars, fueled the young boy's compassion for the idolaters. Above all, Christ-centered parents instilled the love of Jesus in their son, along with a love for any denomination that preached Christ to the world. (see the time outs on page 31 – Andrew Duff: Father of Missiology)

Missiology was initially envisioned and championed by Scottish missionary Alexander Duff but needs to continue to develop and adjust with each new generation, cultural shift and political change. Duff's initial systematic theory of mission was so influential, that it led to his appointment to the newly created Chair of Evangelistic Theology in Edinburgh. It is from that date (1867) that all subsequent generations of missionaries have been the beneficiaries; including local church SR&F missionaries.

Duff's forward thinking about how to systematically conceive of world-wide mission began The Church on a path to understand how to envision, plan for, organize, administrate and implement successful missional activities that continues today.[2]

B. Missiology Today

On one hand, it is staggering to think The Church waited so long to articulate a systematic theology of missions but on the other hand, it makes complete sense because it was always assumed that evangelism was why The Church existed. Therefore The Church always engaged in missional evangelism; never in any theological debate about its pre-eminence.

Thus, for millennia, The Church knew it existed to evangelize, and by and large, was engaged in gospel-centric, *Evangelistic-Disciplemaking* activity. That the purpose of The Church was to win the world to Christ was never in doubt.

---

[1] The following information of Alexander Duff found in these three paragraphs is summarized from the works cited at the end of this chapter.

[2] Missional activities that meet the *4-Fold Evaluative Rubric: Strategically-Relevant* and *Efficiently-Effective, Evangelistic-Disciplemaking* are in constant need of re-evaluation.

TIME OUT

Surrounded by Witnesses
Alexander Duff – Father of Missiology

Born the son of a Gaelic-speaking farm couple, Alexander Duff became the father of missiology upon his return from the mission field of Asia. He first distinguished himself as a Divinity student at St. Andrews University where he was an integral part of founding a student missionary society. After university days Duff was appointed Superintendent of the Church of Scotland's General Assembly in Calcutta, India; arriving in 1830.

Duff immediately set out to create a system of science and letters based in a biblically-based Christian philosophy that empowered him to engage in dialogue with many Hindu philosophers and students that led eventually to many Hindus converting to Christianity. While his time in India was cut short due to ill health, the Lord greatly used his inspired address to the General Assembly that raised missions to new prominence.

Duff's subsequent travels throughout Scotland served to build an infrastructure that mobilized a growing commitment to world missions. Through all of his preaching, teaching and sharing of the vision for missions, Duff developed a systematic theology of mission which served as the basis for his lectures and books *(India and Indian Missions - 1834* and *Missions the Chief End of the Christian Church - 1839).* Duff spent significant periods in both India and Scotland from 1840-1863 and even spent time in America and South Africa where he was recognized as a leading strategist for missions. At the end of the era, Duff realized missions needed to become a central foundation of any theological curriculum. He further recommended a professorship be established along with a missionary institute that would study language and culture for the purpose of worldwide missionary evangelism. Eventually, Duff was appointed to the new Chair of Evangelistic Theology at Edinburgh's New College; the first of its kind anywhere in the world. His impact and legacy live on through missiology curriculum and professorships in seminaries throughout the world.*

*Summarized from the Works Cited at the end of this Chapter

While the methods of evangelism may look different in various countries or cultures, and certain aspects of soteriology (the theology of salvation) have been debated, the mission of The Church was always assumed to be to evangelize those far from Jesus and His Church. Thus, since the first century The Church had accepted the reality that evangelism was at the core of, and the reason for, its existence.

Over the course of the last century or two however, evangelism has become a topic for debate within ecclesiastical enclaves (Church and denominational groups). Surprisingly and sadly the debates include whether evangelism is mandated or even moral! Less surprising, missiology includes a proper exploration of the ethics of how missions should be engaged in.

From this late, but much needed start, modern missiology continues to grow in sophistication and effectiveness for the same reasons that it came into existence. Modern day "evangelists" currently struggle with the very same issues missionaries have experienced throughout the centuries.

Encountering various world-views, religions, cultures and ethics, missiological effectiveness has been greatly enhanced by scientific research and theological reflection; all of which inform and empower The Church to accomplish its Great Commission Mandate. Bottom line: a solid theological framework syncretized with credible theoretical research enables the successful "spreading of the Good News."[3]

II. Missiology History and *The SR&F Outreach Community*

The impact of the theology of mission (missiology) is not at the forefront of most SR&F outreach minister's knowledge or understanding. Moreover, I believe not even the Muscular Christian pioneers (featured throughout this book) were fully aware of the impact missiology had on: a) their thinking; b) the way they envisioned and carried out their ministries; and c) how they lived their lives. If the pioneers of integrating faith and sport (who lived during the life of Dr. Duff) remained unaware of missiology's influence on their thinking, call and lives, we can imagine how much less modern day SR&F outreach ministers understand these influences.

Nonetheless, missiology has provided SR&F outreach ministers with a most essential and profound foundation of theological and philosophical thought that enabled what is now taken for granted: outreach ministry in and through sport, recreation and fitness. It's not that the missiology gurus specifically taught sports outreach in their courses or even that they specifically "connected the dots"

---

3   Again, I state: this chapter is written to aid congregational leaders in their attempt to establish a foundation based on Christocentric *Level #1 Theological Truths*, which will inform a set of biblically-based *Level #2 Philosophical Principles*, out of which *Level #3 Methodological Models* can emerge; all with a final goal of shaping effective local church SR&F outreach ministry.

TIMEOUT

Preach the Gospel - Redefined

I once consulted with the leadership of a world renowned congregation that was contemplating engaging in sports ministry.

What the church leadership envisioned was to construct a sports facility with funds they had raised for capital expansion and improvement. Their basic motivation stemmed from the fact that so many other congregations had built such facilities. All went well until...

The Lead Pastor heard that the other churches saw their athletic facilities as a primary way to communicate the gospel and engage in *Evangelistic-Disciplemaking*. At this point he immediately nixed the entire pursuit based on his belief that the gospel only came through the preaching of the Word of God; not through conducting basketball leagues.

I respectfully confirmed my support for the vital importance of preaching the gospel and I affirmed the preaching of this magnificent preacher, but I asked what the pastor's plan was to preach the gospel to those who would never attend one of the church's worship services? I asked if he could embrace the strategy of using athletic facilities and programs as local missions from which to connect the unchurched with the congregation in such a way that those far from Jesus and His Church would eventually feel comfortable enough to willingly and enthusiastically sit under the preaching?

Sadly, the consulting came to an abrupt end and that congregation never engaged in SR&F Outreach!

between sport, faith and mission. Rather, it was that their efforts led The Church to: a) consider what it meant to envision and plan for missions that were strategic and relevant; b) how to efficiently organize and administrate such missional endeavors; and c) what it would take to make such endeavors effective in terms of fulfilling the Great Commission.

At this point in this chapter and book, today's sport or recreation pastor may be thinking their time could be much better spent by reading something that will help them better run their youth leagues or empower their fitness outreach to be more effective than by contemplating some old dusty Celtic relic…and such thinking has a certain validity. However, every SR&F outreach missionary will inevitably encounter a senior pastor, congregational elder, finance chair and/or denominational leader who questions whether or not such mission is based on solid theological and philosophical foundations. Therefore this short chapter is provided to sports pastors for the purpose of arming them with the assurance that their ministry has historical and biblical support, and their outreach is based on a strong academic footing.[4]

In addition, SR&F outreach missionaries all too often take for granted their ability to engage in athletics and fitness activities for missiological purposes. All of us who are fulfilling our calling as SR&F outreach missionaries owe our very existence to the forward thinking of a robust theology of mission. That theology of mission is undergirded by a strong and historic academic foundation that was initiated by Dr. Duff. Similarly, we stand on the shoulders of many who preceded us in both the Muscular Christian Era and *The Sports Outreach Community*. We can rest assured all we engage in is well justified and thus, we have much to thank Duff and others for.

So by all means spend the majority of your time investigating how to improve on your models and methodology but file this chapter away for the day you have the opportunity to share with your lead pastor about how you are fulfilling the missiological goals of your congregation, or when you are able to enlighten an interview committee about how SR&F outreach missions maximize historic missiological principles. All things equal, knowing about the roots of missiology will get you hired.

This also works the other-way-round. The missiologists of the world also have *The Sports Outeach Community* to thank for continuing to push the edge of missiological envelope all through the last two centuries. Yes, there have been

---

4   It is realized that this book, and all of the *Level #1 Ology* books in this series, are written for a specific purpose. Additionally, it is assumed that the books written about the more pragmatic *Level #3* topics have already been read. Thus, the *Ology* books are recommended as additional aids to envisioning a truly effective SR&F outreach mission. While all three levels are foundational to a truly effective mission, it's not likely a sports minister will ever get the chance, or have the need, to talk about missiology and Dr. Duff unless they have already established solid pragmatic outreach missions.

a few ways and areas in which *The SR&F Outreach Community* has pushed too far[5] or has not properly integrated missiological principles into its outreach, but in general, SR&F outreach missions have greatly influenced and shaped the thinking of missiologists. This influence continues to result in cutting edge, strategic and relevant mission-work that in many geo-political places and various times is the only way The Church has to reach a world that is so far from its Savior, Jesus.[6]

III. Summary

The main lessons that emerge from this chapter should be affirming, empowering and convicting for all SR&F outreach ministers.

First, SR&F outreach ministers can rest assured that what they do each and every day is anchored in, has been enabled by, and is undergirded by the theology of mission. Due to the theological and philosophical work done by missiologists SR&F outreach cannot be dismissed as being unbiblical, irrelevant or ineffectual.

Second, *The Sports Outreach Community* should not only be thankful for the Muscular Christians and others who pioneered faith-sport integration in earlier eras for paving the way for what we do today, but more importantly, we should learn from those earlier models.

Third, SR&F outreach ministers should continue to "push the edge of the envelope" in envisioning new ways to reach those far from Jesus and His Church; and thus be actively creating modern missional history.

Finally, we all stand on the shoulders of those who came before us….and if we remain faithful…ours will be the shoulders that will lift and support others that come after us.

Are we willing to be history makers for sports-related, gospel-centric missions? If so, it is imperative we know the missiological biblical basis…the topic of the next chapter. [7]

---

5   A few examples of going too far include: certain Lord's Day abuses; using alcohol as a draw to an event; rewarding uncontrolled competition; embracing eastern religious philosophies and nuances to permeate fitness ministry classes; etc.

6   For a deeper consideration of this I recommend the book *The Life of the Shoe* – book #8 in the Institutes of Sports Outreach series published by Overwhelming Victory Press.

7   More than likely Pastor Simeon (subject of the Time Out found on page 37) would have faded from all memory except for the fact that… in 1796 his honoring of the Lord's Day led to him preaching a sermon that was unrecognizable by all but one of the Scots whose spoken language was quite different than that spoken by the English preacher…and yet that began a revival that led to the conversion of parents who raised a son who became the father of missiology and the world's first professor of missiology! May we all be faithful each moment of each day…we never know who we might influence and what might be the result.

Works Cited for this chapter....

Andrew Walls, "Duff, Alexander," in *Biographical Dictionary of Christian Missions*, ed. Gerald H. Anderson (New York: Macmillan Reference USA, 1998), 187-88. *Biographical Dictionary of Christian Missions*, Macmillan Reference USA, copyright © 1998 Gerald H. Anderson,

Duff, Alexander. *India and India Missions: Including sketches of the gigantic system of Hinduism, both in theory and practice; also notices of some of the principal agencies employed in conducting the process of Indian evangelization.* Edinburgh: J. Johnstone, 1839.

Paton, William. *Alexander Duff: Pioneer Missionary of Education.* New York: George H. Doran, 1923.

Smith, George. *Twelve Pioneer Missionaries.* London: Thomas Nelson and Sons, 1900.

_____. *The Life of Alexander Duff.* New York: A.C. Armstrong, 1879.

Vermilye, Elizabeth B. *The Life of Alexander Duff.* New York: Revell, 1890.

Walsh, W. Pakenham. *Modern Heroes of the Mission Field.* New York: Revell, 1915.

_____. *Missions the Chief End of the Church.* Edinburgh: J. Johnstone, 1839.

TIMEOUT

Surrounded by Witnesses
What if…..

In the year 1796, Mr. Simeon a clergyman from Cambridge, England was enjoying a tour in the Scottish Highlands and had to make a decision about returning to England from his Inn in Dunkeld. To leave on the Saturday would mean traveling on the Lord's Day. His decision to remain until Monday enabled him to engage in a "ramble" through the pass of Killikrankie where he called at the manse of the village of Moulin. Upon his impromptu arrival Simeon was warmly welcomed by the Pastor (Mr. Stewart) of whom it was said did not possess a true comprehension of the gospel. Stewart politely extended the common curtesy of opening his Moulin church pulpit to the visiting cleric for the following morning.

Now what must be understood is that normally the likelihood of an Englishman being warmly received into a Scottish pulpit, let alone being understood due to dialect, accent and other language barriers, was very remote…and this was certainly the case for that morning. Only one person in attendance that morning heard the gospel! The lone exception was the Pastor himself: Mr. Stewart! In a sense, this Scottish pastor had entertained a stranger whom became his "angel unawares" (Hebrews 13.2). From that day forward, Mr. Stewart embraced the gospel and determined his people would know Jesus Christ! This resulted in the Word of God having a mighty impact on that parish and the wider area.

One couple was deeply impacted by this revival as they sat continuously under the teaching of the re-ignited ministry of Pastor Stewart. In due time this couple became the parents of a son they named Alexander. Their son (Alexander Duff) fondly remembered being raised in a thoroughly Christian environment that rooted him in a fervent faith in Jesus that enabled him to become the father of missiology!*

* Summarized from the Works Cited at the end of this Chapter.

continued on page 38

TIMEOUT

continued from page 37

What if....
Mr. Simeon had traveled on rather than honoring the Lord's Day?

What if...
Mr. Stewart had not willingly given up his pulpit....and never heard the gospel?

What if....
Alexander's parents had not heard the gospel; did not regularly attend Moulin church; and did not raise their son in and by the Word of God?

What if...
Alex had not heeded his call to missions and had not called The Church to incorporate missiology into its seminary curriculum or he had not pioneered the missionary society of the denomination he was a member of?

What if...
SR&F outreach ministers are not faithful to: a) call people in their churches to become local missionaries; b) train, equip and empower them; and c) send them to go and make disciples?

SECTION 2: The Theological, Philosophical, Historical and Biblical Foundations of Missiology

Chapter 5

Biblical Foundation of Missiology for SR&F Outreach Ministry

I. Biblical Principles – Incarnational Missions - 40
    A. Incarnational Missions – Based in the Gospels - 40
        1. The Model of Jesus – 40
    B. Incarnational Missions – Based in The Acts of the Apostles - 42
        1. The Model of Barnabas, Paul and Others – 42
    C. Incarnational Missions – Based in the Epistles - 43
        1. Incarnational Missions – A Colossians Model – 43
            a. Praying for Open Doors – To Empower Gospel Mission
            b. Walking in Wisdom – To Win the Right to Share the Gospel
            c. Redeeming Time - To Live Out the Gospel
            d. Engaging in Gracious and seasoned conversation –
                To be Able to Discuss the Gospel
            e. Answering Each Person – To be able to Explain the Gospel
            f. Summary of a Colossian model of incarnational missions

II. Summary of Biblical Principles – Incarnational Missions – 55

> "God grant that we may go on prospering, and...give us friends who will help us to win young men all over the world for Christ." *
>
> Sir George Williams

---

* J. E. Hodder Williams, *The Life of Sir George Williams* (London: Hodder & Stoughton, 1906) p. 29.

I. Biblical Principles – Incarnational Missions

Theology informs and guides philosophy, and methodology emerges out of philosophy.[1] With that as the foundational undergirding, the following overview of biblical principles is designed to engage readers in a process of determining a Christo-centric missiology out of which both an organizational structure and effective pragmatic models can be developed and employed. Specifically, missiology is based in what has been described as Incarnational outreach.

A. Incarnational Missions Based in the Gospels[2]

The Apostle John was inspired to write in the first chapter of his Gospel: "The Word became Flesh."[3] By this he communicated that God (Jesus) came to earth in a human form (in the flesh).

In addition Luke, who wrote a Gospel closely associated with the Apostle Paul and under the inspiration of the Holy Spirit, states that Jesus came to "seek and save the lost."[4] Thus, the reason Jesus came in the flesh was to seek the lost (those far from Him and His Church) for the purpose of saving them.

The entirety of all four Gospels tells the story of the Incarnation: the birth, life, teaching, death, resurrection and ascension of Jesus. The Gospel accounts of the Christ lay out the fulfillment of all the Old Testament prophecies, predictions and preparations for Jesus's coming.

This theme continued in Luke's account of the Acts of the Apostles which recorded the incarnational approach of the early church fathers and subsequent generations of those they discipled. Incarnational ministry was affirmed and taught in the Epistles. While this synopsis is but an overview, it is offered to show the biblical foundation for the theology of incarnational missions.

So, incarnational ministry was first modeled by God Himself and subsequently by the Disciples He called, trained and sent out. The Disciples in turn called, trained and sent out ensuing generations of gospel men and women. A deeper exploration of incarnational theology follows.

1. The Model of Jesus

No greater message has ever been given to human-kind than the "Good News" of John 3.16. This is probably the best known verse of the entire Bible and begins

---

1   The working premise of the entire Institutes of Sports Outreach book series is that Christo-centric, *Level #1 Theological-Truths* are the foundations from which the biblically-based, organizational infrastructures of *Level #2 Philosophical-Principles* can be created, and such infrastructures will enable and empower *Level #3 Methodological-Models* that are *Strategically-Relevant and Efficiently-Effective*. So, understanding the doctrine of the Incarnation is a foundational and necessary *Theological-Truth* to build all SR&F outreach missions on.

2   I'm not certain when, where or by whom the term incarnational ministry originated. My first exposure to it was when I was dually trained by Young Life and the YMCA. Both ministries had a basic missiology that was rooted in the Incarnation.

3   John 1.14. From the Latin word: *Carnem*.

4   Luke 19.10. Part of the criteria for determining if a Gospel was canonical (the divinely, inspired Word of God) was that it had a strong Apostolic connection. Two of the Gospels were written by Disciples of Jesus (Matthew and John), and the other two were strongly associated with Peter (the Gospel of Mark) and Paul (the Gospel of Luke).

> # SCOREBOARD
> ## Is Your Ministry Incarnational?
>
> The theological word incarnational has an etymological root of "carne," defined as flesh. Thus, incarnational has to do with being "in the flesh." Theologically speaking, incarnational refers primarily to the fact that the God of the universe (Jesus) appeared "in the flesh" (a *Level #1 Theological Truth*).
>
> Secondarily it refers to the fact that all disciples of Jesus are to "flesh out the gospel" of Jesus Christ (a *Level #2 Philosophical Principle*). It is out of these truths and principles that specific expressions of ministry are to emerge (*Level #3 Methodological Models*).

with… "For God so loved the world that He gave His only Son…" Even a large number of secularized non-Christians could recite the end of that verse: "and whoever believes in Him shall not perish but have everlasting life." It is truly good news because it communicates that the Lord Who created and sustains every far-flung galaxy and each sub-atomic particle in each of those galaxies, came to earth, "in the flesh" for the purpose of reconciling humankind to Himself and thus enabling eternal life!

This incarnational coming, in and of itself, communicates God's way of reaching people with His message of love and salvation. He did so by not just entering into the very existence of humankind but more so, by taking on flesh as a man. The coming of God in "the flesh" strongly suggests a similar approach for His disciples to live out their faith.

Not only does the example of God taking on flesh suggest a *Theological-Truth* of incarnational-based outreaches, but the life and teachings of Jesus also support such a theology. Jesus modeled incarnational ministry as He: a) personally related to people as He walked, talked and mentored His disciples (Luke 11.1-13); b) healed those with physical maladies (Luke 11.17-19); c) defended the woman caught in adultery (John 8.1-11); d) associated with tax collectors (Mark 2.13-17) & Luke 19.1-10); e) engaged the woman at the well (John 4.4-26); f) fed the multitudes (Matthew 14 & 15 & Mark 8); g) resuscitated Lazarus (John 11-38-44); and h) praised Mary for her lavish outpouring of love (John 12.1-8).[5] More than just coming to earth, Jesus was the consummate example of living out the gospel "in the flesh." His example is worth emulating and was affirmed, verified and

---

[5] While normal OVP protocol requires all Bible referenced to be cited by a footnote, in-text biblical references are employed here for easier reading and to conserve the space taken by multiple footnotes.

subsequently expanded by His Disciples, the Apostles (like Paul) and ensuing generations of Christians.

B. Incarnational Missions - Based in The Acts of The Apostles

The four Gospels were then followed by Luke's inspired book - The Acts of the Apostles - which related how the early church incarnationally evangelized the world with the gospel of Jesus.

1. The Model of Barnabas, Paul and Others

The Apostle Paul began life as a man named Saul and lived in the same time and place as Jesus. Saul was a fervent adherent to, and defender of, traditional Jewish faith and tradition. Saul persecuted followers of Jesus and attempted to eradicate the growing movement Jesus inspired. What was it that changed Saul from his firmly established Jewish beliefs and life, to Paul, the man who planted more churches, mentored more early Christian leaders and wrote a large portion of the New Testament? His transformation was a direct result of Jesus appearing to him "in the flesh" while he was on the road to Damascus.[6] Thus, Paul understood from his own conversion experience the importance of the incarnation.

In addition, Paul was influenced by the mentors in his own life. Initially, Paul learned from Barnabas who modeled and taught him about incarnational, *Evangelistic-Disciplemaking*. Although Paul at times chaffed under Barnabas's leadership and eventually broke away from him, it became increasingly obvious how Paul grew to embrace and emulate Barnabas' model more and more each successive year of his ministry. For it was Barnabas who went "in the flesh" to seek Paul out,[7] and it was Barnabas who continued modeling incarnational ministry for Paul over the course of their first missionary journey together.[8]

It should be of little surprise therefore, that Paul became the consummate example of going "in the flesh" to cities throughout the world to live out, as well as preach, the good news of Jesus Christ. His example followed the model of his main mentor Barnabas who, in turn, learned incarnational ministry from his Savior Jesus. Paul incarnationally engaged individuals, leading many of them into a personal relationship with Jesus such as Timothy; and he relationally mentored fellow gospel workers such as Titus, Luke and many others.[9]

Paul was also open to receiving incarnational mentorship from people like Aquila and Priscilla who opened up their lives and home as an oasis of retreat, renewal and restoration for their weary gospel missionary friend. Their mentorship is perhaps best observed from the fact that it was only after dialoguing around their table and leatherworking shop that Paul began to talk about "going to Rome." Whereas Rome was an anathema to all committed Jews, nonetheless

---

6   Acts 9.1-22.
7   Acts 11.25.
8   Acts 12.25-15.35.
9   Consult with the lists of these people Paul mentions at the end of many of his Epistles.

Paul heeded the wisdom of Aquila and Priscilla as they shared a vision for how, if the gospel could take root in this most influential city of the world; Rome would make world evangelism possible.

Paul not only modeled an incarnational approach to ministry but he also taught it. Perhaps the most powerful text in this regard is found in I Corinthians 9 where Paul teaches incarnational outreach. Paul's Holy-Spirit-inspired-writings have reverberated through the millennia: "to the Jews, I became a Jew... to the weak I became weak...I have become all things to all people that by all means I might save some."[10] This teaching takes on a much deeper poignancy and significance when the next few verses provide a powerful case in point. By using a sporting analogy in verses 24-27, Paul models that sport can qualify as one of the myriad "all means" used to "save some;" giving a powerful apologetic and rationale for incarnational sports-based outreach.

Thus, the model of Jesus, Barnabas, Paul and others of the early Church all share a common foundation: incarnational ministry on a mission; a model of ministry that "incarnates" the gospel by going into the world with a mission of seeking and saving those who are lost. Missional ministry "goes" in the flesh.

C. Incarnational Missions - Based in the Epistles

The book of Acts was followed by a series of Epistles (letters) that communicated how to believe on, live like, and share Jesus. For the purposes of this book we will focus on one such passage found in the Epistle to the Colossians.

1. Incarnational Missions - A Colossian Model

There are a number of passages in various Epistles that speak to mission; to reaching those far from Jesus and His Church. A common philosophical theme in all of them centers on the missiological truth of "fleshing out" the gospel (incarnational *Evangelistic-Disciplemaking).* The following missiological discussion will be based on a passage found in Colossians chapter 4.

> Continue steadfastly in prayer, being watchful in it with thanksgiving. At the same time, pray also for us, that God may open to us a door for the word, to declare the mystery of Christ, on account of which I am in prison – that I may make it clear, which is how I ought to speak. Walk in wisdom toward outsiders, making the best use of the time. Let your speech always be gracious, seasoned with salt, so that you may know how you ought to answer each person.[11]

---

10   I Corinthians 9.19-23.
11   Colossians 4.1-6.

SCOREBOARD

Sports Ministry, The Ultimate Incarnational Tool

As I discuss in my book (*The Life of the Shoe: Sports Outreach for the World*), sports ministry allows a local church anywhere in the world to become incarnational as it steps outside of its walls to plant *Missional Sports Communities* through *Sports Parables*. This is based upon the belief that sport is a common language of the world. It can bring together a community, a country, or even the world. Many people of all ages watch, read about, or participate in sports on a regular basis. Maybe you have witnessed huge outdoor television screens being placed in public areas so people can join together to cheer on their team. Or perhaps you have been to a park or sports hall in your own community that is crowded with people enjoying basketball, soccer, running, exercising, skateboarding, climbing on a climbing wall or tower, or jumping on trampolines. Sports and recreation are everywhere.

It is time that congregations no matter their size stop depending on their facilities, or lack thereof, to reach their communities. The term *Missional-Communities* is now used by many organizations around the world to describe The Church's response to the current spiritual condition in the world. The basic concept is that believers need to get out of their local church buildings and into their neighborhoods with the gospel to live, serve, witness, and build community. In addition to the attractional model of expecting people to come to a worship service or other activity congregations are wise to encourage and empower their members to embrace the incarnational example of Jesus of "going to make disciples." The phrase *Missional-Sports-Communities* is now used to describe thriving sports ministry communities of people who are working together to be The Church as a visible witness for Jesus and establish an ongoing movement of *Evangelistic-Disciplemaking*.

While *Missional Sports Communities* are the incarnational response for taking The Church to the community, *Sports Parables* are a programmatic response to make the message of the gospel and discipleship incarnationally relevant. *Sports Parables* are following the model of how Jesus taught by creating word pictures through the use of cultural analogies that would have been familiar to His listeners. To add to this is the concept of "Redemptive Analogies" which was a term coined by missionary Don Richardson in his book *Peace*

SCOREBOARD

Sports Ministry, The Ultimate Incarnational Tool cont.

Child.* In 1962 Richardson and his family moved to what was then known as Dutch New Guinea to work among the Sawi tribe who were violent cannibalistic headhunters. Initially resistant to the Gospel, the tribe came to faith in Jesus as one village made peace with another after young children were exchanged among families from opposing villages. Richardson wrote: "If a man would actually give his own son to his enemies, that man could be trusted!" Richardson then used this analogy to explain that the Creator God did the same thing when He sent His Son, Jesus, God incarnate, to earth to make peace with (to redeem) humanity through his death and resurrection. Subsequently Richardson also promoted the idea that God has allowed Redemptive Analogies to exist hidden among primitive, unreached tribes and cultures throughout the world as way to contextualize the Gospel among them. To that end, sport analogies can be used to powerfully communicate the Gospel as they unlock the hidden Gospel truth in all cultures.

While SR&F in and of itself is not a Redemptive Analogy, the concept of using sport and fitness as relevant tools to share the gospel in every community, country, and culture throughout the world is one and the same whenever communicated through *Missional Sports Communities* and *Sports Parables*. Sports missions are the ultimate incarnational tool that God has given us to reach this generation with the gospel!

* Richardson, Don. *Peace Child: An Unforgettable Story of Primitive Jungle Treachery in the 20th Century*. Bloomington, MN: Bethany House Publishers, 2005. To further explore the concepts discussed here, consult with the Nxtmove organization (www.Nxtmove.nl) that has further developed this concept of *Missional Sports Communities* in The Netherlands and around the world and *The Life of the Shoe: Sports Outreach for the World*.

— *P. F. Myers, CSRM International Director*

This Colossian passage is built upon the missiological foundation of incarnating the gospel and provides both a philosophical structure and also suggests a methodological pragmatism that will mobilize, enable and empower effective gospel outreach. If incorporated into the DNA of local church SR&F outreach ministry and integrated into the individual lives of the leaders and participants of such ministries the applied principles offered in this passage can revolutionize the way SR&F outreach mission is done. It has a few basic components: a) praying for open doors - so the gospel can be heard (vv. 2-4); b) walking in wisdom - winning the right to be heard (v. 5a); c) redeeming the time - seeking a time so the gospel can be heard (v. 5b); d) engaging in gracious and seasoned conversation - how to be heard (v. 6a); e) answering each person - being heard (v. 6b).

a. Praying for Open Doors – To Empower Gospel Mission

All effective *Evangelistic-Disciplemaking* begins with, is undergirded with, and is empowered by the continuous prayers of believers. This is seen through a study of some of the words in Colossians 4.2-4.[12]

The word used for prayer (*proseuxe'*) is the normal word for going to, and communicating with God, and when combined with two other descriptive words the Holy Spirit's message is enhanced and made clear.

The first descriptive Greek word is *proskartereite* which communicates prayer is to be steadfast and continuous. The second descriptive word *gregorountes* communicates this prayer is to be watchful, attentive and vigilant.

---

12 All references to Greek word meanings come from *The Analytical Greek Lexicon Revised*. Edited by Harold K. Moulton. Grand Rapids, MI: Zondervan, 1982.

SCOREBOARD
Praying for Missions

Are the Prayers for your SR&F Mission...

- Habitual
- Regular
- Consistent
- Vigilant
- For Open Doors
- For Evangelists
- For Gospel Clarity

Thus the main thing being communicated is that prayer is necessary and to be offered for all outreach efforts. Rather than being a special or one time prayer, it is to be habitual, regular, consistent and vigilant.

The Holy Spirit wasn't done with the directions and mandates for prayer however. He believed prayer to be so vital, that He had Paul write a second directive about prayer in Colossians 4.3&4. These verses gave even more specific mandates. Not only was the Apostle Paul inspired to encourage the Colossians to pray consistently and diligently but also that their prayers should be strategic (for evangelistic doors to be opened) and directed (for specific evangelists and the clarity of their communication).

b. Walking in Wisdom – To Win the Right to Share the Gospel[13]

The second step in incarnational outreach ministry has to do with "walking in wisdom towards outsiders." This means not initially preaching at them.

Walking in wisdom is clear in and of itself but when combined with other passages the concept of incarnational ministry becomes ever more-clear.

> Give no offense….[14]

> Do all things without grumbling or disputing, that you may be blameless and innocent, children of God without blemish in the midst of a crooked and twisted generation, among whom you shine as lights in the world…[15]

> …aspire to live quietly and to mind your own affairs and to work with your hands, as we instructed you, so that you may walk properly before outsiders…[16]

> …be well thought of by outsiders…[17]

> Show yourself in all respects to be a model of good works, and in your teaching show integrity, dignity, and sound speech that cannot be condemned, so that an opponent may be put to shame, having nothing evil to say about us.[18]

---

13 I first learned of the "Winning the right to be heard" concept when I was on the urban Young Life Staff. The basic concept is that incarnational evangelism begins with developing relationships with those far from Jesus and His Church. A major tenet of winning the right to be heard is that the gospel can't be "preached" until it has first been lived out with such authenticity that it creates a willingness of those on the "outside" to listen to a verbal affirmation of the gospel.
14   1 Corinthians 10.32.
15   Philippians 2.14f.
16   1 Thessalonians 4.11f.
17   1 Timothy 3.7.
18   Titus 2.7f.

SCOREBOARD

"Walking in Wisdom"

Are we and our local church Sports Outreach missionaries.....

- Offensive
- Grumblers
- Disputers
- Blameless
- Innocent
- Children of God
- Without Blemish
- Lights in a Crooked World
- Living Quietly
- Minding our own Affairs
- Working with our Hands
- Walking Properly
- Well Thought of
- Models of Good Works
- Known for having Integrity
- Known for having Dignity
- Known for Sound Speech

If not, then…. let us each determine what needs to change!

After looking at this list, I fall far short of the goal and cannot "cast the first stone."[19] If we wonder why we personally, and our SR&F outreach ministry collectively, are not fulfilling our mission to reach those far from Jesus and His Church….incorporating this list into our lives would be the first step in rectifying the situation. Until we (me included) "walk in wisdom towards outsiders" we will not be effective or successful in our mission. Missiology starts when those who have been redeemed by Jesus begin to live like it.

c. Redeeming Time – To Live Out the Gospel

Living as redeemed people includes redeeming each and every moment, situation and opportunity the Lord graces us with. This Colossian passage continues with encouraging each of us to "make the best use of the time."[20] While this has many applications let us concentrate on just the following…

Applied corporately this would implore SR&F outreach missions to think strategically about the time of year, month, week and even the time of day to offer their ministries. It also would encourage strategic wisdom in how to conduct church services/meetings and how, what and when to preach on certain passages or topics. (See the Time Out Sidebar on Right Message on page 50.) To that end, there are four occasions that unchurched people are most likely to enter into a church building: weddings; funerals; and possibly Christmas and Easter.[21] Each

---

19   John 8.7.
20   Colossians 4.5.
21   While it is not a normal expectation that sports ministers will perform funerals, weddings or conduct or preach at Holiday services, they are encouraged to remind their senior pastors and service leaders to remember there may well be those who are in attendance who were invited by the SR&F outreach ministry and/or have no relationship with the congregation or Jesus.

of these afford congregational leaders the opportunity to "make the best use of the time" by preparing liturgies; eulogies; music; testimonies and messages that are encouraging, uplifting and inspiring. It is wise to plan each element of each of these services with the unchurched in mind.

Applied personally the concept of redeeming the time has many manifestations. Daily prayer for those who are far from Jesus and His Church (see point "a" above) is a must and "walking in wisdom" (point "b") entails avoiding any kind of activity, associations or involvements that are open to misinterpretation. It also includes actions and activities that communicate concern, love and thoughtfulness such as gifts, phone calls and invitations to socialize.

Investing in initiating and deepening relationships always redeems the time. SR&F outreach ministers are encouraged to model this by personally engaging in "walking in wisdom towards those without" and also urged to encourage all their SR&F volunteer missionaries and participants to do the same.

d. Engaging in Gracious and Seasoned Conversation – To be Able to Discuss the Gospel

So you and your SR&F outreach ministry volunteers and participants have engaged in the first steps of an incarnational outreach by praying for open doors, walking in wisdom towards those without, and actively redeeming the time by initiating and deepening relationships with those who are far from Jesus and His Church. Now comes a major opportunity to communicate the gospel through our speech. Yet, surprisingly enough this reference to speech does not mean we are to talk about our faith! In fact it's just the opposite. It's more often what we don't say that truly expresses our faith! Not talking about our faith is one of the most overlooked and underappreciated ways Christians have to express their faith.

"What?" You may ask… "Are you saying I'm being a witness by not saying anything about faith." Yes, but think it through. There are two ways in which "not saying anything" works to "open doors" for the gospel.

First, you communicate an authentic and sensitive love for your friend or family member by not verbally "forcing" your faith and religious beliefs on those who aren't yet wanting to hear anything about "religion." This cannot be undervalued. You will create a warm, welcoming and receptive heart if you wait until your friends and family members are ready to hear the gospel.[22]

Second, the "what isn't said" also refers to the actual words and language you don't use and/or the content you don't engage in! I believe you'll find you'll have a far greater impact if your conversations are winsome, upbeat, encouraging and non-profane. So yes, what you don't say can often be more of a witness than

---

22 In essence this is an outworking of identifying the Person of Peace as outlined in Chapter 8 of P. F. Myers book *The Life of the Shoe: Sports Ministry for the World.*

TIMEOUT

Right Message – Wrong Time

I once attended a Christmas Eve Service at a local church that was a committed Bible-believing, Christ-centered and demonstratively loving community. The service was upbeat, even joyous and engaging but then….there was the sermon.

The sermon was on stewardship and giving financially to the church. The pastor explained Christmas was the perfect time to talk about stewardship because it was at Christmas that God gave us the greatest gift of all.

Most of the regular attenders understood and yet had very uncomfortable conversations after the service with their unchurched loved ones who had attended what they thought was a Christmas service rather than a fund raising event!

---

what you do say. (See the Side Bar Time Out on page 53).

It's important to remember you are still "winning the right to be heard" and to rush any verbal gospel presentations is often counter-productive. Keep in mind that until someone is ready to hear the gospel, the gospel still needs to be proclaimed by what and how you live and love; and this is often communicated more so by what you don't do or say. Yes, giving verbal affirmations of the gospel is important but first comes what you don't say….or better understood, how you communicate and talk gets the attention of those you are reaching out to because it is absent of all the negative, profane and crass words, topics and dialogues… and is "gracious and seasoned with salt." So, each of us must ask if our conversations and language are in fact: "seasoned." (See the Side Bar Scoreboard "Seasoned Language" on page 51)

In general, the main point here is that before we can talk about our faith, our faith should already have been communicated by what and how we talk, and sometimes more so by what and how we don't talk. Any forthcoming evangelistic conversation is dependent on whether or not our previous words and conversations have been winsome, wholesome and enjoyable. If "those who are without" don't generally enjoy conversing with us they will certainly be much less likely to engage with us in the final step of incarnational outreach. They will be much less likely to ask us any questions about our faith if they don't see anything about our faith that is worth asking about!

SCOREBOARD

"Seasoned Language"

Are our words and conversations....	Or are they...
• Honoring	• Profane
• Uplifting	• Critical
• Encouraging	• Discouraging
• Affirming	• Disheartening
• Inspiring	• Condemning
• Enjoyable	• Depressing

e. Answering Each Person – To be Able to Explain the Gospel

So we come to that last stage of incarnational mission: answering questions that are asked of us by those we are "walking in wisdom" and "redeeming the time" with. This is the ultimate goal and hope of incarnational Christian missions: to be able to answer the questions being asked by those who are far from Jesus and His Church. Paul's admonition in Colossians chapter 4 to be ready to answer those who ask us questions concerning matters of faith is affirmed by The Apostle Peter who also received Holy Spirit inspiration to write about incarnational mission as seen in the following passage.

> But in your hearts honor Christ the Lord as holy, always being prepared to make a defense to anyone who asks you for the hope that is in you, yet do it with gentleness and respect... 1 Peter 3.15

To better understand being "always prepared to make a defense to anyone who asks you for the hope that is in you," stop and reflect a moment...

Generally speaking, are you more engaged, interested and attentive to what another person is saying to you when: a) they are trying to convince you of something that you have no interest in; or b) when you asked them to explain something to you and/or when you've asked their opinion or insight about something? Now apply this to your desire to share the gospel with someone. Those whom you've been praying for, and been lovingly building ever deepening relationships with, are no different. They may tolerate an unsolicited "sermon" from you about your faith but when they ask your advice, insight or wisdom about something, they will be much more open.

This specific point and this entire chapter are best understood by the phrase

Proclamation-Affirmation that is a concept that coined by Jim Peterson in his book *Living Proof.*

Proclamation – Affirmation[23] is the term that describes the missional process of "incarnating the gospel" and it is imperative that local church SR&F outreach ministers (and all whom they equip[24]) will have prayed, lived, worked and conversed in such ways so as to "proclaim" the gospel by who they are and what they do; all with the hope and goal to be able to verbally "affirm" the gospel in words. That verbal affirmation is best received by those far from Jesus and His Church when it is an answer to a question.

You might say however: "Well what if no one ever asks me a question?" I offer three responses…

The first response has to do with the possibility that the reason you never get asked a question about your faith is because you have no meaningful relationship with anyone who is currently far from Jesus and His Church. If this be the case, then it's high time to see who it is you are positioned to reach and begin a mission to build an ever deepening relationship with them.

The second response is, perhaps the reason you're never asked a question about your faith is because you haven't lived out an authentic faith that is intriguing, inspiring or interesting enough for others to make such inquiries. If this be the case, it would warrant an introspective assessment of your life. If this be the case, may God empower you and me to live our faith in such warm and winsome ways so as to attract questions.

The third response is that you may in fact have been asked a question but you missed it because you didn't recognize it as a faith related question! In fact we shouldn't expect to receive questions that are directly related to our faith. Yes, there may be a time when someone will ask you the same question the Philippian jailer asked Paul: "What must I do to be saved;"[25] but don't expect such a direct question very often, if at all. You may be slightly more likely to be asked a question like the one Philip received from the Ethiopian Eunuch who had been reading the Bible,[26] but even this kind of inquiry will be rare because the Ethiopian's questions came about because he was reading the Bible, and most unchurched people don't even have a Bible; let alone read it. The encouraging thing about this story is that Philip's answers to the Ethiopian's questions resulted in Philip leading the Eunuch to faith in Jesus, and…wait for it…baptizing him!

---

23 This concept is found in Jim Peterson's books entitled *Church Without Walls* and *Living Proof.* For a deeper understanding of the Proclamation-Affirmation transferable concept and its application to SR&F outreach ministry I recommend the fifth chapter, especially page 58, of the second book in *The Institutes of Sports Outreach – The Fundamentals of Sports Outreach.* Also, consult the Glossary of this book.

24 This equipping is based upon what is referred to as the *3-I's* of CSRM: *Inform* (share the basic information of missional work); *Instruct* (teach and train missional work); *Inspire* (model, mentor and motivate missional work).

25 Acts 16.25-40.

26 Acts 8. 26-40.

TIMEOUT

Muscular Christianity Models
It's What They Didn't Say

George Williams was the founder and lifelong heart of the YMCA. At age 13 he was apprenticed to a "draper" (textile worker). The man he was apprenticed to and all of his fellow employees made a great impression on the young George....

One of the first things George Williams became aware of was that all of his fellow workers were "religious" and attended church weekly but what made the biggest impression on him was their language! To be clear, it was not what they said but rather what they didn't say that impressed him! Their language was affirming rather than critical and completely void of any profanity

George committed his life to the Lord while employed at the draper's shop, largely because he witnessed authentic faith being lived out by his fellow workers whose conversations were always gracious and "seasoned with salt."

George went on to found and lead one of the greatest and most effective evangelistic ministries the world has ever seen (the YMCA)... and it all started by what they didn't say!

This is an excerpt from the unpublished and forthcoming book by Dr. Greg Linville: *Sports Ministry Pioneers: 19th Century Models for 21st Century Sports Outreach*. This one is from the chapter entitled – The Founder of a Movement

SCOREBOARD
Questions that "open a door"

What follows are the kind of questions a Christian who is on a mission to bring salvation to others might anticipate hearing.

- How did you keep your cool during that heated game?
- Why didn't you knock that guy's head off?
- What's the secret to a happy marriage?
- How come I've never seen you drunk?
- My kid's driving me nuts! What can I do?
- How come I never hear you curse? Don't you ever get mad?
- Why do you always go to church?
- I just lost my job....what should I do?

"Go into all the world....making disciples....and baptizing them...."

So yes, you might be asked direct questions about faith, especially after a relationship with a non-believer has matured over many years, but it's much more likely for the questions to be about more "earthly" concerns. Such questions may include those found in the Questions that "open a door" Scoreboard above and such questions typically don't directly ask about faith in Jesus. Nonetheless, such questions are the answer to all the prayers for "open doors."

When these earthly questions are asked it is wise to initially respond with understandable "earthly" answers rather than immediately launching into incomprehensible theological verbiage. Yes, at some point biblically-based concepts are important to communicate but being able to use words, analogies and metaphors that are understood by all are far more important; especially in the initial stages of such conversations.

For example, when asked about how to keep calm during a highly competitive game it is wise to be vulnerable and share it's not always easy for you and such calmness only comes after years of practice. Also, sharing a couple of pragmatic, earthly "how-to's"...like: "I take a deep breath," or "I don't say one word to a person until I've said a few in prayer to God," is advised. However, it's also appropriate to say something like: "I'm only able to remain calm because of the strength that comes from God." The main point is to be as Peter wrote: "always being prepared to make a defense to anyone who asks you for the hope that is in you, yet do it with gentleness and respect."[27]

---

27   1 Peter 3.15.

f. Summary of a Colossian Model of Incarnational Mission

So, the summary of the entire incarnational mission process found in the Epistle to the 1st Century church of Colosse is still extremely relevant and practical for the 21st Century Church. The process suggested by this passage consists of: i) consistent, vigilant and continuous prayer for "open doors;" ii) years (more than likely) of "walking in wisdom;" iii) strategically "making the most of the opportunities;" iv) many, many, "gracious" and "seasoned" conversations;" and v) being ready to share "the hope that is in us!"

After having proclaimed the gospel with our lives we stand ready to offer a verbal defense and affirmation of the gospel. Even though it might take years for a person to come to faith in Jesus, SR&F outreach ministry provides its local church "missionaries" opportunities to proclaim their faith through sports leagues, recreational activities and/or fitness and wellness classes. The hope is the proclamation of the gospel through incarnational outreach[28] will eventually result in SR&F missionaries having a chance to verbally affirm their faith to anyone who is inquisitive about Jesus. Does this describe your SR&F outreach ministry mission model? If not, read on for ongoing discussion and proposals.

II. Summary of Biblical Principles - Incarnational Missions

The incarnational approach for SR&F outreach missions really comes down to three basic words: go; dwell and love. Go to those who are far from Jesus, dwell (live) in their world and while dwelling there, love them as Jesus would. When the gospel is lived out in loving ways it is irrepressible, undeniable and irresistible. An acquaintance may start in a fitness class or on a softball team. From there, hopefully, a friendship will begin that eventually grows into a deeper relationship in which the gospel can be lived out and become real to someone who has yet to accept Jesus as their Lord and Savior. Participating in a church's sport, recreation and fitness programs is the way to begin to incarnate the gospel; continued involvement and deepening relationships enables the gospel to be understood and received.

The Quaker approach to "going and making disciples" offers helpful insight. The technical terms they use to explain their evangelistic approach is not to "coerce," but rather "convince." To coerce means to pressure people into praying a prayer to become a Christian; whereas to convince means taking the time to engage in "gracious" and "seasoned" conversations. It is believed that such gospel conversation and interactions are more effective in producing life-long Dedicated-Disciples. Furthermore, the Quakers encourage "evangelists" to not be deceived into equating the power of the gospel preacher with the power of the gospel itself.

---

28   What is referred to in this book series as the *3-R-Model (Repeated, Redemptive and Relational)*.

TIME OUT

Surrounded by Witnesses
George Williams

Little notice was taken when George Williams was born October 11, 1821 the youngest of 8 sons to a farming family in Somerset, England. Williams has fared little better in the 21st century as few take notice of him now. He lived an obscure & nondescript life through his early teen years and obscurity has returned as he has faded from recognition again. While quite well known in England during the latter half of the 19th century - including being Knighted by Queen Victoria in 1884 on the 50th anniversary of the founding of the YMCA - Williams is not currently recognized nor does he receive his just due for his role in pioneering the methodologies which are the heart and soul of most sports-related, para-ministries and local church SR&F outreach ministries since then. Moreover, his influence is wielded far beyond sports ministries and can be detected in nearly every para-ministry that exists today. While those who serve in ministry at the beginning of the third millennium probably don't recognize the name of George Williams and certainly cannot articulate his contributions to ministry, there are few people who have had more of an influence upon ministry, evangelistic efforts and society in general. This obscure farm boy and his ministry principles need to be revisited by anyone engaged in SR& F outreach ministry, or any other ministry for that matter; in the 21st century and beyond

George Williams was the founder and lifelong heart of the YMCA. Early in life he realized reaching men for Christ took time. He wrote to one of the secretaries explaining bringing one man to Christ was the result of one good year's work. He practiced long term relationships with people, preferring to win them to Christ no matter how long it might take. One must remember during the 60+ years George Williams was the driving force behind the YMCA he remained a full time businessman. Not only did the YMCA become

TIMEOUT

Surrounded by Witnesses
George Williams

a worldwide organization under his leadership, but in addition his business was extremely profitable. Part of the reason for this was George worked incredibly long hours and seemed to have an inexhaustible supply of energy, yet when asked the secret to his being successful in both the business and the YMCA, he responded that he managed the men who managed the business. He learned early on to depend upon the II Timothy 2.2 principle of surrounding yourself with reliable men and this was as much a reason for his success as anything else.

This is an excerpt from the unpublished and forthcoming book by Dr. Greg Linville: *Sports Ministry Pioneers: 19th Century Models for 21st Century Sports Outreach*. This one is from the chapter entitled – The Founder of a Movement

SECTION 2: The Theological, Philosophical, Historical and Biblical Foundations of Missiology

Chapter 6

Missiological Foundations for SR&F Outreach Ministry

I. Definitions and Explanations - 60
   A. Vision, Mission, Strategies, Activities, Outcomes - 60
   B. Vision - Mission Illustration - 63
   C. Missiology Redefined - 64
   D. Missiology's Underlying Premise - 64

II. The Current Missiological Model of Sports Outreach - 66
   A. Mega-Models: Featuring Platform-Proclamation - 66
   B. Repetitive-Redemptive-Relational (3-R-Model) - 66

III. Local Mission Redefined - 67
   A. Redefining Coaches - 68
      1. Volunteers or Missionaries – 69
   B. Redefining SR&F Outreach Ministry - 70
      1. Local Missions in a Post-Christian World - 71
      2. Local Mission in a Post-Secular World - 72

IV. Summary of Missiological Foundations - 73

SCOREBOARD

Vision / Mission Template

Vision: States the goal / purpose

Mission: Identifies the general effort needed to accomplish the goals and purpose of the vision

Strategy: Describes the master plan of the mission

Output: Outlines the specific activities that are employed to carry out the strategies

Outcome: Assesses the end result that either affirms or denies the vision was accomplished

> "How true it is that if a Christian ceases to be evangelistic, sooner or later he will cease to be Evangelical"*
>
> John R. Mott

* Mott, *Confronting Young Men with the Living Christ*, p. 35

I. Definitions and Explanations

A number of terms will be used in this and other chapters. Establishing working definitions of them will ease comprehension and application of the subject matter. Understanding the following set of terms will enable SR&F outreach ministers to be better prepared to know how to define mission, mission success and also how to attain it.

A. Vision, Mission, Strategies, Activities, Outcomes[1]

Vision and Mission are often misunderstood and are often used interchangeably. They are also sometimes confused with strategies and/or activities. The following definitions will provide a common language and a unified approach to comprehend and apply a basic organizational structure for effective mission. They will reinforce the vital importance of understanding the tenets of missiology as well as give clear guidance for what congregations can do to accomplish their Great Commission goals.

Vision is best explained by the word accomplishment. It is a noun that names or describes people, places and things. It is not a verb which describes an action or activity. So for the purposes of this chapter, vision describes intended results; not effort or activity. A vision is what is seen at the completion of a mission; not what is done during the mission. A vision also suggests what a ministry should evaluate in terms of determining the effectiveness of its endeavors.[2] To use a nautical metaphor, vision describes the shore being sailed to. Using a building metaphor, vision describes the blueprints of a facility that is envisioned to be erected. Vision essentially defines and describes what the mission hopes to accomplish and/or the reason it exists.

Mission is best explained by a comprehensive and united effort towards the meeting of a goal (vision). It is a verb that describes action or activity, and it is not a noun that describes accomplishment. A mission is the effort that brings about the accomplishment of a vision. Returning to the sailing metaphor, mission describes the comprehensive effort to move the ship towards its ultimate goal. Returning again to the building metaphor, mission describes the actual overall effort to bring the blue prints into the reality of erecting the facility. Mission is essentially the ongoing process of accomplishing the purpose/vision of the ministry.

By establishing a clear vision and mission, a congregation or ministry is able

---

1 I owe a great deal of my understanding of Vision, Mission and Strategies etc. to my dear friend Jay Martin. Jay served as a personal and professional consultant to me and CSRM, and it was his insights and wisdom that revolutionized my thinking. In addition, it was through Jay's catalytic influence that CSRM has been empowered to equip local church SR&F outreach ministers throughout the world with gospel-centric, local-church-based, *Methodological-Models*! While I take full responsibility for any errors or any misapplication of the principles Jay shared with us, Jay deserves all the credit for all the positives that have resulted from our time spent together.

2 The term used in this series of books for evaluating mission effectiveness is *Success-Statistics*. For a full explanation read pages 32-34 and 55-84 in *The Saving of Sports Ministry: The Soteriology of Sports Ministry* book.

TIMEOUT

Muscular Christianity Models
Maintaining Evangelistic-Missionary Character

"If the Young Men's Christian Association is to increase its spiritual vitality and fruitfulness, it must maintain at all costs its distinctively Christian, pronouncedly evangelistic and aggressively missionary character . . . . it must preserve its clear Christian aim, its unshakable Christian foundation, and its genuinely Christian control; that it must hold in proper prominence its Christian program and be animated by a genuinely Christians spirit. The (YMCA) Association must steadfastly resist the danger of becoming a mere human institution - in a general sense religious but not emphatically, pervasively, and contagiously Christian. This essential must never be compromised, obscured, or abandoned for the sake of any plausible outward success or worldly advantage; for such a course would mark the beginning of the end. Wherever an Association lacks world-conquering power, it is because it has to some extent been conquered by the world."*

---
*John R. Mott, *Confronting Young Men with the Living Christ*, p.72f.

---

to know: *Why* they do what they do; *Where* they are going; and ultimately *What* they are to do. The next step is to determine strategies for organizing a mission that effectively reaches those far from Jesus and His Church.[3]

Strategy is best explained as a plan to execute a mission for the purpose of achieving a desired goal/vision. Strategy is a noun that describes and defines a verb. It describes a plan; in fact, a master plan. Such a master plan determines the most pragmatic, efficient and relevant engagement of all resources that will best ensure/assure the mission accomplishes the overall vision. Nautically speaking, strategy refers to determining what would be the best mode of propelling the ship to its intended shore. Such propulsion could be powered by oar, wind, engines or even by swimming. Referring to building, strategy asks if the facility should be made of brick, stone, wood or steel and should it be erected by hand

---
3 A well-formed set of *Level #1 Theological-Truths* will inform, guide and shape biblically-based, *Level #2 Philosophical-Principles* from which *Strategically-Relevant* and Efficiently-Effective, *Level #3 Methodological-Models* can emerge. The organizational structures of *Philosophical-Principles* (*Why, When, Where, With Whom*) are defined and explained more fully in the third chapter of the second book in this series: *Sports Ministry Fundamentals*.

TIMEOUT

Surrounded by Witnesses
Maintaining a Personal Experience of Jesus

"If the (YMCA) Association Movement is to preserve and augment its spiritual vitality, it is absolutely essential that its leaders and controlling members maintain a genuinely personal experience of Jesus Christ . . . the character and spirit of any movement rests ultimately with its leaders. It does not rise or maintain itself above the level of the hidden life that is the real life, of its leaders and guiding members."*

*John R. Mott, *Confronting Young Men with the Living Christ*, p.74f.

---

or power tools. Strategy is essentially concerned with relevance, efficiency and pragmatics…all with an overall goal to empower and ensure effectiveness.

Outputs/Activity is best explained as the implementation of the individual endeavors of the strategy. Activity is a verb that describes a specific endeavor of the overall mission. Sometimes called outputs, activities describe basic actions to accomplish the master plan. So, to keep the metaphorical imagery going…if wind power is envisioned to be the most *Efficiently-Effective* strategy to "reach the shore" (accomplish the vision), then the subsequent activities are those that have to do with choosing, hoisting and adjusting sails that will maximize the wind to move the vessel towards its chosen destination. Keeping with the building metaphor, strategy refers to the digging of the footers; pouring cement; constructing walls; installing plumbing, heating and cooling; and covering it all with a roof. Activity is essentially concerned with the specific tasks called for in the strategy to accomplish the vision.

Outcome is best explained as the cumulative end result of all the individual activities. Outcome is a noun that describes what actually occurred or came into existence as a result of the mission. Outcome is not what was hoped for but rather what actually happened. Keeping with the nautical theme…the outcome is: either the ship actually got to the shore or it didn't. As to the building metaphor, either the facility was completed or it wasn't. Thus essentially, the outcome is actually an evaluation…did all the activities work together to accomplish the original vision?

TIME OUT

Muscular Christian Models
Maintaining Spiritual Vitality

"Well may we ask ourselves, Are there evidences of vitality in us as leaders? Have we the abounding life: are men and boys being saved through us? . . . . Have we the quality of spiritual life and the habits for its maintenance which we would like to see reproduced among the youthful members throughout the Movement? Spiritual vitality comes only from the source of Spiritual Vitality Himself."*

---

*John R. Mott, *Confronting Young Men with the Living Christ*, p.75.

B. Vision-Mission Illustration

The Association of Church Sports and Recreation Ministers (CSRM) is a missiologically based para-ministry.[4] CSRM's **vision** is: a **changed life**. This **changed life** is best described as a person who is a growing disciple of Jesus; one who is continually growing in Christlikeness; and thus becoming a better Christian, spouse, parent/child, employer/employee, citizen, church member etc. CSRM's **mission** is to **equip and empower local churches** to be engaged in efforts to change lives. CSRM's **"4-C-Strategy** consists of: **Consulting; Credentialing; Connecting;** and **Conferencing**. CSRM's **activities/outputs** include specific actions to envision, plan for, organize, administrate and expedite any of the "4-C's." The intended **outcomes** would be congregational-based SR&F staff and volunteers who are equipped[5] to accomplish their Great Commission efforts (*changed lives* for Jesus). So CSRM's evaluates its effectiveness by charting how many congregations are equipped to change lives and how many are actually changing lives.[6]

Therefore, the guiding principle and ultimate goal for CSRM is to "see" the entire world "won" to Christ, and it is CSRM's intention to enhance, expand and

---

[4] See the Glossary for a definition of and the theological rationale for using para-ministry rather than para-church.

[5] CSRM understands there are three basic aspects necessary to fully mobilize and empower congregations for the equipping of their SR&F outreach missionaries. The first is to provide information, the second is to conduct instruction and the third is to engender inspiration. Thus the 3-I's of CSRM are: *Informed, Instructed* and *Inspired* local church missionaries.

[6] This would be what CSRM's *Success-Statistics* are based on. The most recent CSRM *Success-Statistics* revealed that the staff and volunteers of CSRM equipped 900+ churches during the year of 2019.

empower The Church and its congregations to accomplish its **vision** of winning all to Jesus Christ.

C. Missiology Redefined

Missiology, when fully understood, serves to enable churches, denominations and ministries to not only identify their vision, mission, strategies and activities, but more importantly empowers them to fulfill their Great Commission goals. This is because missiology is rooted in what scholars consider interdependent components that include:

- Theology - that provides biblical foundations for mission
- Social Sciences - that reveal the cultural, political, financial and psychological arenas of human existence into which Christian mission engages and penetrates
- Strategy - that envisions the most *Strategically-Relevant* and *Efficiently-Effective* philosophies and methodologies of mission[7]
- History - of how missions have been done in the past, and are currently being done; which are assessed and evaluated for the purpose of envisioning and engaging in long-lasting, significant mission work based on what is learned from the assessments and evaluations of previous mission endeavors

Thus, missiology can be summarized as The Church's endeavors to accomplish the Great Commission (which is the mandate and theological foundation for mission); as lived out through the Great Commandments (which is the moral/philosophical ethos and ethic for mission); and as understood and conceived of in the activities of the Apostles (which provides models and methodological examples of mission as observed in the book the Acts of the Apostles and gleaned from the subsequent Epistles of the Apostles). Thus, the rationale for; the means of; and the way to engage in missiology is biblically mandated, explained and expected. Yet, unless missiological endeavors are also envisioned through the lens of social science research and historical reflection, they will not be *Strategically-Relevant* or *Efficiently-Effective,* and therefore any Great Commission efforts not based in missiology will be extremely frustrating to all attempting to bring the "good news" of Jesus Christ to the world.

D. Missiology's Underlying Premise

Missiology assumes and is predicated upon the belief that people who do not receive Jesus as their personal Lord and Savior (become His disciples) will spend eternity separated from Him in what the Bible calls hell. This is the most com-

---

7   Johannes Verkuyl states, "Missiology's task in every age is to investigate scientifically and critically the presuppositions, motives, structures, methods, patterns of cooperation and leadership which the churches bring to their mandate."

TIMEOUT

Muscular Christian Models
Maintaining Purpose

"Let us summon our active members, one and all, to that most highly multiplying work, the introducing of men and boys to Jesus Christ."*

*John R. Mott, Confronting Young Men with the Living Christ, p.78.

pelling rationale for becoming engaged in any SR&F Outreach *Evangelistic-Disciplemaking* endeavors.

Thus, it naturally follows that any group, congregation, denomination, ministry, seminary, chaplain or individual that agrees with one of the following beliefs would not be compelled to engage in gospel-centric, *Evangelistic-Disciplemaking*:

- ✔ **Universalism** – a soteriology (theology of salvation) that believes all people go to heaven
- ✔ **Non-eternal-tormentism** – a belief that a loving God would not create an eternal hell
- ✔ **Agnosticism** - either...
  - ✔ **Atheistic-agnosticism** of not knowing if a God exists
  - ✔ **Theistic-agnosticism** which believes there is a God but doesn't know which religion's God is the true God
- ✔ **Atheism** - a belief that there is no God[8]

Christian mission is only important and compelling for those who believe: a) there is a God; b) there is a hell; and c) that hell is reserved for all who do not receive Jesus as Lord and Savior.[9]

However, one thing that can be agreed upon by all – even by Christians who don't believe in hell - is that unless the Christian Church reaches those outside itself, it is only one generation removed from extinction. So even if the perpetuation of The Church is the only motivation of some within Christianity, it still

---

8 It is not assumed that the latter two categories would fit within a Christian world view or be ascribed to by anyone in ministry. However there are both denominations and individuals who align with the first categories.
9 This is not stated with any relish or joy. It is not critical but rather analytical. If the Bible is correct, then the Great Commission is not only mandated but becomes the motivation for Christian mission.

would be cause for contemplating missiological concepts.

So then, what are the current missiological models being used in *The Sports Outreach Community*?

II. The Current Missiological Models of Sports Outreach

There are two current missiological strategies that pre-dominate *The Sports Outreach Community*: *Mega-Models* and the *3-R-Model*.

A. Mega-Models: Featuring Platform-Proclamation[10]

The two most popular *Evangelistic-Disciplemaking* strategies engaged in by *The SR&F Outreach Community* are based in mass evangelism.[11] Both are built upon the premise that the gospel is best presented via a verbal testimony or speech.[12] This often occurs at a large gathering[13] or through written or digital formats that are distributed to wide audiences.[14] The vast majority of such outreaches utilize the testimonies of "celebrity" athletes and coaches. In other words, the testimonies of elite athletes and coaches are shared by themselves or their stories are retold by other speakers and writers. These testimonies are communicated through live gatherings, written blogs, articles and books; or through an increasing array of audio-video/ digital formats.

For the most part, these initiatives are positive and can be a most effective tool for gospel-centric, *Evangelistic-Disciplemaking* endeavors. Caution is advised however if the only or primary model of outreach is based in these methodologies. The reason for the caution becomes obvious as this chapter and book unfold, but in essence the full implications of the gospel are impossible to communicate in a 10-30 minute *Mega-Event* or through a 300-word *Mega-Media* blog.

B. Repetitive-Redemptive-Relational (3-R-Model)

The second major way *The SR&F Outreach Community* engages in mis-

---

10   Mega-Models (*Mega-Event*; *Mega-Media*), the *3-R-Model* and *Platform-Proclamation* are all examples of *Level #2 Philosophical-Principles*, and are defined in the Glossary of this book. They are informed and shaped by *Level #1 –Theological-Truths*. In this case, if a *Level #1 Theological-Truth* of missiology believes that the most effective way to reach those far from Jesus and His Church is to "preach" the Word verbally, then the resultant organizational structure (*Philosophical-Principles*) will be to create *Mega-Model* opportunities for celebrity athletes and coaches to verbally share their faith either in live settings or through various media outlets. The reader is referred to previous and subsequent books in this series that explore the related *Sports Outreach Ologies* such as T*he Saving of Sports Ministry: The Soteriology of Sports Outreach*; *Putting The Church Back in the Game: The Ecclesiology of Sports Outreach*; and *The Christ of Sports Ministry: The Christology of Sports Outreach* (yet to be published) which all help to inform and guide the creation of the organizational structures of SR&F outreach ministry.

11   These are referred to in this book series as *Mega-Models*. The first is *Mega-Event* and the second is *Mega-Media*.

12   This is referred to in this book series as a *Platform-Proclamation* and is best defined as the delivery of a verbal or written communication of the gospel by an elite athlete or coach.

13   This is referred to in this book series as a *Mega-Event*.

14   This is referred to in this book series as *Mega-Media*. *Mega-Event* and *Mega-Media* are the "platforms" of *Platform-Proclamations*.

TIMEOUT

Muscular Christianity Models
Maintaining the Cross

"Movements and organizations, like men, must learn the deep meaning of the Cross and . . . . a life of self-denial."*

*John R. Mott, Confronting Young Men with the Living Christ, p.81.

sion-oriented, evangelistic efforts is best described as missional endeavors that focus on three main components: a) *Repetitive* activities that are…; b) *Redemptive* in purpose and are expressed in…; c) *Relational* endeavors. Rather than utilizing a *Mega-Model*, the *3-R-Model* seeks to use incarnational[15] models that enable and empower individual Christians to build ongoing relationships with those who are far from Jesus and His Church.

Another model is based on building and nurturing long term relationships and is a most positive and effective tool for gospel-centric, *Evangelistic-Disciplemaking* endeavors.[16] However, there is also a caution for anyone who only utilizes this model at the total exclusion of integrating the *Platform-Proclamation* models of *Mega-Event* or *Mega-Media*. *Mega-Models*, when properly envisioned, planned for and integrated with a *3-R-Model* into a holistic SR&F outreach ministry maximizes the strengths of both models.[17]

III. Local Mission Redefined

For many, the two words…"local" and…"mission" don't go together because the concept of mission always refers to some faraway place; somewhere overseas in another country. It is to this misunderstanding that this book and chapter now turn. It is believed that this redefinition may in fact be one of the most overlooked and underappreciated concepts for catalyzing Church growth and expansion… regardless of the continent, country or culture.

This chapter assumes that: a) the collective organization of Great Commission efforts of The Church (missions); b) the individual sacrifices and generosity of those who financially and prayerfully support the Great Commission efforts of

---

15 See chapter five of this book for an in depth explanation of incarnational ministry.
16 This is what is referred to in this book series as the *3-R-Model* that is based on *Repetitive, Redemptive, Relationships*.
17 Examples of this integration can be found in the proposals in Chapter 10 of this book.

the Church (missionary funders); and c) the personal ministries of those engaged in Great Commission efforts of The Church (missionaries); cannot be solely relegated to "foreign missions." Rather, the assumption of this chapter is: mission needs to be redefined to encompass all missional activity and would thus include both local missions as well as international (foreign) mission.

This redefinition is more fully understood when it is applied to specific SR&F staff and volunteers who serve in missional roles to a local geographic community.

A. Redefining Coaches

So, are the coaches in church leagues: a) sports volunteers; b) sports ministers; or c) sports missionaries? Your answer is?

One of the primary emphases of the redefinitions addressed in this chapter focuses on all who serve in the SR&F outreach mission of local churches or sports-related, para-ministries. More specifically, this chapter addresses how those who serve in the ministry are perceived and how they are to be related to.

A number of congregations and para-ministry groups such as FCA consider their staff to be "ministers"…but not all. This is easily determined by looking at the large numbers of churches and para-ministry groups that do not require any kind of ministerial training, accreditation or recognition for their SR&F outreach staff.[18] While some congregations and denominations may call them pastors and a few others entitle them sports ministers, many choose rather to give them the title of sports directors or fitness instructors. So taking this trend one step further, if not all SR&F staff members are designated as, or considered to be ministers, how much more true is it that those who are volunteer coaches, referees or league directors are not seen as being ministers…let alone missionaries?

So, what is being proposed here is that each SR&F staff person and all SR&F volunteers be redefined not only as ministers, but more to the point, as missionaries! Perceiving, designating and commissioning each staff member and all volunteers as missionaries is practically unheard of, and yet, that is exactly what they are: missionaries of the Gospel of Jesus Christ to a local unreached community. So it is well worth asking: "how would the Great Commission endeavors of congregations and ministries change if coaches were considered missionaries rather than volunteers?" The shift in the priority would move from winning games, to winning souls!

Just imagine the catalytic change in focus that would ensue if every coach in your local church sports outreach would understand what they do to be the work of a missionary, rather than being the coach of a team! (See the Scoreboard: "A Coach Is! on page 74)"

---

18 Most denominations use the word "ordained" for their clergy whereas the modern day Quakers (now known as Evangelical Friends) use the word "recorded." In addition, almost all denominations will also license staff members if they are not ordained or recorded.

1. Volunteers or Missionaries

Congregations and para-ministries that are willing to move beyond recruiting volunteers and embrace a new vision for attracting and deploying SR&F missionaries would be well served to consider the following changes.

Change in Purpose - It is imperative for all leagues, clinics, activities and fitness classes to move from solely seeking athletic success or physical health and fitness goals to dually seeking both athletic/fitness excellence but also achieving spiritual progress and growth for all participants. (Scoreboard: A Checklist on page 70)

Change in Recruiting – A change in recruiting may require only a subtle shift and yet there may not be a more important shift on this entire checklist. Rather than assuming any church member in good standing who has an athletic background to be a prime candidate for coaching a team in your sports ministry, it is recommended that the priority changes to seeking church members who are ordained by God and feel a call to mission as well as having a passion for sports.

Change in Terminology is necessary to shift the culture from sports activity, or even sports ministry, to sports missions. It is recommended for all league directors, fitness class instructors, recreation leaders and coaches to be called missionaries which not only elevates how they are viewed but more importantly motivates the individual to aspire to fulfill the ultimate goal of the mission they are engaged in.

Change in Training – The change in training moves from being solely focused (or primarily focused) on sport-specific strategies and insights to equipping all local sports missionaries in: a) how to initiate and engage in gospel-centric, conversations; b) how to lead a person into a personal relationship with Jesus; and c) how to begin the discipling process; among other needed aspects of the mission. Notice, this mission training is an addition to, rather than a replacement for, sports or fitness related training. While it is imperative to add the spiritual training to the athletic training, unless both are present, neither will be effective.

Change in Recognition – The move to call a volunteer a local missionary goes beyond a name change. It begins by initiating a formal commissioning service of all sports missionaries in ways that are similar to the commissioning of Sunday School teachers, youth ministry leaders and elders etc. but also includes ongoing private and public communications of expectations as well as affirmations about the spiritual progress being made.

Change in Accountability – Accountability is another area where something is added, not subtracted. Wherever assessments and evaluations are made, it is important to include reports on spiritual activities along with the traditional reports on the number of teams, players, practices and athletic or fitness

SCOREBOARD
Local Church Sports Outreach Missionaries: A Checklist

- ✔ **Change in Purpose and Goals**
  - ✔ Maintaining dual objectives
    - ✔ Spiritual growth
    - ✔ Athletic excellence & physical health
- ✔ **Change in Recruiting**
  - ✔ Recruiting mission-minded, sports-people
  - ✔ Rather than sports-minded, Christians
- ✔ **Change in Terminology**
  - ✔ From: League director, coach or fitness instructor
  - ✔ To: Sport and fitness missionary
- ✔ **Change in Training/Equipping**
  - ✔ Maintain all sports-related, strategies and insights
  - ✔ Add *Evangelistic-Disciplemaking* strategies and insights
- ✔ **Change in Recognition**
  - ✔ Regular times for public commissioning
- ✔ **Change in Accountability**
  - ✔ Require weekly/monthly/yearly reports on
    - ✔ Spiritual conversations
    - ✔ Conversions
    - ✔ Traditional worship attendance
    - ✔ Small group/Bible study attendance

activities. This would include recording how many conversations were engaged in that had specific spiritual content and/or if anyone prayed to receive Jesus as Lord and Savior; or if anyone committed to attending a traditional worship service or small group Bible study.

Change Summary - Perhaps the single-most important change a local church or sports-related, para-ministry could make to enhance and expand their *Evangelistic-Disciplemaking* efforts would begin to recognize, train, and treat all staff, league directors, coaches and instructors as missionaries and expect them to fulfill their mission as such.

B. Redefining SR&F Outreach Ministry

The second redefinition that is needed is SR&F Outreach itself. Historically, local church sponsored leisure and recreation pursuits were originally seen as a way to provide health, fitness and/or recreation to congregational members for

CHAPTER 6: Missiological Foundations for SR&F Outreach Ministry   71

health or fellowship purposes.[19] A few decades later, in response to the desire to ramp up the spiritual development side of such activities, such endeavors became known as sports and recreation ministry.[20] More recently such ministries have often been further re-envisioned, and thus re-titled as sports outreach as many churches embraced a more intentional focus on reaching those outside of The Church.

These attempts to transform programs and facilities into more gospel-centric endeavors are to be applauded. However what is being advocated by this book takes yet a further step in that progression by redefining all such efforts as: mission; sport, recreation and fitness oriented mission. The primary rationale for this has to do with how all such activity and effort will empower more effective *Evangelistic-Disciplemaking* and thus fulfill The Great Commission mandate. Such SR&F outreach efforts will become more effective if envisioned, planned for, organized, administrated and conducted as a mission rather than as an activity; program; ministry; or even an outreach.[21]

However, as exciting and strategic as the proposed change to make SR&F more missional, such mission-driven, Great Commission endeavors are marching towards a head on collision with a world that is increasingly antagonistic and even hostile to anything Christian. Just when The Church begins to contemplate SR&F as a mission, the world culture has changed again.

1. Local Missions in a Post-Christian World

Since the first century A.D.[22] the world became increasingly Christian (at least in culture) as evidenced by such things as the change in name from the Roman Empire to the Holy Roman Empire. This progress of a Christian culture continued well into a second millennia but was derailed in the West by the shifting winds of, among other things, the Enlightenment; all of which eventually led to increasing secularism.

Christian culture also experienced ongoing confrontations (sometimes

---

19   A good example of this, and possibly the first book for Church Recreation, was T. B. Maston's classic: *A Handbook for Church Recreation Leaders*. Nashville: Sunday School Board of the Southern Baptist Convention, 1937, which was released over 80 years ago.

20   Bob Sessom wrote a number of books that focused on recreation ministry including: (with Carolyn Sessom) *52 Complete Recreation Programs For Senior Adults -1979*; (with E.O. Harbin) *The New Fun Encyclopedia Set: A Guide to Using Sports and Games in the Life of the Church – 1976*; and *The Volunteer Coach – 1978*. (See Works Consulted for complete entries).

21   While maximizing sport, recreation and fitness activities for gospel ends, it must be noted that sport is not biblically justified because it can be used as a tool for evangelism or discipleship. Sport is, in and of itself, intrinsically and inherently biblically justifiable. For a more in depth consideration of these concepts, see the first book in this Institutes of Sports Outreach book series: Linville, Greg. *Christmanship: A Theology of Competition and Sport*.

22   The use of A. D. exhibits an editorial core value of Overwhelming Victory Press (OVP) to use the traditional designation of historic dates (B. C. = Before Christ and A. D. = Anno Domini = in the year of our Lord). This represents OVP's commitment to honor the Incarnation of Jesus Christ as the dividing marker of human history on earth. Even this discussion about dating is a proof in and of itself of the dilemma discussed here…a world that is becoming ever more resistant and even hostile to anything to do with Jesus.

deadly, i.e.: The Crusades) with Eastern philosophies and religions. This "post-Christian" culture struck first in Continental Europe, swept through England, Canada, Australia and New Zealand and America. At first, even when personal piety was waning, a mutated Christian social piety remained culturally intact. In other words, much of Western culture remained largely within an overall Christian ethic even though many individuals stopped practicing their faith and no longer personally held to a Christian ethic.

During this most recent era, SR&F outreach ministries were still respected and appreciated, and gospel-centric activities remained in high esteem. This esteem was evidenced by the fact that many secularized, non-churched individuals continued to participate in local church sports leagues, FCA sports camps, congregational sponsored fitness classes and/or camps that operated in a Christian ethic and for evangelistic purposes.

An interesting phenomena occurred however. Secularism replaced Christianity as the prevailing cultural structure for Western society (and much of the East as well). This social phenomenon moved the needle away from respecting and valuing a Christian ethic and culture into an ever deepening non-toleration of anything to do with Jesus.

However, a most interesting trend became more and more evident. Many of those who abandoned their Christian faith and embraced secularism soon discovered total secularism didn't answer their meta-physical[23] questions and longings.

Such people while resolute in their rejection of religion eventually recognized they still had spiritual questions, needs, concerns and passions. The result was that much of the West had come to a place where not only were its people "post-Christian," but also had become "post-secular," and subsequently began to embrace a humanistic-based, spiritualism to fill the void. This shift is currently in full view as the "New Age" world of crystals, séances, and non-Christian meditation is being increasingly experienced and embraced. Regardless of the reasons or evidences, the so-called Christian world gave way to secularism, and secularism is now giving way to spiritualism, the end result is it all now poses a glaring question for The Church in general, and specifically for SR&F outreach mission: how to engage in local mission in a post-secular world.

2. Local Mission in a Post-Secular World

Whereas, *Evangelistic-Disciplemaking* strategies morphed during the post-Christian era, it now enters into a new chapter to know how to best engage the Western post-secular world. In other words, what is important to ascertain is how to envision a mission to those who have rejected the Christian religion but

---

23 Metaphysical is defined as referencing anything beyond the physical, anything concerning first principles, issues of being, and or ultimate purpose for life.

who have also rejected a secular worldview and replaced it with a humanistic spiritualism.

There is both a "pro" and a "con" to this new post-secular reality. The pro has to do with the general population once again being open and receptive to many things "Christian" where Christianity is "spiritual." This pro has a striking caveat however. The true "spiritualist" has a mindset that all religious and spiritual beliefs and philosophies are equal, and they are to be equally respected. So they don't mind if someone from "1st Church" believes in Jesus for themselves; but the spiritualist strongly protests any assertions that Jesus is the only way.

At the very least, contemporary SR&F outreach missionaries are advised to contemplate both their gospel proclamation (how they and their local missionaries live their lives and conduct their missional outreaches) and their gospel affirmations (how they verbally affirm and communicate the gospel).[24] Verbally sharing the gospel (affirmation) has historically always been fraught with minefields, but new age spirituality has increased the odds of: a) misperception (Christianity is good but equal to Buddhism, Hinduism etc.); b) miscommunication (Jesus is one of a myriad of ways to heaven); and c) even angry misinterpretation (Christians are narrow-minded, intolerant bigots).

As has been stated throughout this book series, the "winds have shifted" and The Church in general, and SR&F outreach missions specifically "need to adjust the sails." The future of The Church and thousands of congregations are at stake. Such sail adjustments for local churches are no longer recommended...they have become absolutes!

The next chapter builds on what has been explored in this chapter as it explains the five questions to ensure local church SR&F outreach mission effectiveness.

IV. Summary of Missiological Foundations

The primary foundation for the comprehension and application of the theology of mission (missiology) has to do with understanding the purpose for which a church, para-ministry or mission agency exists. Answering the "why does it exist," or "what is its purpose and goal" question, is an absolute necessity.

If a congregation is confused about whether its purpose is to: a) reach those far from Jesus; b) to worship God; or c) to engage in bringing about social justice; it will never be able to determine if it is effectively accomplishing its goal. Likewise, a para-ministry will never know if its activities are accomplishing the purpose for which it was created if it isn't clear on who they are to reach and/or what they are

---

[24] The transferable concept of gospel proclamation and affirmation is fully explained in the second book of this Institutes of Sports Outreach book series, Greg Linville's *Sports Outreach Fundamentals* (especially pp. 58-61); and in the eighth book of the series: P.F. Myer's *The Life of the Shoe*, Chapter 10 (especially p. 124); The concept originated with Jim Petersen and can be found in his two books: *Living Proof*, Grand Rapids: Zondervan, 1997 and *Church Without Walls*, Colorado Springs: NavPress, 1999.

SCOREBOARD

A Coach is ... A Missionary is ...

✔ **A coach is:**
 ✔ Concerned about winning games

✔ **A missionary is:**
 ✔ Concerned about winning souls

✔ **A coach:**
 ✔ Contemplates athletic development

✔ **A missionary:**
 ✔ Contemplates spiritual development

✔ **A coach:**
 ✔ Envisions sporting strategies

✔ **A missionary:**
 ✔ Envisions ministry strategies

✔ **A coach is:**
 ✔ A church volunteer serving a congregation

✔ **A missionary is:**
 ✔ "A local church missionary serving to expand & enhance The Church"

Do you have...
 Volunteer Coaches
  Or
 Commissioned Missionaries?

reaching out for. Missionaries will be hopelessly frustrated if they are unclear as to whether they are called to end hunger, poverty and/or exploitation or call people into a personal relationship with Jesus.[25]

Once the purpose of a congregation or ministry has been clearly identified and crystalized into a compelling **vision,** and the **mission** to accomplish the **vision** has been determined, then the various **strategies** and **outputs** will result in Christo-centric **outcomes.**

A major reimagining of local mission is needed however…

Sources consulted for this chapter include:
Matthews, Basil. John R. Mott: World Citizen. Harper & Brothers. New York: 1934.

Mott, John. Confronting Young Men with the Living Christ. John H. Doran Company. New York: 1923.

_____. Evangelization of the World in this Generation. Student Volunteer Movement For Foreign Missions. New York: 1900.

_____. Strategic Points in the World's Conquest. Fleming H. Revell Company. New York: 1897.

Other resources found…

In the Yale Divinity School Library which holds the WSCF and John R. Mott Collections

Archives of YMCA connection in the Browne Historical Library of the National Council of YMCA's in New York City

---

[25] It should not be assumed the author believes it need be an either/or in regards to these purposes and goals. Rather, and most often the different options cannot occur without full integration of each of these goals. It's nearly impossible to have an evangelistic conversation with someone who is starving and it is much more likely that long-term poverty/hunger/exploitation will end when the gospel regenerates individual lives who will then transform cultures and communities as did the Quaker women of the original women's liberation movement and Quaker, Presbyterian and Methodist abolitionists prior to America's Civil War. It was gospel-transformed lives that transformed society to be more gospel oriented.

TIME OUT

Muscular Christianity Models
John R. Mott – World Citizen

John R. Mott may be the most unknown of all the Muscular Christian Pioneers and yet remains one of the most influential leaders in the history of The Church.

Born, raised and educated in New York, Mott came to faith under the influence of another Muscular Christian (Kynaston Studd) during Studd's visit to Cornell University in 1885. From there Mott attended Moody's Northfield Conference and became committed to the Student Volunteer Movement (SVM). He also was elected the President of the Cornell YMCA, which was the largest in the world at the time.

Mott became known as "World Citizen" and traveled domestically over 40,000 miles by train each year. He also embarked on over a 100 trans-Atlantic journeys. The travel was all done for the gospel. Mott spoke to an untold number of young people the world over in what he called addresses (not sermons), but nonetheless each address carried the gospel message of committing one's life to Jesus and a strong appeal to become a missionary.

Mott was offered many prestigious positions that included the Presidency of Yale and Oberlin Colleges and the Ambassadorship of China, but he remained the head of the YMCA for his entire career. He respectfully turned down President Woodrow Wilson's invitation as Ambassador because he believed he was already an Ambassador for a higher Sovereign! His other titles and roles included:

1901 - Director of foreign expansion of the North American YMCA
1910 - Chaired Edinburgh World Missionary Conference
1914 - Became involved in relief to POW's
1915 - National Executive of the American YMCA & through his influence 26,000 people served soldiers & prisoners through YMCA the National War Work Council
1916 - Helped to raise $200 million for the final war relief - largest sum ever raised at that time and at Versailles he pleaded for religious freedom of all countries
1921 - Left leadership of SVM & WSCF & assumed leadership of International Missionary Council

CHAPTER 6: Missiological Foundations for SR&F Outreach Ministry

TIME OUT

Muscular Christianity Models
John R. Mott – World Citizen cont.

Mott was clear about his vision (win the world to Jesus) and his mission (mobilize the evangelistic efforts of the YMCA and SVM). His was the original "Purpose Driven Life." His relentless pursuit of His Savior Jesus and his constant drive to ensure the YMCA maintained its commitment to Christo-centric evangelism is a model for all SR&F outreach ministries and ministers.*

---

* Excerpts from the unpublished and forthcoming book by Dr. Greg Linville: *Sports Ministry Pioneers: 19th Century Models for 21st Century Sports Outreach* and the chapter entitled: John R. Mott – World Citizen

SECTION 3: Missiological Applications for SR&F Outreach Missions

Chapter 7

Missiological Applications for Local Church SR&F Outreach Ministry

I. Five Questions to Ensure Local Church SR&F Outreach Ministry Effectiveness - 80
    A. Does It Accomplish the Vision - 80
        1. Program or Missional Program – 80
    B. Does It Have Called and Sent Leaders Who Can Execute the Mission - 81
        1. Committed – 81
        2. Connected – 82
        3. Continuously-reproducing – 84
        4. Summary of Does It Have Leaders – 84
    C. Does It Have Funding - 84
        1. Country Club Model – 85
        2. Congregational Mission Model – 85
        3. Combo Model – 85
        4. Summary of Funding SR&F Outreach Missions – 87
    D. Does It Fit the Overall Congregational Culture, Ethos and Calendar - 87
        1. Fitting the Congregational Culture – 88
        2. Fitting the Congregational Ethos – 89
        3. Fitting the Congregational Calendar – 95
    E. Does it Meet the Unintended Consequences Test – 97
        1. Individual Initiative – 97
        2. Congregational Outreaches – 98
        3. Summary of The Law of Unintended Consequences – 100

II. Summary of the 5-Questions – 100

> "A church that is not a missionary church is contradicting itself and quenching the Spirit." *

* *Lausanne Covenant*

I. Five questions to Ensure Local Church SR&F Outreach Ministry Effectiveness

A local church SR&F outreach minister often receives suggestions and recommendations for "exciting programs" to add to the SR&F ministry. All of these recommendations are well intentioned but not all are equally able to accomplish the vision of the congregation.[1] Most of the recommendations emerge out of a recent fad/trend, but not all such proposals fit within the overall mission of the SR&F outreach ministry.[2] Furthermore, even those that do fit the vision/mission, will do so at varying levels with varying degrees of being effective. So how can a local church SR&F outreach minister decide between what is truly based in missiology (the theology of missions) and that which is not? The following five questions are offered to ensure the successful accomplishing of the missional goals of going and making disciples; growing The Church and individual congregations; and being a redemptive force in sport and society.

A. Does It Accomplish The Vision

The first question to be asked when entertaining the possibility of adding any new outreach, program or ministry is: will this new activity significantly help the SR&F outreach ministry accomplish its vision? Asking the same question about all existing activities may be an even more important exercise as it often reveals the effectiveness (or lack) of even the most cherished and historic initiatives. No matter how many years a program has operated, or how many people it serves, all activities could benefit from a regular "critique." It is certainly prudent and wise to consider the significance of any long-lived outreach, and/or the total number of people a beloved activity has involved or will impact. However, a realistic assessment of the ongoing *Strategic-Relevance* of any activities as well as the ultimate *Efficient-Effectiveness* of all endeavors exhibits sound stewardship of resources and people's efforts. To that end, it is recommended that each and every activity not be easily dismissed but be submitted to a regular "critique" to ensure the accomplishing of a congregation's vision.

1. Program or Missional Program

A most helpful way to evaluate a newly proposed or existing activity is to ask: is it a "missional" program? If it's not missional, meaning its activities do not lead to accomplishing the vision, then it's just a program. Programs always have some value but only programs based in the mission truly accomplish The Church's mandate called the Great Commission! But! If what is being critisized is a truly missional program then a SR&F outreach minister can move to the second question which concerns leadership.

---

[1] This is because they are not either *Strategically-Relevant* or *Efficiently-Effective* in their ability to accomplish the vision.

[2] This is referred to in this book series as the *Defining Purpose* of Sports Outreach: *Evangelistic-Disciplemaking*.

B. Does It Have Called and Sent Leaders Who Can Execute the Mission[3]

Assuming the congregation has:

✔ Envisioned a SR&F missional strategy that fulfills the vision/mission statements of a congregation for accomplishing Great Commission goals

Then it can progress on to answering the second question…

After any proposed new endeavor, and all existing activities, are deemed to meet the missiological goal of accomplishing the Great Commission (the vision), the next most important question is: are there called and sent leaders for the missional outreach.

Even if a proposed outreach has great missional potential to accomplish the vision of a congregation or ministry, that potential will not be realized unless there are missional leaders. The total roles that need to be filled by mission-guided leaders include not only the overall leader (league director; event coordinator; mission coordinator; fitness director; etc.) but also but also supplemental, missional, leaders (coaches; instructors; volunteers). Warm bodies are not enough. Just having a pulse and loving a particular sport or activity does not equate to being a missional leader. To ensure mission actually occurs, the ministry needs leaders who are 1) committed; 2) connected; and 3) continuously-reproducing.

1. Committed Leaders

Effective missional outreach requires truly committed leaders who are: a) called; b) passionate; c) trained; d) resourced; e) Christ-honoring; f) Spirit-led; and g) available.

a. Called to the Missional Activity

Yes, it's possible a person may not understand they have a "call" to a specific SR&F Outreach until they've been involved for a season or two, but at the very least each outreach needs to have a core of leaders that feel a definite call on their life to be a leader in a specific SR&F outreach mission. We're not talking about a nice volunteer who wants to help out, but rather a congregational member who is called to be a sent local church missionary.

b. Passionate About the Missional Activity

Again, it's possible to have one or two leaders of a sports league who are more passionate about the sport of the league than the mission of the league, but missional goals will only be attained when there is a core of leaders that are passionate about missionally reaching those who are far from Jesus and His Church.

---

3 Consult other books in the Institutes of Sports Outreach series including: *Putting The Church Back in the Game* pp. 125f (for an overview of the spiritual criteria for congregational leadership) and pages 85-91 in *The Life of the Shoe* (for an overview of the 2-2-T-2 leadership concept).

c. Trained in Missional Activity

Local church sports, rec and fitness missionaries don't need a Master's degree is sports outreach but their missional effectiveness will be greatly expanded and enhanced with even a couple of hours of basic training in gospel-centric, outreach principles and ministry specifics.[4]

d. Resourced for Missional Activity

The effectiveness of outreach leaders can be increased when they receive quality sports equipment that ensures a high level of sport. Likewise their missional outreach can also be expanded and enhanced when they receive quality devotional and other ministerial resources.

e. Christ-honoring Missionaries

Let me be blunt! If the leaders of any SR&F outreach ministry are not Christ-centered and Christ-honoring, whatever program they lead will not be missional! Missiology is only possible when it and its leaders are: based on; built upon; and belong to: Jesus.[5]

f. Spirit-led Missionaries

Continuing in the spirit of loving bluntness...the mission of "going and making disciples" will be greatly hindered, if not totally impotent, if leaders are not filled, empowered and guided by the Holy Spirit.

g. Missionaries that are Available

Local church SR&F outreach missionaries may be called, passionate, trained, resourced, deeply in love with Jesus and even empowered by the Holy Spirit, but if they are not available at the time of day, week or year that the outreach is scheduled, or if they are emotionally, psychologically or relationally struggling, they can't be counted on for leadership. Being a leader assumes availability both in time and personal stability.

2. Connected Leaders

Sports outreach missionaries are most effective when they are connected to: a) Jesus; b) the congregation; and c) those far from Jesus and His Church.

a. Connected to Jesus

The overall missional goals (vision) of a congregation's SR&F outreach mission cannot be effectively attained by leaders who are not disciples of Jesus, and thus being a disciple of Jesus is a pre-requisite for anyone taking on a primary role of leadership.

However, this does not mean that non-Christians are prohibited from serving

---

[4] See the Postscript of the book *The Saving of Sports Ministry* for a detailed, step-by-step process for assessing where a person is on their spiritual journey and how to help them take next steps. In addition see Addenda B in the same book for answers to frequently asked questions concerning salvation that would be a bare minimum for such training.

[5] Readers are encouraged to read the next book in The Institutes of Sports Outreach – *The Christ of Sports Ministry: The Christology of Sports Outreach* which was being written at the time this book was released.

SCOREBOARD
Creating A "Laborers List"

Another core value of CSRM is based on the command of Jesus in Matthew 9.37, 38...

"The harvest is plentiful but the laborers are few, therefore pray earnestly to the Lord of the harvest to send out laborers into His harvest."

Thus, we maintain a "Laborers List" of people we "earnestly" pray the Lord will send out.

See Addenda 8 for the Laborers List Work Sheet

---

in non-leadership roles. Not only can such volunteers provide much needed help in certain non-ministry roles but more importantly, as they serve they become part of the community of Christ where they begin to experience the gospel being lived out and over time these volunteers often come to a personal faith in Jesus.[6] Therefore, not only should non-believers be welcomed to serve in a SR&F outreach mission but more importantly they should be prayed for, loved and when gospel "doors are opened"[7] they can be invited to seek Jesus to be their Lord and Savior.

b. Connected to the Congregation

One of the most overlooked and underappreciated criteria for local church SR&F leaders, has to do with the leaders being members of the congregation and regular attenders of the congregation's Lord's Day services. While it is certainly possible to include a few SR&F leaders who come from other congregations, the mission is most effective when the overwhelming core of a congregation's sports outreach leadership are members of and regular participants in the church's worship services, Christian Education and fellowship groups.

This point cannot be overemphasized. One of the most important and strategic philosophies of "making disciples" has to do with mobilizing and empowering church members and attenders to be engaged in SR&F outreach ministry. The *Evangelistic-Disciplemaking* process is enhanced and speeded along when the congregation's local missionaries (coaches etc.) are members of and regular attenders of the church sponsoring the sports outreach. It's much more effective to have the coach or player of a team invite a non-churched person to participate in the broader congregational activities. Personal relationships are

---

[6] This progression is summarized by the *5-B's of Sports Outreach (Belong, Believe; Baptize; Behave; Become)* which is defined and explained in Chapter 5 of *The Fundamentals of Sports Outreach*.

[7] See Chapter 6 of this book – in particular page 43-47 to understand the prayers that open gospel doors.

much more effective at getting a non-churched person to become involved in congregational activities and attend Bible studies and worship services. [8]

c. Connected to Those Far From Jesus

While it is not a pre-requisite for SR&F outreach ministers to have an extensive number of unchurched friends, family, neighbors and associates, it is vital that they are comfortable interacting with those "outside" the church…and even more important that they are: …"well thought of by outsiders."[9] Since the mission of the SR&F outreach ministry is to reach those who are far from Jesus and His Church, then at the very least mission leaders should be able to connect with and relate to, the very people they are trying to build relationships with.

There is one further and most important criterion for selecting a leadership team: being a reproducer.

3. Continuously-Reproducing

The ultimate goal of the leadership question is developing leaders who can embrace and execute the vision to reproduce themselves.[10] The future of any *Missional Program* depends upon developing a growing core of leaders. Local churches most often experience success when their goal is to have a leader in every position who is assisted by 1-2 *Missionaries-In-Training (MIT's)*. These *MIT's* understand they are being groomed to be a future league director, head coach, league official, event director, and/or class leader etc., and the SR&F outreach minister works in conjunction with the current leaders to empower, enable and encourage those they envision to be the future leaders of the ministry.

4. Summary of Does It Have Leaders

Thus, the bottom line is…even if a new program is proposed, or an old program's potential to accomplish the vision of the SR&F mission is reviewed and critiqued; having connected leaders is an absolute necessity. If there is not a sufficient leadership pool from the congregation, the newly proposed, and all existing activities, should be postponed until God raises up the necessary leaders.

However, if such a program is flush with strong leadership, then the third question (does it have funding) can be raised and answered.

C. Does It Have Funding[11]

Assuming the congregation has:

✔ Envisioned a SR&F missional strategy that fulfills the vision/mission statements of a congregation for accomplishing Great Commission goals

---

8   What is referred to in this book series as getting the unchurched person over the second *Sports Outreach Dysconnect*. See Chapter 2 of *Fundamentals of Sports Outreach* for a full understanding of the *2-Dysconnects*.
9   1 Timothy 3.7.
10 What is referred to in this book series as *Producing, Reproducing, Reproducers*.
11 For a deeper look into funding SR&F outreach ministry, see Chapter 7 in *Putting The Church Back In The Game* where some of the material in this section originated.

CHAPTER 7: Missiological Applications for Local Church SR&F Outreach Ministry

✔ Assembled the necessary leaders needed for their Great Commission endeavors

Then the third question to be answered is: "how do we pay for it?" The answer on how to fund a congregation's SR&F mission however, is different for different churches. Answering the "does it have funding" question begins with understanding the various philosophies of how to finance SR&F outreach missions. There are three basic models: 1) Country Club Model; 2) Congregational Mission Model; 3) Combo Model.

1. Country Club Model

When it comes to financing SR&F endeavors and facilities, leaders of some churches perceive their SR&F activities to be a service to congregational members and others living in the general community. Therefore they expect those participating in the activities, utilizing the equipment and frequenting the facilities to pay fees and/or purchase memberships that totally cover the cost of all staff, facilities, equipment and programming. At the one extreme of this philosophy even the cost of the building and maintenance of the facility is to be paid by fees and/or memberships. At the other end, the congregation pays for the building of the facility but then expects all facility maintenance and program expenses to be covered by participant fees. This philosophy typically views the athletic centers of their congregation as being a Christian health club, Community Rec Center or Country Club, and assumes it should be funded in similar ways.

2. Congregational Mission Model

A second philosophy sees the SR&F as a missional outreach of the church and *a Strategically-Relevant* way to "go and make disciples" in the very community the congregation's ministry site is found. This financial model believes the congregational budget should pay for all expenses associated with the facility, staffing and programming because it is one of, if not the primary, mission outreach of the church. This model is consistent with the overall view that the church pays for all missions (foreign, national and local) out of its mission budget. So, the bottom line of the Congregational Mission Model is for the church to pay for everything and the participant not have to pay for anything.

3. Combo Model

A third view fully understands and supports the local mission philosophy but also understands that a combination of funding sources for SR&F outreach ministry has strategic and financial merit. So, even though the outreaches are envisioned as local missionary activity and the bulk of the budget should come out of the congregation's budget, the missionary endeavors can be greatly enhanced and expanded if supplementary funding comes from sources outside of the church budget. This philosophy works on the premise that missionary

SCOREBOARD

Financing SR&F Outreach... How Does Your Church Stack Up?

Church Mission Budget Pays For All Permanent Expenses Including:
- Facilities – construction, maintenance and utilities
- Permanent Equipment – such as goals, bleachers, fitness machines and scoring devices
- Staff – year round full and part time staff

Activity Fees and Memberships Pays For All Short Term Expenses Including:
- Short-term Equipment – balls, nets, etc.
- Staff – short term, part time staff such as officials, referees, umpires and league directors

---

endeavors are enhanced and expanded because of two major financial realities and one participation reality. The first financial reality has to do with the additional revenues secure better facilities, equipment and programming, whereas the second creates authentic trustworthiness in the church by eliminating any concerns about financial mismanagement. There is also a significant non-financial reason for having participants "pay to play."

Additional Revenues

Whether additional revenues come from facility memberships, fitness class or league fees, and/or sports team sponsorships from local businesses, all of these funds enable the purchase and maintenance of high quality facilities and equipment, which attracts and keeps an ever-widening base of participants.

Authentic Trustworthiness

Participants in the various leagues, classes and activities expect to pay reasonable participation fees for the privilege of utilizing the equipment and participating in activities of the church's athletic ministry. What they don't expect, and in fact, have a negative reaction to, is anything that would lead them to believe the church is taking their participation fees and using them to pay for the church's overall budget.

Full financial transparency is recommended and congregations are encouraged to communicate the financial policies and budgets for their SR&F outreach missions. This helps manage any questions that might arise by demonstrating full financial accountability. When finances are managed well the ministry objectives are unimpeded and the effectiveness of the outreach is greatly enhanced. When not handled well, the ministry is hindered, if not totally destroyed. When there are unresolved financial concerns, any chance for reaching the unchurched is lost, and the very purpose for which the mission was created is not realized.

Participant Reality

To understand the benefit of requiring the participant to have a financial stake may seem counter-intuitive at first, but remains an undeniable truth. When participants pay to play in a league or take a fitness class, they are most likely to think: "Gotta get my money's worth." Whereas, if it's free, people don't make the same effort to participate, or even believe the league or class is free because it's inferior in some way.

The Financial Goal: Break-even Budgeting

The goal of funding a newly proposed or established local church SR&F *Missional Program* is to "break even." Thus, a planning sheet (see Appendix 9) that encompasses anticipated expenses and expenditures will provide a church with both a picture of what it costs to administer such an activity and also a relatively safe assurance of keeping everything within a reasonable budget. The basic premise is such a budget will predict how many people will register for the activity, what the cost of the activity will be for that number of people and then how much each participant will be assessed to take part. The congregation's financial stewards are reassured by the fact that the proposed outreach will be cancelled if a certain number of participants don't register.

4. Summary of Funding SR&F Outreach Missions

Most churches ascribe to the third view that includes the congregational budget paying for all permanent facilities, equipment and staff but use participation fees to cover all temporary items such as short-term staff, balls and all equipment that needs replaced once every season or two. It is usually these temporary expenses that are in question when a congregation assesses the cost of proposed or reviewed *Missional Programs* and therefore are what is addressed here. The bottom line is, the most *Efficiently-Effective* SR&F outreach missions are funded by a combination of congregational revenues and participation fees.

So, if answers to questions 1-3 are all affirmative, move to question #4…

D. Does it Fit the Overall Congregational Culture, Ethos and Calendar

Assuming the congregation has:

- ✔ Envisioned a SR&F missional strategy that fulfills the vision/mission statements of a congregation for accomplishing Great Commission goals
- ✔ Assembled the necessary called and sent leaders needed for their Great Commission endeavors
- ✔ Secured the financing needed for such Great Commission endeavors

The next step is to synchronize the SR&F mission with the over-arching culture; ethos; and schedule of the congregation. This would include…

1. Fitting the Overall Congregational Culture

Culture is defined here as: the distinctive characteristics of a defined people group. In this case, each congregation is recognized for exhibiting an overall character for which it is known. Some may be known for their social justice activity; a few for ministering to children through hosting a pre-school and other regular missional programming for younger kids; and still others for their fellowship hall which hosts community socials such as parties and weddings; fish fries; and the list goes on.

Thus, a SR&F outreach would be most *Strategically-Relevant* and *Efficiently-Effective* if it is envisioned to easily coordinate and be integrated with the overall culture of the congregation. For example if a church is strongly connected to a social justice effort to assimilate new immigrants, a *Strategically-Relevant* model may be to incorporate athletic leagues that feature sports relevant to the country and culture from which the new immigrant communities come from. If a church is already known for its quality children's schools, services and activities it would make great sense to incorporate sports leagues and recreation opportunities geared for children and/or young families. For a church whose "hall" is well known by community people it would make great sense to sponsor social events such as ethnic dinners and style shows, or perhaps hold concerts, live theater and forums. Holding dance classes and other regular social events would also be well received. Lenten fish fries are labor intensive but lucrative financially and usually untapped evangelistically.

Addressing the Cultural Worship Wars.[12] Another part of fitting the SR&F outreach ministry into the overall culture of a congregation is often not discussed because of the sensitive and often misunderstood nature of race and ethnicity, yet, at the risk of being misinterpreted, and misappropriated, it must be addressed.

The stark reality is, the most segregated time of the week is Sunday morning, and the simple fact remains: different ethnic and racial groups, and even different generations prefer different styles of worship, preaching, teaching and congregational organization. This is more true for the baby-boomer generation, but all age groups experience similar realities. Thus, all worship, preaching, teaching and organizational styles that are biblically-based and Christ-honoring are to be appreciated and applauded. However, local congregations must recognize their SR&F outreaches will have more limited effectiveness if the sports or rec ministry is reaching people who are unable to appreciate, understand and relate to the prevailing culture of the traditional worship and educational services

---

12   The book: *Worship Wars* by CSRM Executive Director David Waddell is highly recommended.

of the host congregation. The real problem is experienced when the current "how" and "what" of the music, liturgy and overall way a congregation functions becomes an overwhelming obstacle to incorporate any potential members into the body life of the church. If the culture of the sponsoring congregation is so foreign to those the SR&F mission is reaching, a reconciling of this issue is recommended.

To fit the SR&F outreach mission to the culture of a local congregation, one of two things are suggested: a) adapt the SR&F to be attractive to people more likely to assimilate into the overall life of the congregation; or b) do the hard and uncomfortable work of adapting the basics of how the congregation functions and conducts traditional worship services to fit the cultural preferences of those the SR&F is reaching. This adaptation is very difficult because by necessity, it includes changing the make-up of the congregation's leadership so as to mirror the culture, race and ethnicity of those the congregation is positioned and called to reach!

Yes, the universal Church is truly multi-ethnic and consists of all races and people but most congregations remain mono-cultural. The key principle for effective SR&F outreach mission is to build upon the culture a local church is known for, and at the right time and in a proper way, congregations should envision, plan for and expedite a church planting effort that will truly "go to the world."

Regardless of how this opportunity is resolved, the hard, cold reality must be faced and dealt with. Hopefully most congregations will see this as a wonderful opportunity to grow culturally, spiritually and numerically.

2. Fitting the Overall Congregational Ethos

In this context ethos is defined as the organizational and operational way in which a congregation functions and what it values. This point is most relevant to competitive sport rather than recreation, fitness or leisure ministries because sports ministry is unique in having to deal with competition. In this regard, there are two specific areas in which a congregation's ethos should be assessed and addressed: a) *The Competition Continuum;* and b) *The Evangelism – Discipleship Continuum.*

a. Competition Continuum[13]

Within the realm of local church SR&F outreach, sport can be organized along a continuum of varying competition levels. This *Competition Continuum* ranges from leisure (no discernable competition) and recreation (moderate

---

13 See each of three other books in this series in regards to determining a theology of competition and appropriate levels of competition: *Christmanship: A Theology of Competition and Sport* (where I have written more extensively on the theology of competition); Chapter 3 of *The Fundamentals of Sports Outreach* (which explains the *3-Tier Paradigm of Level #1 Theological-Truths; Level #2 Philosophical-Principles* and *Level #3 Methodological-Models*); and pages 59-62 of *The Saving of Sports Ministry* (that examine *Competition-Gone-Berserk* and *Competition-Gone-Soft*).

TIMEOUT

Worship Wars

There may be nothing as close to partisan politics as the different views on worship in the modern church. Is worship supposed to be traditional or contemporary (and by the way, contemporary worship is now 40+ years old!)? Should the aim or worship be contemplative or celebratory? Is the dress code classy or casual? The differences in feelings about worship have created some feuds worse than the Hatfield and McCoy ordeal. The topic has split families and separated long friendships. Since the war generally centers on music style, I like to refer to the Worship Wars as "The gunfight at the O.K. Chorale."*

If your sports, recreation, and fitness ministries attract new people to the church, the leaders must determine how to assimilate the new people into discipleship, study, and worship. Some would say the new people need to understand and accept how we do things in the church. Others would argue that the message must remain biblical, but the worship methods can differ to meet the culture. The Apostle Paul gave the same truth about grace in the gospel, but he altered his technique depending on whether he spoke to Jews or Gentiles. When Paul went to Athens, he talked about the statue of the "unknown god" and related what the Greeks knew into the message of what they didn't know. Our churches must do the same thing. (Acts 17:16-34)

My home church had operated a neighborhood summer day camp and after school program for several years when the leadership realized that the families they were reaching felt out of place in the traditional worship services. The new families felt intimidated by the suits and nice outfits that people wore to worship. With this understanding, the church decided to do an additional service in the recreation center and had the minister that led the summer and after school programs to do the preaching. Families saw a familiar face delivering the message, the dress was much more casual, limiting any clothing intimidation, and the format was more relaxed and contemporary. Worship, after all, is about the "Who" rather than the "with."

Later, when I served at another church that wanted to reach new people, decided to hold two different services; a traditional service

TIME OUT

and a separate contemporary service. In making the decision, there was much partisan discussion about the two worship styles. I refer to this incident in the book, *Worship Wars: The Kings Lead the Battle to Spirit and Truth.*** (You'll find the story behind the chapter in 1 Kings 3:16-28). During this debate...

"One man at this church had the best take on all the worship wars. During the period of discussing the possible move to hosting one of each style of service, he said, 'If holding a contemporary service can help someone meet Jesus and turn them into a worshipping believer, then we must change the direction of one of the services.' I think he must be related to Solomon."***

The principle was laid out by the Apostle Paul when he said: "I have become all things to all people so that by all possible means I might save some." (1 Corinthians 9:22b NIV) The message of the gospel doesn't change, but we can adjust our methods to incorporate people into the body of Christ. I believe it behooves us to do just that.

*   *Worship Wars*, p. 14.
**   *Worship Wars* In the chapter titled, "Let the Baby Live."
***   *Worship Wars*, p. 264.

> — **David Waddell** is a Professor at Ole Miss, the Executive Director of CSRM and a former local church sports ministers. He is the author of 3 books including *Worship Wars*.

competition) to high level sport (intense competition). All three positions on the *Competition Continuum* are biblically defensible.[14] So, if all three can be justified biblically, where should a church position its SR&F outreach? The answer usually lies at whatever level a congregation feels the most comfortable. Once a congregation's ethos has been determined, its sports offerings can be organized to fit within that ethos.

For example, if the overall ethos of a congregation is uncomfortable with highly competitive sports or any kind of interactions or activities that involve "winning and losing," then its SR&F outreach mission would be well served to organize sports leagues from a leisure philosophy (i.e. not keeping scores/wins/standings, having officials etc. See A Case for Non-Competitive Sport Time Out on page 93). Or, moving across the *Competition-Continuum*, if a congregation is more comfortable at the recreational level, then it is encouraged to: a) organize games but not hold tournaments; b) have all games / contests be self-officiated; and c) not keep any records or statistics.

Conversely, if the ethos of a congregation affirms and values accomplishments of succeeding and competition, then the SR&F outreach mission is encouraged to host highly competitive leagues and tournaments complete with officials, standings and awards for winners.

Of course it's not an either/or scenario. Some early childhood games could be played within the non-competitive model; senior adult leagues could be organized as recreational activities, and young adult flag football leagues could be conducted as highly competitive leagues.

Astute SR&F outreach ministers will assess their congregation's competitive "temperature" and organize their outreaches to match where the church falls on the *Competition-Continuum*.

b. Evangelism, Discipleship Continuum

The *Evangelism, Discipleship Continuum* should not be confused with the *Evangelistic-Disciplemaking Concept*. The relevant difference here has to do with assessing what a congregation is more comfortable with: evangelism or discipleship.

SR&F outreach ministers need to know if their congregation's ethos is more in tune with "seeking to reach the lost" or "making disciples." For example, if a congregation's highest value is to "evangelize the lost," it will not be satisfied with youth leagues that only serve kids whose families are already in the church. They will be however, strongly supportive when they hear that 90% of all participants don't have a relationship with Jesus or a church.

Conversely, if the ethos of a congregation focuses on the spiritual development of their parishioners, it will not be satisfied if the vast majority of participants

---

14   As established from *Level #1 Theological Truths* as outlined in *Christmanship* and other books in this series.

TIMEOUT

A Case for Non-Competitive Youth Sports

I served as the League Director of our children's basketball program at our church for 16 years. Now, one would think, it being a "church league," coaches would understand that sure, it's nice to win, but that is not the most important thing. We want to have the kids learn the game, improve their skills, make new friends and have fun doing it. Unfortunately there are always a couple of coaches trying to get their team to the "final four" by running up the score and you guessed it... their teams were scheduled to play each other next week. Other than eliminating the scoreboard, what could we do?!!?!

Well, I am here to tell you, that is exactly what we did. We did away with the scoreboards, but not just for their game. We eliminated the scoreboard for every game that Saturday and guess what? The kids still played as hard and everyone had a great time. You can imagine how pleased I was when other coaches said:

"Hey Mike! Can we do this all the time?" "What's that?" I asked. "Keep the scoreboard out of the game" was their reply! I of course was happy to hear this unsolicited agreement with what we did, but I wanted to know why this one coach felt that way as he was not one of the coaches that I ever needed to be worried about.

He told me that it was about half way through the first period and his girls' team was playing with reckless abandonment...but in a good way. They were actually hustling and running the plays and getting everyone involved in the game and scoring baskets. As I said, he was a coach I never had to worry about and being that kind of coach, after being amazed as to how well his girls were playing, he decided he had better check the scoreboard at center court to make sure that his team wasn't overly running away with the game. That was when he first noticed that there was NOT a scoreboard to check.

"That is why I don't want you to bring back the scoreboard," he told me. As we wound up our brief conversation, it became apparent that the problem with keeping score was, how much pressure it put on our kids. Our young round-ballers felt that they needed to score every time they brought the ball down the court and if they didn't, they were failures. This explains what I believe is wrong with children's sports in

continued on page 94

TIMEOUT

continued from page 93

today's world. Kids are judged on how many games they have won, how many points they scored, how many all-star teams they made, and how many trophies are on their shelf at home, etc., etc. Nowhere do they have a place to play anymore, simply for the joy and fun of playing a sport.

Well, we as a league, kept the scoreboards in the closet the rest of the season and every season after that...and you know what? It didn't seem to make much difference in the energy in the gym every Saturday. Kids were still playing hard. Kids were hustling and parents were rooting them on. But with the pressure to score removed from the game, they were also learning how to play basketball without the pressure to win at all costs or be considered a loser. They were improving their skills, making new friends and the best part was they were having fun doing it.

Now I would be sure to explain at our parent's meetings at the beginning of every season why we didn't keep score and I would relate the story I just shared above with them, closing by saying, "I know there are great lessons to be learned in winning and losing. One must be a gracious winner, not boastful, and one must learn that one can't always win and except that fact as well. As kids grow and continue in sports, they will have plenty of opportunity to learn those lessons." Then I would share with them a story from one of my college coaches who used to say: "The fun in climbing a mountain is in the climbing. When you get to the top it is just cold and windy." Finally, I would tell them that I have played a lot of basketball in my lifetime, from my elementary school team all the way through to four years of college and then some...and I can't tell you the score of one single game that I ever played in. I can tell you however, that I had a lot of fun playing the game of basketball.

One final thought...scoreboard or no scoreboard, there are always going to be some parents keeping score on their own in the stands. As I would tell them at out parent's meeting. "We'll keep you in our prayers..."

— **Mike Maloney** – Former Sports Minister
Sandia Presbyterian Church and CSRM Board of Trustee

SCOREBOARD
You & Who

An effective model for reaching those far from Jesus and His Church is called the "You & Who" model.

The "you" refers to current church members and attenders

The "who" refers to anyone not currently attending the church.

This model is most effective when the "you's" of the congregation are encouraged to invite a "who" to join one of the church's sports leagues, recreational activities or fitness classes.

Some churches have even mandated that their "who's" cannot play or participate unless they bring a "who!"

---

are not members of the church and furthermore, these "outsiders" main, or only, reason for participation is competition or physical fitness. However, a church focused on spiritual formation will greatly affirm adult sports and recreational activities that connect such endeavors with spiritual lessons that emerge from the sporting or recreational activity.

In summary, wise SR&F ministers will adapt their outreach missions to fit the ethos of their congregation's *Evangelism-Discipleship Continuum.*

3. Fitting the Overall Congregational Calendar

Fitting a SR&F outreach mission into the overall schedule of a local church means more than just making sure the needed facilities, staff and equipment are available…although this is certainly vital. The more important part of fitting in has to do with strategically thinking about how to maximize SR&F outreach effectiveness. The following is one model of an *Efficiently-Effective* scheduling of missional SR&F activity within the congregation's yearly calendar of seasons and events…

"First Church Integrates Sports Outreach."

Step #1 At the end of a summer's softball league, each coach at "First Church" encourages all church attending players (the you's) on the team they coach to invite a non-church member (the who's) to join them for the church sponsored

"Vespers in the Park" in September.[15] These church members continue to follow up each week of September, inviting their non-churched friends to attend these weekly times that include: a different recreational opportunity each week; a special meal created by the church "barbeque bubbas;"[16] and a 5-10 minute "thought for the week" delivered by a church staff member or pastor.

Step #2 The second step First Church initiated for fitting its SR&F mission into the overall schedule of the congregation was to invite all in attendance of the weekly "Vespers in the Park" to attend the congregation's Fall Festival. The festival consisted of outdoor activities with a fall flair that include children's games such as bowling with pumpkins; face painting; bluegrass music; apple cider etc.[17]

Step #3 All who attended First Church's Fall Festival received information about attending the church's community thanksgiving dinner and participating in the church's Fall sports leagues, recreation activities, fitness classes and social events.

Step #4 Anyone attending any of the Fall leagues or activities received personal and corporate invitations to special Christmas services…especially the Christmas Eve candlelight service.

Step #5 All who attended the Christmas Eve service and/or other SR&F activities were encouraged to make a "New Year's Resolution" that included joining a 4-6 week Alpha course or Christianity Explored class that is held in homes of SR&F leaders, coaches and fitness instructors.

Step #6 Next up? During Lent, "First Church" invited everyone participating in SR&F outreaches to a 4-week series of meals at the congregation's ministry site for a "meet and greet" to hear about all the congregation has to offer and a chance to meet staff and other church members.

Step #7 This "meet and greet" was followed up each week with Lenten meals and included information about the Easter Egg Hunt on Holy Saturday and Easter Resurrection Day services. "First Church" continued providing information about other SR&F opportunities during Lenten and Easter services…including a special invitation to sign up for the summer softball leagues and invite a friend (a *who*).[18]

The point should be clear. It's one thing, a good thing in fact, to schedule a

---

15 This assumes a "you and who" approach to a church softball league. The "you" refers to church members and the "who" refers to the non-churched person the "you" invited to play softball. See the You and Who Scoreboard on page 95.
16 What do you mean you don't have any barbeque bubbas?! This is a powerful ministry for men, and all churches are encouraged to "fire up the grill" and get your men involved in this way.
17 Substitute the musical style and activities that fit your congregation's culture. Bluegrass was chosen because it is not typically the musical style of most churches and thus is an example of how to adapt to the culture of those a congregation is trying to reach.
18 The *Producing-Reproducing-Reproducers* transferable concept starts immediately.

SR&F event, league or activity that fits into a church calendar as far as having facilities and equipment available, but it is far more effective to envision a year round strategy that fits into the church calendar. Transferring whole families from the gym, field or pitch, from the leagues and events to the sanctuary, Bible studies and fellowship groups is one of the most vital objectives of the entire *Evangelistic-Disciplemaking* efforts of a congregation. SR&F outreach cannot be considered missional unless this kind of coordinated scheduling, transfer and integration occurs. Anything less can only be considered running programs and the SR&F mission will only have limited success. Unless *Evangelistic-Disciplemaking* is intentional, it will be accidental at best.

E. Does it Meet the "Unintended Consequences" Test

The fifth question to be answered has to do with the Law of Unintended Consequences. This law is found to be true in many different spheres of life, but what is a surprising reality to many SR&F leaders is how it is found to be true in a few key SR&F outreach mission endeavors. In general, the Law of Unintended Consequences is realized whenever the actual results of any endeavor, activity or action greatly differs from what was hoped the activity would achieve. One specific in local church SR&F mission has to do with how The Law of Unintended Consequences is often experienced in relationship to outreaches conducted on the Lord's Day. In these specific cases, The Law's fruit is witnessed when the exact opposite of the hopes and intended goals of such outreaches occur.[19] In fact, the sobering reality is the results of many well-intentioned efforts often bring about the exact opposite of what was intended!

For example, most of the time, the motive for engaging in sports outreach on the Lord's Day is good and pure because the rationale is based on reaching people who are far from Jesus and His Church. Yet, the undeniable reality remains: Lord's Day sports outreach endeavors are often abysmal failures because, while the theory of playing sports on the Lord's Day seems a wise and logical way to engage in evangelistic efforts, the end results simply do not produce the desired outcomes or goals. However, it must be understood, The Law of Unintended Consequences does not cause the results but rather only reveals them.[20] Such specific pragmatic outreaches that emerge out of these insufficient theological and philosophical foundations originate from one of two sources: 1) individual player or coach initiatives; and 2) corporate congregational outreaches.

1. Individual Initiatives

Conventional wisdom would suggest that competing/playing on the Lord's

---

19 For example, the prologue and epilogue of this book, illustrates how Harold's Lord's Day efforts simply did not accomplish what was intended and hoped for.

20 What causes the unintended results has much more to with the faulty *Level # 1 Theological Truths* on which such *Level #2 Philosophical Principles* are structured and organized; and from which the subsequent *Level #3 Methodological Models* are operated.

Day (even Sunday morning) for the purpose of reaching teammates who are far from Christ would be a good thing…and it is up to a point. Yet, and even more insidiously, what is subtly, yet convincingly, communicated to those far from Christ is, that church participation is non-important, or at least not as important as playing sport! Thus, the actual results of these efforts have been shown to be not only much less effective than hoped for, but worse, are often antithetical to the intended purpose. It would be similar to what would be communicated to: a) drug addicts…if the person reaching out to the addicts takes drugs with those she is trying to reach; or b) the men who frequent the burlesque if they were accompanied by a Christian friend.[21]

2. Congregational Outreaches

Lord's Day outreaches sponsored by a local church are similar to individual initiatives in that they are well intentioned and yet can suffer from the same negative Law of Unintended Consequences results. However, with a true theological foundation, and a proper philosophical plan, congregational-based SR&F outreaches operated on a Lord's Day can overcome the dreaded Law of Unintended Consequences and fulfill the goal of reaching people for Christ and subsequently, growing their congregations.

The key to whether a Lord's Day SR&F mission will be effective or not, is based on comprehending and implementing the necessary theological and philosophical underpinnings of the Lord's Day doctrine. Typically many of these outreaches are not based on biblically-based theology and philosophy, but only on the "conventional wisdom" of running Lord's Day SR&F activities, and thus, will suffer from the results of the Law of Unintended Consequences. However, if the activities are envisioned, planned for and expedited according to theological truths and biblical principles, congregations will experience great *Evangelistic-Disciplemaking* success! What makes the difference is one key *Level #2 Philosophical Principle* which is based on a few *Level #1 Theological Truths*.

The theological foundations for determining Lord's Day sports, recreation and fitness activities emerge out of the contemplation of many different specific doctrines. These include among others: a) soteriology (doctrine of salvation; b) ecclesiology (doctrine of The Church); c) missiology (doctrine of missions); and d) Christology (doctrine of Jesus, the Christ/Messiah). In specific, the key questions for whether or not a local church SR&F outreach should engage in Lord's Day activities would include: what is believed about being "saved" (are disciples required to attend church); what is believed about The Church (can disciples grow deeper in their faith if they don't participate in a local church on

---

21   I am not equating playing sport with taking drugs, but rather, I am equating non-adherence to Lord's Day principles and non-participation in a local church body with taking drugs. The distinction is vital to any proper understanding of a theology of sport participation.

CHAPTER 7: Missiological Applications for Local Church SR&F Outreach Ministry

at least a weekly basis); what is believed about being sent (does being sent mean to abandon any/all associations with a local church); and what did Jesus practice and teach about the Sabbath (would Jesus participate in a basketball game held on a Sunday).[22]

The philosophical principle that is informed by this theological foundation is therefore, to design and organize all activities in ways that motivate people to want to go deeper in their faith and are conducive to people being able to partake in both SR&F and traditional church activities.

While most denominations, theologians and everyday Christians would agree one's salvation is not dependent upon church membership and participation, most know the obvious truth is, church participation is a key indicator of, and enhancement of, spiritual formation, growth and long-term discipleship. This *Level #1 Theological Truth* informs the *Level #2 Philosophical Principle* that suggests traditional congregational activities such as corporate worship, Christian Education classes, fellowship/accountability groups and other involvements are foundational, irreplaceable commitments. Thus, all SR&F endeavors should be organized in such a way so as to ultimately engage all SR&F participants in these traditional church activities.[23] Therefore, *Level #3 Methodological Models* that enhance and maximize the ability of all SR&F participants to engage deeply in traditional, congregational Lord's Day activities will experience results congruent with the original intent and goal of such outreaches and steer clear of The Law of Unintended Consequences. There is one interesting wrinkle on the corporate congregational outreaches that needs explained however.

The previous two paragraphs should be seriously considered but should not be taken to mean that all SR&F programming on a Lord's Day should be avoided. Rather, I strongly suggest that when such SR&F mission activities are properly envisioned, wisely planned, and strategically implemented, a most effective confluence of SR&F and traditional congregational activities can be devised. For example…

- A "20-something" Ultimate Frisbee league could be combined with a young adult Bible study on a Lord's Day evening with the result being an expansion in attendance and an enhancement of the quality of the disciplemaking born out of the "teachable moments" experienced in the Frisbee league.

---

22   See books 3 & 4 in the Institutes of Sports Outreach book series for a complete explanation of soteriology and ecclesiology and their relevance to this and many other local church SR&F outreach ministry endeavors.

23   This should not negate what I have written elsewhere that affirms SR&F ministries are in themselves powerful tools for discipleship and spiritual growth. Here, I am simply affirming the "both/and" principle of combining traditional corporate worship, Bible study and other disciplemaking efforts with SR&F related worship and disciplemaking activities. Such a synchronization of efforts is amazingly effective and make for a truly winning combination.

- An intergenerational bicycle club could conclude with a time of corporate family devotions on a Lord's Day afternoon. Such an activity would provide unique opportunities for spiritual lessons gleaned from "influence moments" experienced on the bike ride and it also provides the opportunity for kids and adults (you's) alike to invite friends and neighbors (who's) to an attractive "church" event.
- A summer long "Vespers in a Park," can be envisioned. Such an activity could take place each Lord's Day evening and would include a picnic cooked up by the congregation's "grill bubbas," and a different recreational activity at the various parks visited. One week it's intergenerational kickball, the second week co-ed volleyball, and a third week the activity would be water skiing. Such engagement empowers church members with a winsome series of events to invite family and colleagues to, and provides those invited to hear a 5-minute "vesper thought for the week" delivered by the church pastor or other staff.

Such examples of combining recreational activities with more traditional Lord's Day endeavors most often produce higher attendance and more significant spiritual growth.

3. Summary of The Law of Unintended Consequences

Individuals and congregations have a sense that reaching those far from Jesus through Lord's Day SR&F endeavors is right, and are thus surprised and confused about why such efforts are more often ineffective. It is only after they have come to understand ecclesiological, soteriological and missional *Level #1 Theological Truths* that inform how to shape a biblically-based organizational structure that is founded on *Level #2 Philosophical Principles,* that they will be able to envision, plan for and expedite a truly effective *Level #3 Methodological Model* of Lord's Day SR&F activities and avoid the repercussions of The Law of Unintended Consequences.

II. Summary of the Five Missiological Questions

The potential for congregations to ask and answer the five questions raised in this chapter will ensure significantly more *Strategically-Relevant* and *Efficiently-Effective* SR&F outreach missions.

Has the time come for your congregation to re-evaluate your missiological underpinnings?

SECTION 3: Missiological Applications for SR&F Outreach Missions

Chapter 8

Missiological Applications for Sports-related, Para-Ministries and Sports Chaplaincy

I. The General Proposals - 104
    A. Maximizing Missional Endeavors #1 – Uniting Local Church & Para-Ministry Missions – 104
        1. Two Vital Missiological Questions – 105
        2. One Ultimate Goal – 105
    B. Maximizing Missional Endeavors #2 – Integrating the Mega-Models and the 3-R-Models of Missions – 105
        1. Option #1: Mega-Event & 3-R-Model – 107
        2. Option #2: Mega-Media & 3-R-Model – 109
        3. Option #3: Mega-Event & Mega-Media Model – 109
    C. Vital Missiological Questions Revisited – 109
    D. Summary of the General Proposals – 112

II. Final Thoughts on the Integration of the Local Church and Para-ministries - 113

> "The best thing for you and for me is to engage in earnest Christian work for the bodies and the souls of men."*
>
> *Robert Ross McBurney*

---

* Lawrence Locke Doggett, *The Life of Robert R. McBurney*, Cleveland: F.M. Barton, 1902, pp. 146f. All Muscular Christian Model quotations in this chapter are from the two pages referenced here and thus each has the footnote #1. McBurney's focus on men throughout these quotes should not be misinterpreted as being sexist. Rather, the YMCA at the time of McBurney existed only to reach and disciple men. The YWCA was created to focus exclusively on reaching women.

TIME OUT

Muscular Christian Models
Robert Ross McBurney
The Model of the Para-ministry as an Outreach Arm of the Local Church

Although George Williams was the founder of the movement, Robert McBurney was the man who envisioned and shaped what the YMCA came to be and personally became the model for all YMCA secretaries (executive director). The genius of Williams was to create a vision and passion within young men to reach other young men for Christ whereas the genius of McBurney was to give to those men pragmatic models of how to reach young men for Christ. He expanded Williams's methods of using fitness, physical activity and amusements to proportions Williams initially never dreamed of. Nevertheless all of McBurney's endeavors never forsook the YMCA'S purpose of winning young men to Christ. Where Williams saw the buying of Exeter Hall in which to hold crusades as the crowning achievement of the London YMCA, McBurney saw the myriads of facilities he built, bought and renovated as the means to the Y's end of attracting young men to Christ. It is safe to say no other figure had a more significant influence upon the YMCA than Robert Ross McBurney. He more than any other individual defined the General Secretary's role and his philosophies continued to influence the Y over a century after he last worked for the Y.

EARLY LIFE
Robert Ross McBurney was born an Ulster Scot in Northern Ireland to a prominent Physician and surgeon. His mother (nee Ross) was an ardent Methodist. His mother instilled in him a rich love for Church singing and hymns, but died when Robert was but a "wee bairn" of only six. Robert was raised in the Church and had a zest for Christian service for his entire life as a result of this early upbringing. His father, mother and step mother (another fervent Methodist) were all instrumental in instilling in Robert a firm biblical and ecclesiastical foundation which served him the rest of his life.

EARLY ADULTHOOD
In 1854, at the age of 18, Robert came to America as one of the

TIMEOUT

hundreds of thousands of poor Irish immigrants who were escaping the potato famine or who were searching for a better life. Upon his arrival in New York City he found his first lodging at the newly organized YMCA (which was only in its second year of existence at the time) and his first employment was secured with Henry Harrison a friend of his father. The Harrison family was well connected in the American political and business worlds including family members who became president and served in Congress. He worked in Harrison's hat establishment and may have continued in that business except for the fact that it went bankrupt during the Civil War. During his work in the hat business, he found time to become a leader of a noonday prayer meeting at the North Dutch Church on Fulton Street in New York City (where he was greatly influenced by the preaching ministry of Theodore Cuyler) and joined the Mulberry Street Methodist Episcopal Church (later St. Paul's) of which he remained a member until his death. He also became involved with many of the area Sunday Schools and other Church ministries. The noonday prayer meeting was the impetus of a very influential and renowned revival.

ASSOCIATION WITH THE YMCA

From there, McBurney connected with the newly formed YMCA of which he became its first employed officer in 1862. His first salary was a paltry $5 per week. This sum and the fact that he remained a bachelor throughout his life in order to better serve the Y were two indications of the level of his commitment to his calling. In fact he often had to be persuaded by the board to take a salary increase. He was a man totally committed to reaching men for Christ and arranged his entire life so he could serve in Christian ministry. The words of his biographer describe McBurney best: "He made all his decisions in the light of full surrender to the one end of his life." To be continued…

This is an excerpt from the unpublished and forthcoming book by Dr. Greg Linville: *Sports Ministry Pioneers: 19th Century Models for 21st Century Sports Outreach*. This one is from the chapter entitled – The Heir of a Movement.

I. The General Proposals

This chapter outlines two general proposals; all for the purpose of aiding *The Sports Outreach Community* to establish foundational transferable concepts to mobilize, enable and empower gospel-centric missiology. The first is uniting local congregations and sport-related, para-ministries for full mission integration. The second is integrating the *Mega-Models* and *3-R-Model of Evangelistic-Disciplemaking* in SR&F outreach.

A. Maximizing Missional Endeavors #1 – Uniting Local Church & Para-Ministry Missions

The bottom line reality is that most congregations struggle to reach those outside the church and would benefit from the strategic methods, connections and relationships the para-ministry world has developed. By contrast, most para-ministries struggle to connect those they are reaching to a congregation that can shepherd long-term spiritual growth and maturity.

I am convinced The Church would experience an unprecedented expansion and increased relevance if local congregations and para-ministries would unite in synergistic, gospel-centric, *Evangelistic-Disciplemaking* collaborations. Both the local church and each para-ministry have great strengths, but both also have limitations. If united, their strengths would be enhanced and their shortcomings would be mitigated; if not eliminated. Unprecedented potential awaits any brave, creative and willing parties.

To that end, this chapter explores the why, what and how, of uniting the local church and para-ministry worlds. Therefore, this chapter will also propose a few models and feature quotes from, this chapter's Muscular Christian Model historical vignette, Robert Ross McBurney. (See Scoreboard: Integration Models on page 113) McBurney personally embodied, and corporately integrated, an excellent local church/para-ministry model 150 years ago when he became the visionary leader of the mission-oriented American YMCA.

As to these concepts and models, specific proposals for these integrated and collaborative sports outreach endeavors are featured in other books in this series[1] and those specifics will not be repeated here. However, one of the main points of this chapter is an encouragement for: a) para-ministries to consider aligning their outreaches under the auspices of a local church; and b) local churches to embrace, empower and enhance para-ministries in any of the ways outlined in the The Mission Integration Models Scoreboard on page 113…or in other creative ways.

Such unification and integration of the para-ministry and local church worlds

---

1 For additional thoughts about envisioning collaborative models for local church, sports chaplaincies and para-ministries see the following three Institutes of Sports Outreach books: pages 89-91 in the second book - *Sports Outreach Fundamentals*; Chapter 8 in the fourth book in the series - *The Saving of Sports Ministry: The Soteriology of Sports Outreach*; and Chapter 4 in the eighth book in the series - *The Life of The Shoe: Sports Outreach for the World*.

will not come without some risk and difficulty. It will require a willingness to lay down many "sacred cows" and will require systemic change and such collaborations will very likely cause organizational, financial and methodological upheaval. The major obstacle may well be however, ego and ownership issues or the ever present: "But we've always done it that way." Yet, I believe the benefits will far outweigh the pain of change. Who is willing to risk for the gospel?

This process of change starts by asking two vital missiological questions…one for local churches and the second for para-ministries…all for the purpose of accomplishing one ultimate goal.

1. Two Vital Missiological Questions

The question for local churches is: are they effective in reaching those far from Jesus and His Church? The fact is; most congregations tell me they are evangelistically unsuccessful. Thus, it is highly recommended for these congregations to synergistically unite with sports-related, para-ministries that have a proven record of reaching those far from Jesus.

The question for sports-related, para-ministries has to do with, being effective in bringing the individuals they reach to full spiritual maturity.

Most para-ministry leaders that I've talked with indicate they feel inadequate in successfully "making disciples." They tell me that the athletes they reach out to most often struggle spiritually unless they join their staff or become rooted in a Bible-based congregation. Thus, it is highly recommended for these para-ministries to synergistically unite with local congregations that are far more likely to empower new or immature believers to attain full spiritual maturity.

2. One Ultimate Goal

The ultimate goal of the entire Church (individual Christians, local congregations, mission agencies, denominations and para-ministries) is to "go and make disciples." To that end, a united, synergistic, co-laboring in ministry would produce great *Evangelistic-Disciplemaking* results. Isn't it time for The Church (local congregations and para-ministries) to come together to accomplish the ultimate goal? Isn't it time for individual congregations and para-ministries to unite and integrate their efforts?

So, the first general proposal for maximizing gospel-centric missiology is a unified integration of the local church and para-ministries. The second has to do with understanding the strategic power of uniting and integrating two basic models of outreach.[2]

B. Maximizing Missional Endeavors #2 – Integrating the *Mega-Models* and the *3-R-Models* of Missions

This is not an either/or debate. Rather it is a both/and exploration. When

---

[2] Such models are *Level #3 Methodological-Models* that meet the *4-Fold Evaluative Rubric (Strategically-Relevant* and *Efficiently-Effective)*. Refer to Chapter 4 in the *Sports Outreach Fundamentals* book for a full description and details.

TIMEOUT

First Church & Baseball Chapel

First Church received the good news that a minor league baseball team was coming to their town. The congregation began to pray and envision how to reach out to the team's players, management, coaches and other personnel.

The congregation began the outreach on their own but after a couple of years gratefully welcomed the help of Baseball Chapel when it offered its insights and connections to the overall outreach that included connecting the chapel leadership with the chaplains of other teams within both the minor and major league systems. Together the combined efforts enabled a strong outreach over the next decade that impacted thousands of people associated with the team.

Weekly Bible studies strengthened those in attendance, whereas weekly Chapels brought a verbal proclamation of the gospel to players, coaches, stadium workers and even umpires...and yet the real ministry occurred each day in ways only a local church could provide.

Members of the congregation opened their homes for weekly meals and a few even accommodated a player or two in a spare bedroom for the entire summer. Women in the church reached out to the wives or "significant others" of the players, who were left alone in a strange city when their husbands went on road trips with the team. Childcare was provided during games for player's children; transportation was provided for basic shopping, post office runs and trips to the barbershop or salon.

Perhaps the most important thing that happened was the players and their families became part of a local church and grew in their faith journey.

Not only did First Church and Baseball Chapel unite in their outreach, they also combined the *Mega-Model* of *Platform-Proclamations* that occurred in weekly Chapel services with the *3-R-Model* of daily relational efforts that served the needs of all involved.

The end result was the "making of disciples!"

Batter UP! Who's ready to unite ministries and ministry models?

the two ministries models are integrated and used together in a seamless whole, the overall outreach is even more effective. What follows are two specific proposals for integrating *Mega-Models* and *3-R-Models* of gospel centric, *Evangelistic-Disciplemaking*.

1. Option #1: *Mega-Event & 3-R-Model*

This proposal assumes that one aspect of a local church SR&F outreach mission plan includes reaching adults through league and team sports. It is also assumed that the basic week-to-week, season-to-season and year-to-year outreach[3] philosophy is focused on, using ongoing relational mission[4] for the purpose of mobilizing the congregation's local missionaries to incarnationally reach those far from Jesus and His Church.

So, in such local church sports leagues the primary way the gospel is proclaimed is through the congregational members[5] as they engage in weekly on the court competitions and day-to-day connections with their friends, family members and teammates.[6] It is through these repeated engagements that congregational members exhibit love and live out their faith with those who are far from Jesus and His Church."

While the weekly relational-based proclamation and affirmation of the gospel pays dividends, when it is combined with a one-time, *Mega-Model* outreach a huge benefit for the gospel can be anticipated.[7]

Mega-Event **at the end:** In specific, many first time commitments to Jesus will occur at a *Mega-Event* that comes at a sports league's year end banquet. This event typically includes having an elite athlete and/or coach deliver a verbal affirmation of the gospel that ends with an invitation to receive Jesus as Savior. This integration of a season-long outreach based in a relational, incarnational methodology with a one-time event maximizes the cumulative effect of both models.

Mega-Event **at the beginning:** The other way the *Mega-Event* model can be utilized is as an initial entry into the ministry. For example, if a church sponsors a neighborhood festival that includes "inflatables" for kids to enjoy; live music to dance to; and another delicious BBQ feast provided by the "grill bubbas," it would serve as a great initial contact with community people. If a mission strategy includes a "front-end" *Mega-Event,* there are four major components to understand and employ for such a strategy to work.

First, prayer is an obvious necessity for true gospel effectiveness and congregations are encouraged to form a regular, consistent system of prayer.

---

3 What is referred to in this book series as *Evangelistic-Disciplemaking*.
4 What is referred to in this book series as the *3-R-Model* of creating, *Repetitive-Redemptive-Relational* opportunities.
5 What is referred to in this book series as the missionary *You's* of the congregation.
6 What is referred to in this book series as the *Who's*. See The *You* and *Who* Scoreboard on page 95.
7 What is referred to in this book series as integrating a *3-R-Model* with a *Mega-Event / Platform-Proclamation* of the gospel, and repeating it in multiple seasons; possibly over many years.

TIMEOUT

Muscular Christian Models

Centered on Touching Hearts & Lives

We might discuss creeds till doomsday, and I do not think anybody would be helped by it. It is touching men's hearts and lives for Christ that is our business, since we both believe that we have been redeemed by His precious blood, and that today He is our advocate before the throne.*

— Robert McBurney

---

* This is an excerpt from the unpublished and forthcoming book by Dr. Greg Linville: *Sports Ministry Pioneers: 19th Century Models for 21st Century Sports Outreach*. This one is from the chapter entitled – The Heir of a Movement.

Second, hosting a front-end *Mega-Event* requires (this is an absolute necessity) a church-wide effort that encourages every congregant to invite friends, family, neighbors and/or co-workers to the festival.

Third, it is important to coach congregants on how to interact with guests they invite and/or meet at the festival including recognizing such an event to be an ideal time and place to invite people to join adult leagues, fitness classes and/or youth leagues. Perhaps even more important is to caution church members to initiate and continue in conversations with the invited guests, rather than spending the entire time fellowshipping with other church members!

Fourth, a word of caution is offered. Conventional evangelical wisdom may suggest that since a crowd was gathered, the gospel should be "preached." However, such a forced "preaching" of the gospel may in fact send the church's neighbors running for the hills; never to return. The purpose of the festival is not to deliver a sermon[8], but rather to "proclaim" the gospel by warmly welcoming and engaging with those who are not church members. Verbal affirmations of the gospel may occur in individual dialogues but are best left to later times and occasions. If the festival is envisioned to be a place to winsomely attract people for a first time association with the church, then all who attend the festival can be enthusiastically interacted with, and if they experience warmth and acceptance they

---

8   What is described in this book series as a *Platform-Proclamation* of the gospel.

are usually open to further invitations. Such invitations to participate in other congregational activities are most often well received if a first time guest's experience has been positive. Whereas an invitation to accept Jesus as Lord and Savior is usually not well received for a first time visitor, specific invitations to: join the church's sports leagues and fitness classes; utilize its child care services; attend church sponsored financial or fitness classes and/or divorce recovery groups; are almost always appreciated.

So, by strategically planning a mission that integrates both models into the overall outreach plan, the Great Commission efforts of a congregation is maximized. While a *Mega-Event* can be organized as a stand-alone outreach, it can also be strategically paired with a *Mega-Media* endeavor with good results.

2. Option #2: *Mega-Media & 3-R-Model* [9]

The gospel impact of an outreach based in ongoing and consistent relationship building [10] can also be greatly enhanced if it integrates a relevant and intentional media resource[11] into the overall missional plan. This proposal consists of choosing a specific week to deliver a media-based, verbal affirmation of the gospel to the participants in the various leagues, classes or activities of the congregation. Whether this media piece is a written piece of literature, a C.D. or podcast link to an audio clip; or a social media video connection, such pieces can greatly augment to the ongoing relational ministry that occurs weekly. Such communication pieces can provide many opportunities for "evangelistic conversations" to occur over the ensuing weeks the relational outreach runs.

3. Option #3 – *Mega-Event & Mega-Media Model*

Likewise, the impact of a *Mega-Event* can be maximized if it is combined with a *Mega-Media* component. For example, if First Church hosts the aforementioned Festival at their recreational center, gospel impact can be enhanced by handing out a quality piece of literature or digital file that is relevant, mildly evangelical and well produced. It is highly recommended however, that such *Mega-Media* pieces address topics that are relevant to the community and include invitations and suggestions for how the invited guests can participate in other church-sponsored activities.

Relevant to the community would include having "hometown" athletes share their athletic and spiritual journeys and additional invitations would include a listing of upcoming leagues, fitness classes and other services, events or activities.

C. Vital Missiological Questions Revisited

The question for all para-ministries is: are the functional activities (as opposed to the stated missiological goals) of a para-ministry expanding and enhancing local congregations, or do they only perpetuate the para-ministry.

---

9   Whereas proposal #1 integrated the *Mega-Event* model with the *3-R-Model*, this second proposal integrates the *Mega-Media* model with both the *3-R-Model* and *Mega-Event* model.
10 What is referred to in this book series as the *3-R-Model (Repetitive-Redemptive-Relational)*.
11 What is referred to in this book series as *Mega-Media*.

TIMEOUT

Muscular Christian Models

Centered on Men's Salvation

L. L. Doggett wrote in his introduction to McBurney's biography the following description of McBurney. It is a warm and touching description which accurately portrays a man which should be an example and model to anyone conversing with anyone not currently attending a church.

> Another thing as pre-eminent in this man's life as his dominating love was the ever-present, ever-ready, concern he had for men's salvation. It was hardly possible to come into personal contact with McBurney without feeling his interest in one's eternal welfare. On every hand he made it his business in an engaging and tactful way to establish such relationships as would impress men with this interest. He took advantage of every slight occasion to this end and in a direct and really loving way he made a personal impress upon thousands of young men. His cordial, earnest greeting, his hand, his look, the few words he spoke, however brief or inconsequential otherwise the interview, lifted the life he touched. Multitudes of young men owe to his efforts their personal salvation, and hundreds of others have been led by him to devote themselves to the ministry...*

---

* This is an excerpt from the unpublished and forthcoming book by Dr. Greg Linville: *Sports Ministry Pioneers: 19th Century Models for 21st Century Sports Outreach*. This one is from the chapter entitled – The Heir of a Movement.

TIMEOUT

Muscular Christian Models

Are Our Sports Facilities... Centers of Magnetic Power

It would be difficult to exaggerate the importance of the social element as a factor in winning and holding young men in right paths. Much has been done by the Association (YMCA) in this direction, but much more should be done. If the young stranger is to be helped from falling into bad social surroundings by the Association, its rooms must become a center of magnetic social power."*

— Robert McBurney

---

* This is an excerpt from the unpublished and forthcoming book by Dr. Greg Linville: *Sports Ministry Pioneers: 19th Century Models for 21st Century Sports Outreach*. This one is from the chapter entitled – The Heir of a Movement.

Stated more specifically, do the efforts of the para-ministry result in either: a) planting churches; or b) or in building, growing and strengthening already existing congregations?

The answer to this question reveals the heart and DNA of a para-ministry.

Barnabas and Paul were not comissioned as ministry organizers to initiate and perpetuate a para-ministry! Rather, they were sent to plant and build churches. In essence these two men and all whom they mentored operated as a para-ministry or mission agency, but what their efforts left behind were local assemblies of converts to Jesus (churches). Their legacy was not a para-ministry but rather local churches that planted yet other congregations; which is the ultimate goal of missionaries.

There is no doubt that church planting mission agencies and para-ministries can fulfill a biblcial model for expanding The Church, but all too often these groups end up only enhancing and expanding their own organizations and never plant or grow a church.

The question for all local churches is: are the functional activities (again, as opposed to their stated missiological goals) of a local church expanding and enhancing The Church or are they perpetuating their own congregation? Another

TIMEOUT

Muscular Christian Models

Centered on men who are astray

I would advise you to . . . come into heart-touch with men - lost men, men who are astray, and when you come to make effort to lead such men into right living, you will be more and more impressed with the fact that only by God's spirit, and through a new spirit begotten in them by the Holy Ghost, are they to be really helped.*

— Robert McBurney

---

* This is an excerpt from the unpublished and forthcoming book by Dr. Greg Linville: *Sports Ministry Pioneers: 19th Century Models for 21st Century Sports Outreach*. This one is from the chapter entitled – The Heir of a Movement.

---

way to ask this question is: is the congregation effectively reaching those far from Jesus? If not, then that congregation is not much more than a fellowship group or social club.

Again, there is no doubt the local church is ordained of God and yet all too often its local assemblies fail at the most basic levels to fulfill their call to effectively engage in Great Commission endeavors. Sadly it too often becomes inward focused rather than outward. Sadly, many congregations are content with ministering to those who are already members rather than engaging in a mission to those "who are without."[12]

D. Summary of the General Proposals

It can only be imagined as to what could really happen if local congregations and para-ministries actually embraced each other with a united and integrated Great Commission effort. It is yet to be seen how The Church will grow and expand if local churches and para-ministries unite to conduct outreach methodologies that integrate consistent, ongoing relational endeavors with exciting and attractive one-time outreaches[13] into their overall mission plan.

---

12   Colossians 4.5.
13   What is referred to as integrating *Mega-Models* with The *3-R-Model*.

CHAPTER 8: Missiological Applications for Sports-related, Para-Ministries & Sports Chaplaincy 113

SCOREBOARD

Mission Integration Models

- A local chapter of minor league Baseball Chapel to be led and shepherded by a specific congregation including having their sports minister be the Chaplain, and have the local church cover all Chapel expenses

- A local church hire a youth minister who's job description includes being a FCA staff person at the local high school with an intermediate goal of encouraging student athletes to take part in the church's middle and/or high school ministries

- A local church hire a single's pastor who's job description includes being the AIA staff person for the local college with a goal of encouraging collegiate athletes to get involved in various congregational activities, groups and services

- A residential summer camp partner with a congregation to create a summer's worth of day camps to be held on the campus of the church and utilizing the church's athletic and recreational facilities

Isn't it time to unite around a shared missiology that integrates various outreach models to reach the 4-5 billion people who are still far from a relationship with Jesus and His Church?[14]

II. Final Thoughts on the Integration of the Local Church and Para-Ministries

It's not a question of whether or not a congregation ever leads a person into a personal relationship with Jesus. This has happened repeatedly for millennia. It's also not doubted that sports-related, para-ministries have successfully discipled athletes and coaches. Praise God these goals are met at times and praise Him also for the committed efforts of all within these congregations and ministries who strive for these ends.

The real question however, is not whether new birth and spiritual growth ever occurs within current models of outreach, but rather the question becomes,

---

14 See Addendum #5 for a more detailed list of proposed models for para-ministries and local churches to unite in ministry.

could the ultimate goal of making disciples become ever more successful![15] I believe the answer is yes…**without a doubt, yes.**

I don't pretend to think the unification and integration of efforts will be without cost and great change. I do however strongly believe the end result will catalytically empower the great expansion of The Church! What remains to be seen is who will envision and pioneer the future of mission?

---

15   What is referred to in this book series as being *Strategically-Relevant* and *Efficiently-Effectively.*

TIMEOUT

Muscular Christian Models

Robert Ross McBurney (Continued)

MODEL FOR SPORTS-RELATED, PARA-MINISTRIES
Although McBurney led the YMCA, he remained solidly connected to the local church. He personally attended, remained an active leader in his church throughout his life and always believed the first commitment of each YMCA member was to his local church. Moreover, he personally connected all new believers to a local church.

Truly, Robert Ross McBurney was an exemplary witness for Christ and provides a wonderful model for the current day YMCA worker and sports minister. May his fervor for his Savior and his dedication to winning others to the Savior, be the heart cry and foundation of each and every sports minister and YMCA worker who may read this recapitulation of the life of Robert Ross McBurney.

Leading men to Christ was only the beginning for McBurney. He believed the building up of a new believer to be a foundational aspect of Y work and was accomplished through Bible Study. He fully believed in the inspiration and authority of the scriptures and taught them to men. One of the most popular Bible classes he taught was entitled "Conversations with Jesus." His philosophy of Bible study was twofold. First that it should be practical in nature. He believed that a strictly "critical" study of the Bible would not help the common man and therefore the mission of the association Bible study was to help men in their daily life. His second philosophy of Bible study was that it was to lift up Jesus. He wrote: "the more we lift up Jesus Christ to the gaze of men, the more assuredly will men be drawn to him."

Although McBurney was active in personally leading men to Christ and in leading association Bible Studies, he always believed and promoted the fact that the work was to be done by young men for young men. He believed the role of the secretary was to stay in the background and push the members to the foreground. He worked

continued on page 116

TIMEOUT

continued from page 115

hard at training and directing others to do the work of the association. He was to be the one who cast the vision and the one who supported those who did the work. He believed the YMCA secretary was responsible for:

> ". . .the reaching of young men. He may have a model educational work, a good physical department, large meetings, and a thorough social atmosphere, but if he has not a band of workers who are personally reaching young men and winning them from sin to righteousness, from the world to the Church of Jesus Christ, he is not fulfilling his responsibility."

One last quote gives additional support to the point that personal evangelism was the purpose for which McBurney gave his life. Describing McBurney in his comprehensive volume on the International work of the early YMCA, Kenneth Scott Latourette states:

> *"He was warmly evangelistic, had a genius for friendship, and through personal contacts won many to the Christian faith."* *

*Kenneth Scott Latourette - *World Service*, p. 26.

This excerpt it taken from a CSRM blog which itself is an excerpt from the unpublished and forthcoming book by Dr. Greg Linville: *Sports Ministry Pioneers: 19th Century Models for 21st Century Sports Outreach*. This one is from the Chapter entitled – The Heir of a Movement.

SECTION 3: Application of Missiological Foundations

Chapter 9

Missiological Applications for Sports Outreach in a Multi-Faith World

I. International Mission Redefined – Mission in an Intolerant and Violent World – 118
   A. Redefinition of International Missionary Strategies – 118
      1. "Dispensing with Sacred Cows"… Where Cows are Sacred – 118
      2. Doing it Differently in Places… in Places Where "We've Always Done it This Way" – 119

II. International Mission Insights – 120
   A. From Elitist to Incarnational Missions – 120
      1. Embracing the Needs, Conditions and Culture of Those Served – 121
      2. Partnering with and Learning from Those Being Served – 121
      3. Seeking to Partner With Indigenous People as Equals in Mission – 123
   B. Expecting Suffering and Persecution in Missions – 123
      1. Running To, Not Away From Suffering and Persecution – 123

III. International Mission in Action – 125
   A. Developing an Organizational Structure From Biblically-Based, Philosophical-Principles – 125
      1. Sports Outreach Ministry Training – 125
          a. Conferencing – 125
          b. Consulting – 126
          c. Content Sharing – 127
      2. Sports Outreach Ministry Models – 127
   B. Sharing, Transferring, Working and Releasing the Vision – 130
      1. Share the Vision – 131
      2. Transfer the Vision – 132
      3. Work the Vision – 133
      4. Release the Vision – 134

IV. Summary of the Vision – 135

> "We are all missionaries. Wherever we go we either bring people nearer to Christ or we repel them from Christ."*
>
> *Eric Liddell*

* https://www.azquotes.com/quote/368725#:~:text=Wherever%20we...,we%20repel%20them%20from%20Christ.

I. International Mission - Mission in an Intolerant and Violent World

Yes, mission strategy for the Western world is in need of a redefinition but missionary work in much of the rest of the world is experiencing an even more dire and vulnerable reality because of: a) the virulent, religious-based, persecution of Church buildings and discrimination towards anything Christian; b) political instabilities that lead to societal upheavals and displaced people; c) increasingly intolerant secularism; and d) chaos due to pandemics.

A. Redefinition of International Missionary Strategies

Notwithstanding a few prior periods of time and isolated unfortunate incidences in which international missionaries faced persecution, torture and even death, Christian missionaries have usually been well received for centuries. If for no other reason, such favor was realized because of their willingness to provide humanitarian aid. However, such welcomed reception has diminished in many places around the world with an ever increasing number of missionaries being imprisoned, persecuted and executed. Such developments call for new strategies and redefinitions.

Just as Alexander Duff redefined and revolutionized Christian mission in the 19th century, a new vision for strategic and relevant mission is needed in the 21st century.[1] The intolerance, hatred and violence towards Christians by Taliban radicals, militant and hostile Hindu governments and power hungry tribal leaders, all call for a redefinition of what mission, and what being a missionary, means. New efficient and effective strategies for proclaiming and affirming the gospel to hundreds of unreached people groups are needed. Additional, international missionaries who are trained, supported and equipped are much needed. While there is no "cookie-cutter," "one size fits all" methodology, there is a developing model that is emerging out of the sports ministry world that is achieving gospel-centric success in international missions.

1. Dispensing with Sacred Cows... where Cows are Sacred

At one time, it was thought by some that opening an orphanage, hospital or school were not valid expressions of Christian missions, and yet the proof of their effectiveness continues to be evidenced throughout the decades. As long as such initiatives maintain gospel-centricity, they continue to be highly effective methodologies for expanding and enhancing The Church throughout world. However, there is an ever increasing and sad reality occurring because more and more countries are refusing to allow these much needed social services if they are resolute in being Christo-centric.

On the other hand, some of the resistance to innovative missiological models comes not from hostile Imams or corrupt politicians, but rather from missionary traditionalists within the Christian missionary community itself. While it is

---

1 See chapter 4 of this book that features Duff and his role in revolutionizing international missions and being the catalyst for creating the academic field of missiology.

TIME OUT

Praying for Modern Day Apostle Pauls

One of CSRM's Global Network Partners (GNP's) who serves in a country that actively persecutes Christians requests ongoing prayer that modern day Apostle Pauls will be raised up in each of his country's 200+ unreached people groups…especially among the Islamic terrorist groups active throughout his country.

His prayer request included a reminder that Paul (like those involved in the religious terrorists groups of today) was an enemy of the followers of Jesus; persecuting, imprisoning and even killing Christians. Yet God worked a miracle and Paul became the leading evangelist of the New Testament.

Yes indeed, let us pray that God will raise up the 200+ "Pauls" for that country and thousands more for other countries.

---

indeed sad that Communistic governments refuse a Christian hospital or school to operate, or an Islamic country rejects humanitarian aid for its hungry and hurting people if offered by a Christian group; but it defies logic when mission agencies continue with their "sacred cows" of how mission efforts should operate. It is hard to understand why such creative new missionary endeavors are rejected only because they don't fit the traditional mold.

Thankfully however, these restraints and persecutions haven't totally stopped those engaged in less traditional but oh so effective means to reach those far from Jesus and His Church.

To that end, a case could be made that international, sports-related, missions have indeed "adjusted their sails;" and yet, even more adjustments are needed. The redefinitions that have already occurred in international missions include mission agencies seeking coaches rather than ministers and recruiting entrepreneurs rather than seminarians.[2] So not only do mission strategies need to be redefined but so does the understanding of what it means to be a missionary.

2. Doing it Differently in Places… in Places Where "We've Always Done it This Way"

Doing it differently in this newly redefined world of missions includes using sports-related strategies.

---

2   Uttermost Sports (www.uttermostsports.org) is the world leader in this strategy.

It has become more and more obvious that coaches who can improve sporting excellence are welcomed in many regions and countries; including countries and governments that are otherwise antagonistic to anything Christian. Such countries are increasingly opening their borders to effective coaches, even if the coaches are disciples of Jesus!

Similarly, a Christian business-person who can enhance the economics of a community will be accommodated in areas that are normally resistive to Christianity. More and more missionaries are recognizing that their entrepreneurial gifts and abilities open previously shut doors for the gospel.

These strategies are doubly effective when combined. If a coach is able to improve both the athletics and economics of a particular country, their impact will be wider, greater and more long-lasting. The recognition of this strategy is revolutionizing how missions are envisioned and continues to provide the necessary impetus for adapting how international missions are done and serve as the foundation for what follows (International Insights). The following insights are penned by CSRM's International Director who claims that while there have been great strides made, there is still much more that needs done.

II. International Mission Insights

CSRM's International Director (P. F. Myers) serves two key roles in the Institutes of Sports Outreach book series. Myers is not only the author of the 8th book in this series (*Life of the Shoe: Sports Outreach for the World*) but is also a contributing author for most of the other books in the series where his wisdom frequents the pages in sidebar additions entitled: "International Insights." The bulk of what follows in this chapter is written by Myers for obvious reasons: he simply is a widely-experienced expert in this area of gospel work and thus a world authority on this topic. He writes…

A. From Elitist to Incarnational Missions

Unfortunately, the West for too long has done what I describe as "elitist" or "subordinate" missions. What is meant by this is…most Christians would rather send money to support other's mission trips than to go themselves…unless the mission happens to be in the Caribbean! It is interesting however, that those who actually do go, think Jesus arrives with them, leaves when they leave, and the entire experience and surroundings should mirror those of a wealthy home country and culture!

Authentic missions however, are incarnational outreaches, not recreational holidays. Incarnational assumes the SR&F mission team is willing: 1) to embrace the needs, conditions and culture of those they are serving; 2) to learn from those they serve; and 3) to recognize the importance of partnering with the indigenous people as equals in mission.

International Insights

The sports mission team from "1st Church" travelled to a developing nation to reach the indigenous people with the gospel of Jesus. This mission team spent three days "serving" the local people while each day the mission team had their meals prepared and served by the cook they brought with them so they could eat meals they were familiar with, like back-home.

After their three day mission, they spent four days debriefing at a fancy resort. The reason? They needed time to deal with and overcome the poverty they had just experienced firsthand.

The cost of lodging for one night at the resort equaled an entire month's living expense for many local indigenous families.

As unfortunate as it may be, it would be more beneficial for some Americans to give money rather than go on such a mission trip!

1. Embracing the Needs, Conditions, Language and Culture of Those Served

I came to realize the importance of embracing the needs, conditions and culture of Indigenous people early on in my missionary life.

At the age of 13 I went on my first mission trip to serve the Mayan Indians living on the Yucatan Peninsula of Mexico. We slept in thatched huts where chickens ran under our hammocks as we slept. Our toilet was a hole in the ground, and our shower was nothing more than a bucket of water dumped on our heads. We followed the local pastor's lead as he deployed us to assist (not direct) the building of a facility for their congregation to meet in.

I learned that to reach those far from Jesus, short-term mission teams must, as much as possible, become like those they serve.[3] Of course this often includes the possibility of experiencing some rather uncomfortable situations. It's possible that members of the mission team may well get dysentery or some other "bug." It often means a loss of sleep due to intense heat and humidity; insect infestations; lack of privacy; and/or other inconveniences... but the impact that can be made for Jesus is well worth the risk and sacrifices.

The bottom line is many mission teams from the West need to change their perspective on both short-term and long-term, missions. Mission is not about the short-term missionary. It is about serving Jesus and brothers and sisters (or potential brethren) in the Lord!

---
3   What is referred to as incarnating the gospel based on John 1.14.

Steve Camp (a contemporary Christian singer) has a quote from one of his songs that should challenge us all. It so impacted me that I decided to memorize it: "There is safety in complacency. But God is calling us out of our comfort zone into a life of complete surrender to the cross. To live dangerously is not to live recklessly, but righteously, and it is because of God's radical grace for us that we can risk living a life of radical obedience for Him."[4]

2. Partnering with and Learning from Those Being Served

We must become fellow servants with the indigenous Christians who have invited us to labor alongside of them as they minister to those they have been called to reach. If we short-term missionaries have hearts that are truly willing to serve, then God can use us to take the gospel everywhere. Effective mission flows out of humility and a willingness to learn. However, when we leave our own culture, or even just step into an environment or situation that is uncomfortable for us, the biggest challenge can be overcoming false expectations.

Chuck Swindoll, in his book *Growing Strong in the Seasons of Life*, says:

> "We need to take an honest look at this painful thorn that blurs our vision and conceives our disappointments: expectations. We erect mental images, which are either unrealistic or unfair or biased. Those phantom images become our inner focus, rigidly and traditionally maintained. Leaving no room for flexibility on the part of the other person (allowing no place for circumstantial change or surprise), we set in mental concrete the way things MUST go. When they DON'T, we either tumble or grumble or... both. The result is tragic. As our radius of toleration is reduced, our willingness to accept others' imperfections or a less-than-ideal circumstance is short-circuited."[5]

Swindoll goes on to say that we need to "stop anticipating the IDEAL and start living with the REAL – which is always checkered with failure, imperfection, and even wrong."[6] Expectations will almost always color the way we plan and do ministry. They affect the events and influence the attitudes of those involved in regard to what goals will be fulfilled by the mission. Expectations are often vague, unspoken, and not measurable until the person is placed in a setting that challenges those expectations. This is precisely why missions, local or international, should be such an integral part of *Evangelistic-Disciplemaking*. Many times, a person will be unaware of his expectations until they go unmet. A frontline mission experience often breaks down wrong expectations created by living in the IDEAL with a false sense of cultural reality and allows learning and growth

---

4   Steve Camp; *Justice* (Album) 1988 Sparrow Records; Living Dangerously in the Hands of God (song).
5   Charles R. Swindoll, *Growing Strong in the Seasons of Life*, Grand Rapids, MI; Zondervan Publishers, 1994.
6   Charles R. Swindoll, op. cit..

as the REAL is embraced. For the missionary, the IDEAL can be a culture and tradition that he comes from, and is familiar. The REAL is the culture and tradition they are trying to reach and must learn in order to be most effective.

3. Seeking to Partner With Indigenous People as Equals in Mission

It is crucial to keep in mind that an effective, short-term, sports mission strategy of partnership is dependent upon both those who are going, and also the local churches and para-ministries/mission agencies who host the short-termers. Both have something valuable to offer and contribute. Ultimately engaging in such strategic partnership increases the chances of long-term success. Lasting fruit only occurs when missionaries go incarnationally as learners to partner and unite with local indigenous congregations for the purpose of mobilizing, equipping and empowering effective mission. Only when indigenous congregational believers lead the missionary outreach, participate in the missionary activities, interact with those being reached and become personally involved in disciple-making-follow-up with those who come to know Christ will there be lasting success. This strategic methodology is what I have called the development of a *Missional Sports Community*.[7] These *Communities* are usually not based in a building but can be formed almost anywhere. They are the outworking of direct outreach in a community with individuals who come together around a common interest (SR&F outreach missions).

The commitment to develop *Missional Sports Communities* is key for any effective, long-term, gospel success; and these communities are most effective when implemented through local congregations. The training of congregational leaders (young and old) will enable the perpetuation of ongoing ministry through SR&F missions.[8]

B. Expecting Suffering and Persecution in Missions

The REALITY of life is that most Christians around the world live in poverty and/or under difficult circumstances which often includes suffering and persecution. It shouldn't be surprising then, that short term (or for that matter, long-term) missionaries will also experience such hardships.

1. Running To, Not Away From Suffering and Persecution

Thus, Christians need to stop running away from suffering and persecution and recognize it as a part of a Christian and missionary experience. Suffering is a normal part of the human experience in the fallen world and Jesus warned His followers that they would be hated by the world, just as He was. There is a cosmic spiritual battle and Christians will face opposition because satan wants to destroy Christian lives, families, marriages and churches.

This suffering and persecution should not come as surprise as much of the Bible was written by persecuted and suffering believers…and it was sent to

---

7   As explained in chapter 11 of *The Life of the Shoe: Sports Outreach for the World*.
8   For practical ways to pursue effective partnership, see the International Insights sidebar in Chapter 3 (pg. 25).

SCOREBOARD

Ripken's Insights on How to Survive Persecution

1. They know Jesus intimately because they have faced persecution and are living out the Resurrection

2. They know the power of prayer and fasting (one Chinese believer was held in the same house for 33 years where he spent 4 days every week fasting and intimately knew the presence of God)

3. They can recite large portions of scripture by memory

4. They can sing many hymns and spiritual songs from memory (what they called "heart songs to Jesus"

5. They see their suffering as for Jesus' sake, as the highest calling

6. They know they are prayed for and not forgotten by the Body of Christ around the world

7. The local believer's community cares for their own who are suffering and support them spiritually and physically as they are able

8. They know persecution is normal and yet they try to live with joy

9. They have claimed their freedom in Jesus who has set them free from the bonds of this life

10. They have lost their fear, fear of death, fear of man

11. They have established a genealogy of faith (as one pastor who was imprisoned in the former Soviet Union stated: "If I hear from prison that my family died but did not deny their faith in Jesus, I will be the most proud man!)"

Maybe it would be more beneficial for some Americans to give money rather than go on a mission trip!

other persecuted and suffering believers. It's easy to gloss over Paul's, Peter's and many other 1st Century followers of Jesus and yet they write about being beaten, whipped, robbed, stoned, ship-wrecked, and how they experienced constant danger and hardship for the sake of the gospel.[9] The suffering experience of 1st century missionaries was not the exception for them and it will not be the exception for 21st century missionaries who commit to faithfully follow Jesus.

Being on mission is not just going to a foreign land. Rather, it is living for Jesus wherever He places us to serve, love, and share the gospel. It is living for Jesus with the people we live with or live near. It is living for Jesus with people who live just down the street or across the tracks, or across an ocean. If Christians are truly on mission they should expect some opposition, suffering, and persecution. In this regard, modern day missionaries can learn much from their brothers and sisters who are living as disciples of Jesus in difficult places.

Nik Ripken, author of *The Insanity of God*, recounts meeting house church leaders in China who called prison their seminary. One of the leaders went on to say: "Men go to prison for 2-3 years, and women only for usually 2-3 weeks. God gave the church to men... and to women [He gave] everything else."[10] The point was that it was the women who had to carry on with the daily functions of the Body as the men were away "getting their education." Every member of The Church had to step in and do their part. How do they survive? The answer can be found in the Ripken's Scoreboard on page 124.

III. International Mission in Action
A. Developing an Organizational Structure From Biblically-Based, Philosophical-Principles

All successful missionary endeavors are at their best when rooted in solid theological foundations that inform and shape organizational structures and strategies, out of which emerge truly effective ministry.[11] What follows are overarching philosophies that provide the structure for specific pragmatic models.

1. Sports Outreach Ministry Training

Sports ministry training has three primary manifestations: a) Conferencing; b) Consulting; and c) Content-Sharing. All training is for the purpose of mobilizing, connecting, empowering and enabling indigenous sports ministry leaders in how "to fish," rather being given "fish."

a. Conferencing

Conferencing is one strategy that is designed to simultaneously impact small

---

9   Acts 4:1-31, 7:54-50, 16:16-40; 2 Corinthians 11.24ff.
10 Nik Ripken and Gregg Lewis. *The Insanity of God*, Nashville, TN; B&H Books, 2013. See the Scoreboard on page 124.
11 This is a summary of the *3-Tier Paradigm: Level #1 Theological-Truths; Level #2 Philosophical-Principles; Level #3 Methodological-Models*. See chapter 3 of *Sports Outreach Fundamentals* by Dr. Greg Linville.

to large groups of people. Traditional models of conferencing consisted of gathering trainees together at a common site. In the digital age, newer models utilize ever evolving technology to impact increasingly large groups of trainees via digital formats. Both models can be effective.

Conferencing provides a unique forum for *Informing* and *Instructing*[12] conference attendees with the information that is needed to envision, plan for, organize, administrate and implement truly effective sports outreach missions. In-person conferencing also becomes an efficient way to disseminate training materials and resources that will further train and equip local church sports outreach ministry leaders for effective *Evangelistic-Disciplemaking*. While face-to-face conferences can distribute hard copies of training materials, digital conferencing is able to share electronic files and resources that can be printed and disseminated (with permission) locally.

A major focus of most CSRM sponsored conferences is to teach the principles found in the International Church Sports Ministry Training Manual that serves as a basis for the teaching and training of international leaders.[13] The manual is based on the foundation of CSRM's Institute of Sports Outreach book series[14] and includes a handbook for participants and covers topics such as: a) biblical foundations of SR&F outreach ministry; b) how to cast vision and direct mission; c) how to engage in *Evangelistic-Disciplemaking* through SR&F outreach ministry; and d) how to envision, plan for, organize, administrate and implement a *Strategically-Relevant* sports ministry. This training includes the *WIN, BUILD, SEND, MULTIPLY, Sports Ministry Pyramid* and how to incorporate it into setting up a successful SR&F outreach ministry. Over the last years, thousands of delegates representing hundreds of churches in scores of countries have been trained and equipped for building movements of congregational-based, SR&F outreach ministry.[15]

b. Consulting

Consulting is a second strategy and often comes about as a result of relationships that began at a conference. Whereas, small and large group gatherings have unique and positive gospel influence, and play a most important role in the training of current and future sports ministry leaders, CSRM nonetheless places a high value on mentoring relationships. Such relationships continue to have an

---

12   *Instructing* and *Informing* are two of the main activities that define CSRM's efforts to "Equip the local church to change lives through sport, recreation and fitness outreach ministry." *Inform* has to do with the creation, production and distribution of Christo-centric content and curriculum. *Instruct* has to do with training SR&F outreach ministers in how to most effectively utilize and employ the content and curriculum that has been created. See the Glossary for more detail on the 3-I's of CSRM.
13   This training manual can be ordered at: http://www.csrm.org/overwhelming-victory-press.html.
14   All books of the Institutes of Sports Outreach are a highly recommended pre-requisite for any CSRM training. Books can be ordered at: http://www.csrm.org/overwhelming-victory-press.html.
15   The principles of this training can be found in *The Life of the Shoe – Sports Outreach for the World*.

irreplaceable impact as they empower life-on-life influence. I have called these vital interactions "*2-T-2-2 Relationships.*"[16] Consulting is valuable in something as basic as providing information for how to envision a SR&F outreach mission or suggested rules for a sports league but whenever it develops into having a *Barnabas* who molds a *Paul*; a *Paul* who inspires a peer; or who inspires many *Timothy's*; consulting goes beyond the mere passing on of information to truly impacting and transforming individual lives.

c. Content Sharing

It has never been easier to share content throughout the world. At the touch of the button massive amounts of content can be sent and received within nano-seconds. This is one of the driving reasons CSRM has increased its commitment to an ongoing development of gospel-centric, Christ-honoring, congregation-based SR&F resources.[17] It is very important and necessary to communicate and translate any relevant content into the heart language of those you are seeking to serve and reach.

2. Sports Outreach Models

A wide spectrum of international models that have been tried and found to be highly successful throughout the world can be found in addendum #5.[18]

These resources can become great tools to complement a congregation's *Evangelistic-Disciplemaking* strategy. Please note that the models provided in addendum #5 are not an exhaustive list. You certainly might even have other things to add.

B. Sharing, Transferring, Working and Releasing the Vision

The ultimate goal of all missionary work is to identify, mobilize and empower local, indigenous, congregational, leaders (*Timothy's*)[19] who will carry on the work and in turn "pass it on to other reliable men."[20] The hope is that God will use all short term mission groups to energize a whole new generation of *Paul's* to change lives through SR&F missions. The following four-step process is a tried and proven model for inspiring SR&F missions in a local church throughout

---

16   For a concise explanation of the *2-T-2-2 Relationships* consult page 151 in the Glossary of this book.
17   CSRM does the following among many other things. Through its publishing arm (Overwhelming Victory Press - OVP) it releases numerous books, manuals and blogs each year. Through its production studio (Overwhelming Victory Flix - OVF), CSRM releases weekly pod casts and monthly webinars entitled: Tuesday Talks along with video training series. Through its AGON Institute of Sports Ministry, CSRM has also developed a concentration in sports outreach that can lead to a Master degree and/or be applied towards a sports ministry certification. All of these resources can be accessed via the CSRM website: http://www.csrm.org/overwhelming-victory-press.html.
18   Each of these models meets the *4-Fold Evaluative Rubric* that consists of being *Strategically-Relevant* and *Efficiently-Effective*. For a detailed exploration of this see Chapter 4 of the second book in this series: *Fundamentals of Sports Outreach*.
19   This is referred to in this book series as *Producing, Reproducing, Reproducers*. Consult Chapter 7 in *The Life of the Shoe: Sports Outreach for the World* for a detailed explanation of the concept of Barnabas, Paul, Timothy, reliable men. Also consult Addendum #8 about developing a *Laborers List* – insights into how to identify and recruit Timothy's.
20   2 Timothy 2.2.

the world. What follows is a four-fold check-list of how to go about sharing the vision of how SR&F outreach missions can be integrated into a congregation's Great Commission endeavors. The check-list is provided to aid anyone[21] who is called to share and spread the vision of how sports, recreation and/or fitness based missions can greatly enhance and expand a local church's gospel impact.

1. Share the Vision [22]

Each congregation is at a different place on a continuum of understanding of SR&F missions. On the one end, some congregations and even whole denominations believe competition and sport to be unbiblical; even evil. Others may not believe it to be evil but rather deem it a waste of time and superfluous. Many may value sport for its earthly benefit but don't consider it to have any spiritual or eternal significance. The few congregations that do believe it to be biblically justifiable and even understand sport can be used for gospel purposes are often at a loss for how to specifically utilize sport for any effective spiritual outcomes.

So it is recommended the process for sharing the vision start with connecting with the pastor and other congregational leaders.

- First – Pray and fast that you will find favor with those you are hoping to meet with
- Second - Meet one-on-one with the pastor and afterwards with church leadership for the purpose of determining the congregation's current positioning, status and receptivity to *Evangelistic-Disciplemaking-based* SR&F missions
- Third – During these early sessions, it's important to assess the congregation's understanding of SR&F outreach mission and develop next steps to move forward, remembering it is a long term process more than a short term project
- Fourth – In conjunction with congregational leadership it is vital to identify potential SR&F missionaries (*Timothy's*) in the congregation who can be built into, trained and encouraged[23]

The end goal of this first step is to help the church leaders transfer the vision to a broader spectrum of congregants that would include a more complete understanding of the why, when, where, how and what of SR&F outreach mission.

2. Transfer the Vision

After the initial plan has been established with congregational leaders and

---

21 The checklist is referred to in this book series in the *2-T-2-2 Relationship* model as a *Barnabas* or *Paul*.
22 It is highly recommended to read *The Life of the Shoe: Sports Outreach for the World* for a detailed outline of this section.
23 What is referred to as *2 T 2.2 Relationships*. This is done through the *3-I's*: that provide *Information; Instruction; & Inspiration*.

Timothy's have been identified, the next task is to assist the entire congregation to fully grasp the vision and become equipped through: a) individual meetings/mentoring; b) SR&F mission seminars and c) ongoing training of key leaders, *Timothy's*; and anyone who exhibits any interest in joining the mission. Other objectives include leading the congregation to identify:

- Who the congregation is positioned to reach (target group) from two different perspectives: a) demographic (i.e.: age, gender, culture, language groups etc.) and b) geographic (neighborhood, school system, housing project, zip code etc.).
- Existing congregational resources
    - People – coaches, athletic directors, athletes, referees/officials and sporting goods suppliers
    - Facilities – sports and fitness complexes that are owned by the church and/or could be borrowed, rented or leased by the church
    - Equipment – sports and fitness equipment that is owned or could be borrowed, rented or leased
- The leisure pursuits of the target audience
    - Sports they regularly play
    - Recreational activities they regularly engage in
    - Health and fitness preferences
- Where these three converge, strategic mission can be envisioned, planned for and inaugurated

Once the congregation's resources are compared to the leisure pursuits and sporting needs of the community, a SR&F outreach mission plan can be envisioned.

3. Work the Vision

After the vision is established, it is best if the SR&F missionary serves alongside the congregation to assure effective long term SR&F mission activities and outreaches. This may well be the most important step of them all, and yet it is the one most regularly overlooked and neglected.

Just because someone (a *Timothy*) has been "told" what to do, doesn't mean they know how to do it in real life. Therefore, the equipping is not completed until the *Barnabas* and *Paul* have repeatedly demonstrated how to do the mission…and to the chagrin of many, the equipping of the *Timothy* is often a multi-year endeavor. At the very least it is only truly complete when a Timothy has experienced the full cycle and process. (See the Producing, Reproducing,

Reproducers Scoreboard on page 134)

Here lies the rub for many...

It is often the desire of a motivated *Barnabas* or *Paul* to reach and train thousands of people.[24] However, while this motivation is certainly to be commended, its needs to be balanced with the reality of what can actually be accomplished and passed on in one day or hour of "training." It would in fact be a modern day miracle if a person is considered trained and deemed capable of leading a SR&F mission after attending just one seminar. To say it a different way...does merely providing information about missional outreaches suffice? Is it enough to provide data (head knowledge), or is more needed? While communicating information is an extremely important part of the equipping process (in fact, it is vital); to fully equip aspiring *Timothy's*, the training must include a long term, heart-engaged, hands-on, experiential approach, that is based on modeling, mentoring and motivating.

So, while short term dissemination of data is important, effective and ongoing mission work will only occur when such information is partnered with long term experiential ministry activities that are modeled, mentored and motivated.

In summary, it is imperative to spend as much time as possible, investing in the lives of all the *Timothy's*. This would include scheduling quality time meetings and joining with them during practical outreaches and otherwise assisting the church in hosting a project or event.

The end result of equipping congregational leaders and *Timothy's* will be a multi-faceted approach employing multiple models that will reach those far from Jesus and His Church. One important reminder is important. Make sure that an ongoing, discipling, follow-up is planned for, and carried out with, any new believer. This follow-up with those who are starting their new life in Christ is key to the overall effectiveness of the mission. To that end, connecting them with a local church is imperative.

4. Release the Vision (On-going Sports Ministry and Follow-up)

Of course, the SR&F mission will only endure through one generation if it is not totally released to the next generation...who will in turn, pass it on to future generations. This releasing of the vision includes both you and congregational leaders doing the following:

- Delegating every aspect of planning and implementation of the mission to the *Timothy's*
- Staying in regular contact with congregational leaders and they to their SR&F *Timothy's*

---

24 The term in this book series for training is *Inform*. What is meant by this is to communicate concepts and knowledge. However, this kind of training only provides information or content; it does not fully equip. To fully equip a Timothy would also include *Instruction* and *Inspiration*. Consult the Glossary for full explanations of the 3-I's.

TIME OUT

Sports Outreach Suggestions

- Require members of the congregation to **join the sports outreach team** for specific outreaches including giving them responsibilities to prepare / set up for leagues, events, classes and activities, which has a vital side benefit as it acts to ensure they take ownership of the project
- Ensure the congregation **follows the STRIVE model** as they plan SR&F missional activities
- Ensure the congregation plans for **intentional *Evangelistic-Disciplemaking*** using the *Sports Ministry Pyramid Model*
- Organizing a **Sports Challenge Event** (Addendum 6) to model sports outreach and inform the congregation
- Engage the youth of the congregation and your community through **weekly sports ministry trainings**
- Establish a ***Missional Sports Community***

Check out *The Life of the Shoe: Sports Outreach for the World* for a detailed explanation of the *STRIVE* and *Sports Ministry Pyramid* models.

- Encouraging and assisting them in their ongoing Great Commission endeavors
- Watching to ensure congregational and mission leaders continually pursue *Evangelistic-Disciplemaking* through ongoing SF&R ministry while implementing the *Sports Ministry Pyramid*[25]
- Observing and encouraging as they keep evaluating, pruning, implementing, and pressing on through the journey

IV. Summary of International Missions

As the preceding four steps of passing on the vision for SR&F missions are enacted, it behooves Americans and others to learn from persecuted brothers and sisters instead of imposing on them a Westernized cultural faith perspective. Nonetheless, some of the elements Ripken lists in the Scoreboard on page 124 need to become the norm for The Church as it focuses on and pursues

---

25   See Chapter 4 In *The Life of the Shoe: Sports Outreach for the World.*

Evangelistic-Disciplemaking through SR&F missions in our post-Christian world to enhance the collective quest to win people to Jesus.[26] The syncretization of both cultures can be incredibly impactful.

For example, prayer and fasting (Ripkin list #2) should be a strong focus for leaders, and prayer should be demonstrated and encouraged for all participants. Along with the expected sports components, biblical themes should be taught through scripture memorization competitions and through the singing of songs that are based on those specific passages (Ripkin list #3 & #4). All involved in the program should be supported and encouraged physically and spiritually (Ripkin list #7).

Additionally, regardless of the age of the participant, it is strategic and wise for SR&F mission programs to include testimonies and stories shared by individuals based on personal stories of faith, sacrifice, and suffering. In this way a genealogy of faith (Ripkin list #11) will be intentionally established in the local Body of believers.

The focus of any SR&F mission should be to help all those involved at every level to know Jesus more intimately (Ripken list on page 124). In this way The Body of Christ is assured of being most effective for the present and in the future, no matter what may come.

SCOREBOARD

Producing, Reproducing, Reproducers

- Year/Season #1
    - Model It
        - Watch Me Do It
- Year/Season #2
    - Mentor It
        - Let's Do It Together
- Year/Season #3
    - Motivate It
        - I'll Watch You Do It
- Year/Season #4
    - Monitor It
        - I'm here if you need me

---

26 What is referred to in this book series as *Dedicated-Disciples*.

TIME OUT

Sports Ministry Parable

One day a man was walking through the forest when he came upon an ant hill. He noticed that the ant hill was built in a gulley (ditch), a very dangerous location for a colony of ants to live. It was the dry season now, but in the rainy season when the rains come the hill would be surely flooded and all the ants would die. Because this man loved nature and all creatures in the world including the smallest insects, he wanted to warn the ants of the impending danger.

So he came up with a plan. He stood over the ant hill and yelled out a warning:

"Ants, move your house or you will be destroyed!"

Not getting any response he leaned down as close as he could to the ant hill. Cupping his hands around his mouth he tried yelling even louder.

"Ants, move your house or you will be destroyed! You are in danger."

Still there was no response...

Finally, not knowing what else to do he came up with an idea. He thought: I can become an ant. Then I will speak their language. Then I can warn then. Then they will listen to me.

So this is what he did. He became an ant. Once inside the ant hill he went immediately and found the queen of the colony. Speaking the language of the ants, he shared what he knew and implored the queen to lead her colony to safety. But the queen was not convinced. She shared that she thought this location was best because it was close to the food source. It was also close to a location that would provide all the necessary resources to build a bigger and better ant hill. No, they would not move. They would stay.

Still some ants heard about this man-ant and believed what he was saying. Immediately they packed up their families and moved to a safe location. However, most just laughed at him and called him crazy. Frustrated and discouraged, the man-ant continued to plead his case. After some time the queen become annoyed and ordered her guards to remove the man-ant from her presence. They were told to silence him for good. He was taken outside and killed.

TIMEOUT

Within a few weeks the rains came. Just as the man-ant had warned, the ant hill in the gulley (ditch) was washed away. All the ants that had stayed behind died.

In the same way, God became a man in the person of Jesus to warn us and show us a way to find safety. Jesus said,

"I am the bread of life. He who comes to me will never go hungry, and he who believes in me will never go thirsty... everyone who looks to me shall have eternal life, and I will raise him up on the last day (John 6:35 & 40)."

Jesus did not claim to be a man, a prophet, or just a teacher. He was the Messiah!! He came for all men regardless of your race, religion, or nationality. Won't you listen to him?

P. F. Myers wrote this parable to share the gospel of Jesus with people of other faiths, specifically Muslims. It has turned out to be a relevant parable which Myers shares often with anyone seeking to discover the Truth about Jesus. The goal should be to focus on turning people's attention from religion to realtionship that can only be found in Him.

SECTION 4: Relevance of Missiology for the Broader SR&F Community

Chapter 10

Summary of Missiology in Relationship to SR&F Outreach & Final Proposals

I. Moving From...Moving To – 142
    A. Moving From Sports Activity to Gospel-Centric Mission – 142
    B. Moving From Sports Volunteers to Gospel-Centric Missionaries – 142
    C. Moving From Foreign to Local Missions – 143
    D. Moving From *Mega-* and *3-R-Models* to Integrated Models – 143
    E. Moving From Proclamational Preaching to Incarnational Proclamations – 143
    F. Moving From Membership-Funded to Mission-Funded SR&F Outreach Ministry – 144
    G. Moving From Ministry Silos to Ministry Integration – 145
        1. Creating Engaging Missional SR&F Activities – 145
        2. Creating Bridges to the Congregation – 145
        3. Creating A Conducive Culture – 145

II. General Practical Applications of Incarnational *Evangelistic-Disciplemaking* for SR&F Outreach Missions – 146
    A. Envisioning, Planning For and Administrating SR&F Outreaches for Incarnational *Evangelistic-Disciplemaking* – 147
    B. Resourcing, Training, Equipping and Mentoring Church Members for Incarnational *Evangelistic-Disciplemaking* – 147

III. Does it keep focused on "The Harvest" – 149

IV. Book Summary and Next Steps – 150

> And He called the twelve and began to send them out...so they went out and proclaimed that people should repent.
>
> *Mark 6. 7 & 12*

I. Moving From...Moving To

So what are the pragmatic steps needed to call, train, equip and send local church SR&F outreach missionaries to engage in truly missional endeavors? The lessons gleaned from this book can be summarized by the phrase: "Moving from...Moving To."

A. Moving From Sports Activity to... Gospel-Centric Mission

The first step in moving the ministry from sports activity to gospel-centric mission is absolutely foundational. Unless there is a no-compromise, ruthless dismantling of any sports, recreation or fitness activities that are not rooted in mission, there will be little if any progress in mobilizing and enabling the overall ministry to effectively fulfill The Great Commission. **This needs to be said again in different words so the importance of the statement is not lost.** Sports ministries must be committed to engage in an intentional mission of going to make disciples of those who are far from Jesus and His Church or they will be doomed to provide nothing more than sports activity.

This overall ministry/mission commitment is only effective when it is understood and embraced by Lead Pastors, congregational staff, elders, trustees and finance board members, as well as all church members and it is the foundation from which each of the following emerges.

B. Moving From Sports Volunteers to... Gospel-Centric Missionaries

Once the commitment to change from organizing sports activity to engaging in gospel-centric, SR&F-based mission has been implemented, a key subsequent action includes adjusting the expectation of the role of all who serve in the mission. No longer are they to be viewed as "just volunteers;" but rather held in honor as local missionaries.

This honoring starts with how they're recruited and continues with how they're trained, equipped, recognized and supported. Recruiting includes raising the expectation from "come and coach a few kids in basketball;" to "you're being asked to coach a youth basketball team for the dual purpose of leading the kids and their families into a personal relationship with Jesus as you help them get

SCOREBOARD

Does Your SR&F Outreach Ministry Work to ...

Get people to the church
or
Get the church to people?

better at their sport."

The honoring also includes training and equipping these local church missionaries to know how to succeed in both the spiritual and sports realms. It also entails a public commissioning of all such missionaries and ongoing recognition and prayer support.

If coaches and other "volunteers" are envisioned, treated and honored as missionaries, they will begin to engage in their sports activities as vitally important missionaries, not a replaceable volunteer.

C. Moving From Foreign to... Local Missions

The impact experienced by a congregation when SR&F endeavors are viewed as local missions is truly outstanding. It has an effect, and brings about seismic change that is experienced by each member of the church. Parishioners become aware and are motivated to envision where they can serve as a local missionary. They begin to see the mission opportunities that present themselves at work or school and within their neighborhoods and family. No longer does the individual congregant see their association with a local church to be a one hour per week worship, but rather a 24-7 opportunity to make a gospel impact. Changing from a perspective that to be a missionary is reserved only for "special, Godly, people who go overseas," to a new reality that all church members are to be missionaries in their own community, will prove to be a catalytic gospel powerhouse for Church and congregational expansion.

D. Moving From *Mega-* and *3-R-Models* to... Integrated Models [1]

The model of utilizing mass media and/or mass gatherings has often been used effectively to either initiate a relationship with someone far from Jesus and His Church and to provide an opportunity for someone to pray to receive Jesus as their Savior. The model that emphasizes building long term relationships with unchurched people has also been used effectively. The challenge being proposed in this book is for local church SR&F outreach ministers to envision a new methodology that incorporates the strength, and mitigates the shortcomings, of these two models by combining the two into one seamless continuum. The result will encourage all who are willing to step out and change from relying on only one and fuse the two together.

E. Moving From Proclamational Preaching to... Incarnational Proclamations

The previous change goes hand-in-hand with this one. The recommendation here is to move from relying exclusively on a model of ministry that emphasizes creating gatherings of unchurched people to hear the gospel preached, to a model that encourages proclamation of the gospel in and through incarnational, one-on-one, relationships. The underlying rationale has to do with the understanding that when a good and trusted friend first lives out (proclamation) the gospel, and

---

[1] For an in depth understanding of the *Mega- & 3-R-Models* see Chapter 6.

SCOREBOARD

Integrating Church Ministries

Ways of Integrating Congregational Ministries:
- Children's Pastors deliver weekly devotions to children's sports teams
- Youth Pastors coach high school teams
- Women's Ministry leaders attend fitness classes
- Men's Ministers leaders play in softball leagues
- Family Ministry leaders direct co-gender volleyball league
- Singles Pastors organize ultimate Frisbee "pickup" games prior to Lord's Day evening Bible studies
- Sports Ministers lead a Lord's Day morning Bible study
- Senior Pastors include unchurched SR&F outreach participants in their hospital visits
- Senior Adult Pastors participate in golf or bowling leagues
- Administrative Pastors organize bike and hike groups

---

then verbally shares gospel messages (affirmation) with their unbelieving friends the message is better able to be nuanced and made personal and relevant. It is also assumed that the incarnational gospel messenger is more attuned to a gospel receiver's situation and mindset, and thus, they are able to deliver the message in more personal and less offensive ways.

Moving to incarnational involvements does not necessarily mean never having a preached gospel message but rather encouraging an increased utilization of the incarnational approach to reach those far from Jesus and His Church.

F. Moving From Membership-Funded to... Mission-Funded SR&F Outreach Ministry

Changing to a mission focus also entails changing, or at least adapting the funding plan. It is recommended that SR&F outreach finances be moved to the mission or outreach part of a church's budget. This change maintains a congregation's focus on the mission-based outreach and enables the finance committee to hold the SR&F staff accountable for effective *Evangelistic-Disciplemaking*. This change does not mean participation fees aren't charged to participants but rather these fees supplement the basic budget that comes from the church mission budget. Such a change in basic funding re-emphasizes all endeavors are to be missional.[2]

---

2   For more on funding SR&F outreach mission consult chapter 7 in *Putting The Church Back in the Game*.

G. Moving From Ministry Silos to... Ministry Integration

While this may be the last sub-point, it describes one of the most important and necessary adaptations needed to effectively move a local church SR&F outreach from sports activity to gospel-centric, mission. It entails an intentional integration of all church ministries (See the Scoreboard – Integrating Church Ministries on page 144). This would empower not only the reaching of those far from Jesus and His Church but also enable a systematic incorporation of new believers into congregational life.

The congregations that are most effective in making disciples are those that envision and maintain a systemic missional methodology that not only anticipates, but actually expects to reach and incorporate unchurched people into their church. This intentional integration entails at least three main objectives: 1) creating SR&F activities that engage church staff and members in personally inviting unchurched people to join them in the various outreach ministries;[3] 2) creating bridges from the SR&F missional activities to the overall body life of the congregation;[4] 3) creating a culture within the congregation so its members can winsomely welcome and be sensitive to unchurched people taking part in various church events and services.

1. Creating Engaging Missional SR&F Activities

The most effective SR&F activities are those in which congregational members and staff can confidently invite their unchurched family members, work colleagues and neighbors to. Such activities are both attractive to those outside the church and center on the leisure pursuits of those who participate in congregational studies and services.[5]

2. Creating Bridges to the Congregation

Once the missional outreach activities have been created and congregational members and staff are taking part in them with the guests they have invited, there needs to be easily navigated next steps. Next steps include further invitations to attend congregational social events, Christianity Explored classes and/or Bible studies and life groups where new or not yet believers would receive a warm and open welcome.

3. Creating a Conducive Culture

Congregations would do well to conduct all activities such as a class, course

---

[3] This is a You and Who approach as described in Chapter 7
[4] See Chapter 2 and pages 61-64 in the Sports Outreach Fundamentals book that describes how to overcome sports ministry's 2-*Dysconnects*.
[5] Color coding of all church activities and service is recommended to communicate the intent and content of the various activities. Green indicates the activity would be understood, appreciated and even enjoyed by an unchurched person. Yellow indicates there will Spiritual content that would be understood and appreciated by those showing interest in faith and/or have recently entered into a personal relationship with Jesus. Red indicates the service/activity is geared for committed believers and would not be understood or appreciated by unchurched, unbelievers. I am indebted to John and Glynis Bussell who first introduced me to this concept and to Bryan Mason for introducing them to me.

SCOREBOARD

Creating a Culture to Incorporate the Unchurched

Ways of enhancing and expanding a welcome to the unchurched:
- First Appearances
  - Campus and Building Signage – clear and concise directions...
    - In the parking lot
    - Throughout all facilities

- Welcome Team
  - Clearly designated welcome staff
    - Name tags; vests etc.

- Church Services and Bible Studies
  - Minimize religious language/jargon
  - Provide Bibles and refer to page numbers rather than books of the Bible
  - Assume the message is being heard by unchurched and non-Christians and adapt it to those who may need a bit more explanation

- Follow Up
  - Discreet, personal, non-threatening contact as, and when, appropriate

---

or worship service in such a way as to make unchurched attendees feel welcome, warm and comfortable. This certainly includes an enhanced and expanded process for making guests feel welcomed but more so it entails realistically assessing how various services, Bible studies and other gatherings are perceived and experienced by first time attenders and those who haven't had any exposure to organized religion or Christianity.

II. General Practical Applications of Incarnational *Evangelistic-Disciplemaking* for SR&F Outreach Missions

Two foundational administrative efforts are needed to ensure mission effectiveness: A) envisioning, planning for and administrating SR&F missional outreaches; and B) the calling, resourcing, training, equipping, mentoring and sending of local church members (missionaries). The ultimate goal is to foster incarnational relationships between followers of Christ and those far from Christ for the purpose of reaching them for Christ.

SCOREBOARD

Does Your Church Tell its Members ...

To come to church
or
Go be the church?

A. Envisioning, Planning For and Administrating SR&F Outreaches for Incarnational *Evangelistic-Disciplemaking*

Incarnational ministry requires and assumes relationship....the relationship between disciples of Jesus and those who have not yet entered into a personal relationship with Christ. Thus, it is crucial for local church SR&F leaders to create outreaches that would enable congregational members to participate in long-term, missional-programs for the purpose of initiating and developing ever-deepening relationships with those far from Christ and His Church. Such endeavors would by necessity entail both repeated and ongoing activities, rather than one time stand-alone events. Some examples can be found in the Scoreboard Incarnational Models on page 149.

What should be seen in these examples is how a one-time *Mega-Event* can be combined with repeatable, on-going missional programming for maximum gospel impact, but the heart of incarnational, *Evangelistic-Disciplemaking* remains in creating environments for deepening relationships between the churched and the unchurched. Ongoing, repeatable *Missional-Programs* that enhance incarnational opportunities for congregational members result in the most *Strategically-Relevant* and *Efficiently-Effective* outreaches The Church has.

B. Resourcing, Training, Equipping and Mentoring Church Members for Incarnational *Evangelistic-Disciplemaking*

It's one thing for local church SR&F leaders to envision, plan for and implement outreaches for the purpose of connecting parishioners with unchurched friends, family and associates; it's another thing entirely to empower them to be effective in such outreach endeavors. Such empowerment comes through resourcing, training, equipping and mentoring parishioners.

Resourcing, training, equipping and mentoring are all distinctively different and yet are all interconnected and vital.

Resourcing refers to communicating the knowledge and insights that are necessary for knowing how to reach those far from Jesus and His Church.[6]

---
[6] What is referred to in this book series as the first *I – Information.*

Resourcing includes providing data about trends, research results, theological truths, ministry tips, relational insights and anything else that would increase a local missionary's understanding of the unchurched person and enhance efforts to befriend and minister to them. Resourcing also includes communicating basic information such as schedules and how the specific outreach they are serving in fits in with the big picture of the congregation's efforts to reach those far from Christ and His Church. In its simplest form, resourcing is best conceived of as being nothing more than providing the materials and data to be used in the training and equipping process.

Training takes all of the resource data, and explains its relevance, and ultimately explains how to implement it in strategic and effective ways. Training is best conceived of by envisioning a class room with a teacher (trainer) and students (trainees).[7] It's a sterile environment where resources are explained.

Equipping refers to the demonstration and practice of how applying the knowledge and insights (Information); the training can be best utilized in the various outreaches. Equipping involves modeling and practice. The first step is for the person serving as the resourcer and trainer to demonstrate how to practically engage in SR&F outreach mission by modeling the hoped for approach. Second, equipping also entails providing opportunities for aspiring parishioners to practice what they have been trained in and to receive supportive evaluation of their efforts. Equipping is best conceived of as the living classroom where trainees begin to practice what they've learned. Such practice occurs in a dynamic environment under the supervision of the trainer/equipper who evaluates and critiques the efforts of the trainee for the purpose of making them ever more able to carry out effective incarnational ministry.[8]

Mentoring refers to the ongoing efforts to motivate, encourage, inspire and support those being resourced, trained and equipped.[9]

Mentoring has to do with the ongoing relationship between trainer and trainee where the mentor supports, encourages and motivates all mentees (volunteer missionaries) they supervise. Mentors also perform a most needed role of lovingly challenging those being resourced, trained and equipped to take seriously their role of reaching those far from Christ and His Church. Mentoring assumes a long term interactive relationship that enables the attainment of the long term goal of developing future generations of missionaries.[10]

So, while incarnational-based outreach may be the goal, it does not happen in

---

[7] What is referred to in this book series as the second I – *Instruction*.
[8] The end result is a strong group of incarnational missionaries conducting a truly *Strategically-Relevant* and *Efficiently-Effective* SR&F outreach mission.
[9] What is referred to in this book series as the third I – *Inspiration*.
[10] What is referred to in this book series as *Producing, Reproducing, Reproducers* which is outlined/explained by the *2-T-2-2 Relationships* in chapter 7 of the 8th book in this series: *The Life of the Shoe: Sports Outreach for the World*.

SCOREBOARD

Incarnational Models

- Hosting a 5-k race may serve as a great way to make initial contact with runners, but forming a running club will enable ongoing, repeatable opportunities for the deepening of relationships through having club members engage in regular training runs and also enter races as a team
- Holding a dinner dance provides a great "first step," whereas, hosting ongoing dance classes that rotates the teaching of different ball-room dances provides a year-round environment for friendships to form
- Planning a year round calendar of Summer, Fall and Spring "30 and over" basketball leagues will not only attract men seeking competition and physical fitness but more importantly facilitate the development of friendship and camaraderie through ongoing leagues
- Inviting the public to a "health fair" will certainly attract community members to learn more about diet, exercise and medical services, but providing ongoing fitness classes and wellness activities will enable long term relationships to form and grow

a vacuum or without significant vision, detailed planning and consistent execution of the plan. As I have often said, "unless *Evangelistic-Disciplemaking* is intentional, it is accidental at best." I also believe unless *Evangelistic-Disciplemaking* is incarnational, it is usually ineffective.

III. Does it keep focused on "The Harvest"

The teaching of Jesus about the harvest being ripe was recorded by Matthew. This passage makes it clear that Jesus made reaching people with the gospel to be the priority for His disciples. Thus, the question for modern day SR&F outreach ministers is: is your ministry focused on reaping the harvest? Does this call from Jesus motivate what you do each and every moment of each and every day? Do you have an urgency to call, resource, train, equip, mentor and send your volunteer missionaries to go? Too often, winning games, getting fit or having fun supersedes what should be our main and driving force.

SCOREBOARD
Resourcing, Training, Equipping & Mentoring

Resourcing: is best conceived of as providing the materials to be used in the training and equipping process.
Training: is best conceived of as a class room with a teacher (trainer) and students (trainees)
Equipping: is best conceived of as the living classroom where trainees begin to practice what they've learned
Mentoring: is best conceived of as an ongoing relationship between trainer and trainee

IV. Book Summary and Next Steps

Book Summary - The purpose of this book is to inspire local congregations to re-envision their SR&F outreach ministries for the purpose of molding them into vibrant, missional communities that make disciples who make disciples of those who are currently far from Jesus and His Church. Will your church now embrace such an endeavor?

Next Steps - So far, this Institutes of Sports Outreach book series has explored three theological foundations for SR&F outreach and all have assumed what follows in book #6: *The Christ of Sports Ministry: The Christology of Sports Outreach*. Books #8 and beyond use these sports outreach *Ologies* (ecclesiology; soteriology; missiology; Christology) as foundations for developing pragmatic sport, recreation and fitness models that are truly strategic, relevant, efficient and effective.

SCOREBOARD
Do We Worry or Work?

Do we worry the world will change The Church
or
Will we work to have The Church change the world?

Addendum #1

Glossary

1-Foundational Purpose of Sports Outreach
The first transferable concept and the guiding principle of *The Sports Outreach Community*. It describes the end goal of *The Community*: making *Dedicated-Disciples* of Jesus Christ.

2-Dysconnects of Sports Outreach
The second transferable concept describes and defines the two hurdles SR&F outreach ministries encounter in reaching those far from Christ and His Church. The first *Dysconnect* has to do with attracting people from the general community in which they live, to specific local church SR&F activities. The second *Dysconnect* has to do with moving people from the SR&F activities to the broader congregational activities including becoming active participants in traditional worship and Christian Education opportunities.

2-T-2-2 Relationships
This concept is based on 2 Timothy 2.2 and the model of discipleship that was lived out among the early founders of The Church. Howard Hendricks, esteemed professor at Dallas Theological Seminary, introduced a similar concept but with a different order. The *2-T-2-2 Relationships* transferable concept is based on spiritual relationships that believers have with one another for the purpose of becoming effective followers of Jesus. CSRM's International Director incorporated *2-T-2-2 Relationships* into the *Sports-Ministry-Pyramid* model as a key to *Evangelistic-Disciplemaking*. The essence of this transferable concept is three relationships: 1) a current minister who has intentional and effective relationships with his peers (*Paul-Relationships*), who has 2) been mentored and influenced by an older, more experienced minister (a *Barnabas-Relationship*), and who 3) actively mentors and influences younger, aspiring ministers (*Timothy-Relationships*).

3-I's
The *3-I's* form a *Re-sourcing; Re-training & Re-energizing* continuum for fully equipping SR&F outreach ministers for the purpose of empowering them to envision, plan for, organize, administrate and evaluate a truly *Strategically-Relevant & Efficiently-Effective, Evangelistic-Disciplemaking* sports outreach ministry.
• *Inform* – has to do with the creation, production and distribution of *Re-sources* that are: Christo-centric *Level #1 Theological-Truths*; Biblically-Based *Level #2*

Philosophical-Principles; and *Level #3 Methodological-Models*.
- *Instruct* – has to do with *Re-training* SR&F outreach ministers in how to most effectively utilize and employ the *Re-sources* that have been created, produced and distributed.
- *Inspire* – has to do with *Re-energizing* SR&F outreach ministers with new motivations and inspirations for reaching those far from Jesus and His Church and also has to do with developing ongoing, personal, mentoring, relationships that enables SR&F outreach ministers to become fully equipped for successful Great Commission endeavors.

3-Tier Paradigm Organizational Structure

The third transferable concept outlines the organizational structure of SR&F outreach ministries. Based upon three levels, it builds from a foundation of how to think (theologically); which shapes and informs how to organize (philosophically); out of which *What* to do (methodology) emerges. Moving from *Why* a SR&F ministry exists to *When, Where* and for *Whom* it is organized to *What* is done; this organizational structure ensures *Strategically-Relevant* and *Efficiently-Effective* SR&F outreach ministry.

4-Fold Evaluation Rubric

The fourth transferable concept describes the four necessary components for ensuring a SR&F outreach ministry will accomplish its goals and objectives which include being *Strategically-Relevant* and *Efficiently-Effective*.

5-B's Process of Sports Outreach

The fifth transferable concept explains the process of developing a *Repetitive-Redemptive-Relational* ethos and culture within SR&F outreach ministry for the purpose of making *Dedicated-Disciples* of Jesus. It outlines how a SR&F can envision, plan for and implement an effective outreach ministry.
- *Belong*
- *Believe*
- *Baptize*
- *Behave*
- *Become*

7-Continuums of Tension of the Sports Outreach Movement

The sixth transferable concept outlines the seven most important theological and philosophical issues confronting *The Sports Outreach Movement* as it enters its 8th decade.

Glossary

Accommodation
One of four classical responses and reactions embraced by sport-related individuals who encounter the dilemma of integrating faith and their sport. It describes those who choose sport over faith but try to hold on to both.

Blow-In; Blow-Up; Blow-Out
This *Level #3 Methodological-Model* consists of: a) an American sports team *Blowing-In* to a specific community within a foreign country to play a game against a local or national team; b) having one or more of the athletes verbally share the Gospel (*Blow-Up*) and ask for those in attendance to "accept Jesus;" and then c) *Blow-Out* to the next stop on the short term mission trip. This phrase was first used by sports outreach ministry Pioneer Rodger Oswald who used it to describe the essence of what all too often occurs when American sports teams engage in short term international mission trips. It is based on a soteriology (theology of salvation) that believes the mission's goal is fulfilled and accomplished when a person "raises their hand" or "prays a prayer" with limited regard to "making disciples" or connecting those being reached with a local congregation.

Building-with-Leaders
Building-with-Leaders is a *Level #2 Philosophical-Principle* that emphasizes the importance of investing in leaders and their development for the ultimate purpose of achieving *Strategically-Relevant* and *Efficiently-Effective* SR& F outreach ministry. This philosophy is the true bed-rock of SR&F outreach ministry but should not be used to dismiss the importance of constructing and maintaining high quality athletic and fitness facilities, which greatly enhance and expand local church outreach efforts. *Building-with-Leaders* is a philosophy that seeks to recruit, *Re-Source*; *Re-Train* and *Re-Energize* local church volunteers to build effective *Repetitive-Redemptive-Relational* opportunities with friends, family members and associates for the purpose of *Evangelistic-Disciplemaking*. This phrase is often partnered with its corollary: *Leading-with-Buildings*.

Capitulation
One of four classical responses and reactions embraced by sport-related individuals who encounter the dilemma of integrating faith and sport. It describes those who not only choose sport over faith but totally abandon their faith in favor of sport.

Christmanship
One of three philosophical approaches to competition and sport; *Christmanship* describes a laser-focused and biblically-based, Christ-honoring ethic of

engagement with sport. As compared with gamesmanship that espouses the highest ethic is to win; or sportsmanship which emerges from a philosophy rooted in humanistic relativism and ends with an ethic of fair play etc.; *Christmanship* is an ethic that outlines how to engage in sport for the glory of God and in ways that honors all *Co-Competitors*.

Co-Competitors
A term in the *Christmanship* Ethic used to describe individuals who play on other teams. This descriptive term is used rather than words such as opponent, adversary or enemy.

Competition-Gone-Berserk
Competition-Gone-Berserk is a phrase used to describe how some local church sports ministries have completely abdicated on creating a culture of biblically-based competition (*Christmanship*). Unchecked and unsupervised competition often results in participants experiencing such a negative competitive environment that they choose to not only leave the church league, but more significantly, they decide to have nothing to do with the congregation that sponsors the league. Whether born out of a total lack of any theological structure for competition and sport, or from an underdeveloped *Level #1 Theological-Truth* of competition, the end result of *Competition-Gone-Berserk* is the same…a lost opportunity to reach those far from Jesus and His Church.

Competition-Gone-Soft
Competition-Gone-Soft is a phrase used to describe how some local church sports ministries seek to greatly curtail or totally eliminate competition within all of their leagues and games. This approach is usually born out of an underdeveloped *Level #1 Theological-Truth* that believes competition is intrinsically and inherently evil. This underlying theology leads to a local church sport outreach ministry envisioning and developing a ministry structure that doesn't reward Godly competition and even penalizes anything bordering on competition. Sadly, the organizational structures that emerge out of such *Level #2 Philosophical-Principles* lead to *Level #3 Methodological-Models* that are not appealing to large segments of those who are far from Jesus and His Church; and thus do not attract them to participate in any of the outreach programs a congregation offers. There are however, specific sports outreaches that are rightfully designed to create less intense competition: a) low impact volleyball for beginners; b) Slo-break basketball for seniors; c) basketball clinics for pre-schoolers; and d) various fellowship leagues of all ages. Nonetheless, for the most part, non-competitive sporting activities do not attract or keep people involved. Any local

church that seeks to "go and make disciples" of athletes is encouraged to develop a culture of biblically-based competition (*Christmanship*) that will be managed so as to appeal to, and attract, competitors to participate…all with the end goal of winning them to Jesus.

Core Values

Whereas *Theological-Truths* define and describe the *Why*; *Philosophical-Principles* define and describe the *When, Where* & with *Whom*; and *Methodological-Models* describe and define the *What* of the *3-Tier Paradigm*; the *Core Values* define and describe the *How* of the 3-Tier Paradigm. *Core Values* have to do with creating an environment of organizational and administrative excellence; an atmosphere of warmth, love and encouragement; and a culture of integrity, punctuality, efficiency and safety. *Core Values* consider how participants in SR&F activities feel; and are the bedrock of "proclaiming" the Gospel through the fleshing out the Great Commandment.

Counting-Conversions

Counting-Conversions is a phrase used to summarize how many congregations, denominations, missions and ministries determine the effectiveness of their *Evangelistic-Disciplemaking* (*Success-Statistics*) endeavors. It describes the fact that many ministries and churches believe evangelistic success is complete and finished whenever a person "converts" to Christianity (what is often called getting them "saved"). This end goal of "getting a person saved" is evidenced by one or more of the following: a) raise a hand at the end of a team huddle; b) pray a prayer with a coach or other evangelist; or c) fill out a card in response to a *Platform-Proclamation* of the Gospel at a *Mega-Event*. *Counting-Conversions* is linked with the concept of endeavoring to have people make a *Day's-Decision* for Jesus, rather than seeking to "make" life-long *Dedicated-Disciples* of those who far from Jesus and His Church. The key distinction is the ultimate goal of such endeavors. Is the end and final goal to get a person to make a decision or become a disciple?

Day's-Decision

Day's-Decision is one of the *Double D's* of soteriology. It is used in discussions concerning topics such as salvation, evangelism and outreach. It is used in tandem with *Dedicated-Disciple* and describes the pragmatic end result of SR&F Outreach ministries. Based in a *Level #1 Theological-Truth* of soteriology, it is based in a simplistic theology of evangelism that strives to get a person to "raise a hand;" "pray a prayer;" or "fill out a response card." Any of these end results indicate a person accepted Jesus on a particular day. While proponents of this approach to evangelism would never say they would discourage participation in a local congregation; nor would they state discipleship to be unimportant; nonetheless, this phrase describes those congregations and ministries that tend to not incorporate ongoing disciplemaking methodologies into their overall evangelistic endeavors.

Dedicated-Disciple
Dedicated-Disciple is one of the *Double D's* of soteriology. It is used in discussions concerning topics such as salvation, evangelism and outreach. It is used in tandem with *Day's-Decision* and describes the pragmatic end result of SR&F outreach ministries. Based in a *Level #1 Theological-Truth* of soteriology is the belief that *Evangelistic-Disciplemaking* consists of not only getting a person to "raise a hand;" "pray a prayer" or "fill out a response card." This philosophy believes it is equally important to engage all who have accepted Jesus as Lord and Savior in disciplemaking activities to ensure full spiritual maturity. While proponents of *Evangelistic-Disciplemaking* would never say a *Day's-Decision* is unimportant; nor would they state accepting Jesus as personal Lord and Savior to be irrelevant; they seek to pragmatically incorporate ongoing disciplemaking methodologies into their overall evangelistic endeavors.

Efficiently-Effective
Paired with *Strategically-Relevant*, it is the second half of the *4-Fold Evaluative Rubric*. *Efficiently-Effective* suggests the criteria congregations need to help assess and determine whether or not a local church SR&F outreach ministry is actually accomplishing its goal of making disciples. It defines and describes ultimate effectiveness; and also communicates the importance of basing the organization and administration of SR&F outreach ministry within a strong stewardship ethic.

External Motivational Influences of Competition (EMIC)
EMIC - describes the pressures of competing because of, with, or against external forces such as time, obstacles, challenges of weather or other natural causes, courses (golf, race, etc.) and/or other human beings.

Evangelistic-Disciplemaking
In essence this describes how to reach and disciple those far from Christ and His Church. This term uniquely defines the *1-Defining Purpose* of *The Sports Outreach Community*. It assumes that "to go and make disciples" entails both going to those far from Christ and His Church (evangelistic outreach) as well as nurturing the faith of newly-born believers and maturing the faith of long-time pilgrims (discipling endeavors). Congregations and ministries can best

accomplish their Great Commission goals by envisioning, planning for and implementing; attractive outreaches that connect people to Jesus and His Church. This *Level #2 Philosophical-Principle* of *Evangelistic-Disciplemaking* is informed and shaped by the *Level #1 Theological-Truths* of soteriology. It is from these theological concepts and philosophical organizational principles then that Level #3 *Methodological-Models* emerge.

Evangelistic-Environments
Evangelistic-Environments describe one of the key aspects of the *Core Values* of the *3-Tier Paradigm*. The ultimate goal of a SR&F outreach ministry is to create a winsomely attractive and warm environment that facilitates opportunities for congregational members to build relationships with friends, associates and family members for the purpose of having evangelistic conversations.

Gamesmanship
Gamesmanship (gamesmanship is not italicized because it is not original to CSRM) is one of three philosophical approaches to competition and sport. It is partnered with sportsmanship and *Christmanship*. It describes a philosophy based on a secularized-pragmatic-ethic of engagement in and with sport. Its highest value is to win; regardless of how. As compared with sportsmanship that is based upon an ethic rooted in the humanistic-relativism of playing fair etc.; and *Christmanship* that espouses engaging in sport for the glory of God and in ways that honors all *Co-Competitors*; gamesmanship only prizes winning.

Internal Motivational Influences of Competition (IMIC)
IMIC—describes the pressures of competing because of, or against, internal forces such as one's pride, a personal level of excellence, goal, or a personal unmet ego need.

Leading-with-Buildings
Leading-with-Buildings is a *Level #2 Philosophical-Principle* that emphasizes the "build it and they will come" philosophy for SR&F outreach ministry. This philosophy has some merit and should not be unduly dismissed. High quality athletic and fitness facilities and equipment do attract those far from Jesus and His Church. However, such facilities by themselves are not enough. They must be missionally-programmed by leaders who envision, plan for and expedite *Repititive-Redemptive-Relational* opportunities for church members to initiate and deepen relationships with friends, family members and associates for the purpose of *Evangelistic-Disciplemaking*. This phrase is often partnered with its corollary: *Building-with-Leaders*.

Level #1: Theological-Truths
This *Level #1* foundation for the *3-Tier Paradigm*, both informs and gives shape to *Level #2 Philosophical-Principles*; out which emerge *Level #3 Methodological-Models*. These truths form how SR&F outreach ministers think and what they believe. They are the foundation for *Why* such ministries exist (*Evangelistic-Disciplemaking*) and *How* (*Core Values*) they conduct and operate their outreaches. Key words: think, believe and envision.

Level #2: Philosophical-Principles
This second level of the *3-Tier Paradigm* provides the organizational structure for SR&F outreach ministries. It is shaped and informed by *Level #1 Theological-Truths*; and is what *Level #3 Methodological-Models* emerge from. This organizational structure defines the *When*, *Where* and *With whom* SR&F outreach ministries envision, plan for and administer their outreaches. Key words: organize and administrate.

Level #3: Methodological-Models
This third level of the *3-Tier Paradigm* emerges out of the *Level #2 Philosophical-Principles* that provide the organizational structure for SR&F outreach ministries. Once a SR&F outreach ministry understands the *When*, *Where & With Whom* of their SR&F outreach ministries are to reach, they can then organize, administrate and implement their outreaches. Key words: do and act.

Mega-Event
Mega-Event is the term used to describe one end of the fourth of the *7-Continuums of Sports Outreach*. It describes one of *The Sports Outreach Community's Level #2 Philosophical-Principles*, out of which emerge specific *Level #3 Methodological-Models*. The *Philosophical-Principle* of this model is based on a *Level #1 Theological-Truth* belief that the gospel can be sufficiently and effectively communicated via a verbal *Platform-Proclamation* by a celebrity athlete or coach at a large gathering. *Mega-Event, Platform-Proclamations* take place within, or as an adjunct to, a *3-R-Model (Repetitive-Redemptive-Relational)* methodology. For example, a local church hosts a youth basketball league that is primarily based on a weekly *3-R-Model* but ends the league with a one- time, season-ending *Mega-Event* in which a celebrity athlete shares their faith. Or the church may use a similar kind of *Mega-Event* on the front end of a league or program to attract people to join their activities. A *Mega-Event* could also describe a one-time outreach of a sports-related, para-ministry such as when they sponsor a "Faith at the ballpark" day, where everyone at the game is invited to hear professional athletes share their faith at the conclusion of the game. The common

theme for *Mega-Events* is the use of large and exciting one-time events or activities to attract those far from Christ and His Church for the purpose of hearing a verbal, *Platform-Proclamation* of the Gospel. *Mega-Event* is often paired with a *Mega-Media* outreach and is often juxta-positioned with the *3-R-Model (Repetitive-Redemptive-Relational)* on the fourth sports outreach continuum.

Mega-Media
Mega-Media is the term used to describe one end of the fourth of the *7-Continuums of Sports Outreach*. It describes one of *The Sports Outreach Community's Level #2 Philosophical-Principles,* out of which emerge specific *Level #3 Methodological-Models*. The *Philosophical-Principle* of this model is based on a *Level #1 Theological-Truth* belief that the gospel can be sufficiently communicated via a verbal *Platform-Proclamation* by a celebrity athlete or coach via mass media. *Mega-Media, Platform-Proclamations* take place within, or as an adjunct to, a *3-R-Model (Repetitive-Redemptive-Relational)* methodology. For example, a local church hosts a youth basketball league based on a weekly *3-R-Model* but at some point during that season, will hand each league participant a copy of the written testimony or an audio-visual link of an elite (celebrity) athlete or coach sharing their faith. A *Mega-Media* outreach could also describe a one-time effort of a sports-related, para-ministry. This *Level #3 Methodological-Model* consists of handing out gospel oriented pamphlets, magazines, tracks, videos and/or books that feature the testimonies of elite athletes. These handouts are circulated at *Mega-Events* such as the Olympics, Super Bowl or Final Four games. An increasing example of the use of *Mega-Media Model* is how social media is utilized to distribute the gospel via audio, video and literary outlets. The common theme for *Mega-Media* is the use of a spoken and/or written *Platform-Proclamation* of the gospel in efforts to reach those far from Jesus and His Church. *Mega-Media* is often paired with a *Mega-Event* outreach and is often juxta-positioned with the *3-R-Model (Repetitive-Redemptive-Relational)* of the fourth *Sports Outreach Continuum*.

Mega-Models
Mega-Models is the term used to categorize all *Platform-Proclamations (Mega-Events; Mega-Media)*. The word mega is intentionally used to describe sports outreach ministry that attempts to reach the masses in a "mega" way. These *Level #2 Philosophical-Principles* that drive various *Level #3 Methodological-Models* of sports-based outreaches are informed and guided by a *Level #1 –Theological-Truth* that believes delivering a verbal proclamation of the gospel to mass audiences either at live gatherings (*Mega-Events)*, or through written or recorded audio-visuals (*Mega-Media)* is the most effective way to reach those far from Jesus and His Church.

Missional Programming

As distinguished from programming, the distinctive of *Missional Programming* has to do with programming with a clear Gospel-centered, end-goal. Running a youth basketball league describes a church program. Facilitating a mission to youth through the strategy of a basketball ministry focuses congregational-based coaches on the Gospel-centered, end-goal of *Evangelistic-Disciplemaking*.

Missional-Sports-Communities

The term *Missional-Sports-Communities* is now used by many organizations around the world to describe The Church's response to the current spiritual condition in the world. The basic concept is that believers need to get out of their local church buildings and into their neighborhoods with the Gospel to live, serve, witness, and build community. Instead of the old attractional model of expecting people come to a worship service or other activity just because a congregation advertises all are welcome, congregations must encourage and empower their members to embrace the incarnational example of Jesus of "going to make disciples." The phrase *Missional-Sports-Communities* has been in use since at least 2012. *Missional-Sports-Communities* describes thriving Sports Ministry communities of people who are working together to be The Church as a visible witness for Jesus and establish an ongoing movement of Evangelistic-Disciplemaking. Consult with the Nxtmove organization (www.nxtmove.nl) that has further developed this concept in The Netherlands and around the world.

Muscular Christian Era

The forerunner of *The Sports Outreach Movement*, Muscular Christianity was the term given to describe a particular philosophy that emerged in the early 1800's from Thomas Arnold's Rugby school and George Williams YMCA. It then flourished through the life and ministries of men like Moody, Mott, Naismith, Stagg and the Studd brothers. It culminated in the first few decades of the 1900's when Olympian Eric Liddell inspired the world by both his running to Gold in the 1924 Paris Olympics; but even more so, when he chose not to run on the Lord's Day and thus forfeited at least three other medals. The essence of Muscular Christianity had to do with the integration of faith and sport. It devolved over the decades into more of a cultural ethos rather than a Christ-centered missional community.

Ologies

Short hand for the *Level #1 Theological-Truths* of the *3-Tier Paradigm* that inform and shape *Level #2 Philosophical-Principles*. The key and foundational *Ologies* include: ecclesiology; missiology; soteriology; cosmology; anthropology; and Christology.

Orthodoxy
Orthodoxy (not italicized because this is a common Theological term) refers to the necessity of establishing theological and doctrinal foundations in general; and in specific it serves to undergird the *Ologies* of Sports Outreach that provide the basis for all *Level #1 Theological-Truths*.

Orthopraxy
Orthopraxy (not italicized because this is a common theological term) refers to the necessity of establishing biblically-based philosophies from which pragmatic methodologies can emerge. Orthopraxy has to do with the *When, Where* & with *Whom* of the 2nd level; the *What* of the 3rd level; and the *How* of the *Core Values* of the *3-Tier Paradigm*. In SR&F outreach ministry, a well envisioned orthopraxy will ensure the successful accomplishing of the *4-Fold Evaluative Rubric* that consists of being *Strategically-Relevant* and *Efficiently-Effective*.

Personality-over-Presence
Personality-over-Presence defines a *Level #3 Methodological-Model* based on a *Level #2 Philosophical-Principle* that organizes SR&F outreaches for the purposes of having a "sports personality" give a verbal *Platform-Proclamation* of their faith, rather than envisioning, planning for and expediting outreaches based on creating on-going *Repetitive-Redemptive-Relational* activities that are focused on empowering local church missionaries to have an ever-growing and deepening presence in the lives of those far from Jesus and His Church.

Platform-Proclamation
The word platform is used in reference to a place from which to proclaim the Gospel. Proclamation refers to the verbal proclamation of the Gospel that takes place from various platforms. Such proclamations are almost exclusively delivered to large groups via mass-media. *Platform-Proclamation* is a *Level #3 Methodological-Model* that is most usually associated with Mega-Event-based outreaches. It utilizes the "platforms" associated with the notoriety afforded to elite athletes and coaches; so they can verbally "proclaim" their faith to the masses.

Proclamation-Affirmation
Proclamation-Affirmation (not italicized because this concept was coined by Jim Peterson) is the *Level #2 Philosophical-Principle* that is shaped and formed by *Level #1 Ologies* such as soteriology (theology of salvation); missiology (theology of missions); and ecclesiology (theology of the Church). These *Ologies* suggest the most *Strategically-Relevant* and *Efficiently-Effective* outreaches are those based

in *Repetitive-Redemptive-Relational* SR&F outreaches. Such outreaches are created to attract those far from Christ and His Church to participate in activities (*Belong* – the first of *The 5-B's Process* of sports outreach) in which the Gospel is proclaimed through the organization and implementation of quality missional programming; as well as the Christ-like lives of congregational leaders and members. It is hoped these efforts and relationships result in opportunities for congregational members to "affirm" their faith verbally in ways that will encourage non-Christians to *Believe* (the second of *The 5-B's Process* of sports outreach) in Jesus; accepting as their Lord and Savior.

Progressive Intensity Levels of Competition (PIL's)
PIL is used to describe a concept concerning an ascending progression of seven distinct competitive levels within the *Volatility Scale*. Each level brings an increasing amount of intensity to the competition, and this increasing intensity carries with it an inherent potential exasperation for all involved.

Producing-Reproducing-Reproducers
This phrase summarizes the hope and end-goal of all SR&F outreach ministries. This hope is based in the *Evangelistic-Disciplemaking* transferable concept, and summarizes the end result of reaching those far from Christ and His Church with the Gospel: *Dedicated-Disciples* of Christ who reach others.

Redemption
One of four classical responses and reactions embraced by sport-related individuals who encounter the dilemma of integrating faith and their sport. It describes those who choose faith over sport by attempting to redeem individual sports-people (bring them to faith in Jesus) and also by attempting to redeem (adapt and alter the way sport is organized and participated in) the culture of sport.

Re-energizing
Re-energizing is the third part of the *3-I Continuum* for fully equipping SR&F outreach ministers for the purpose of empowering them to envision, plan for, organize, administrate and evaluate a truly *Strategically-Relevant & Efficiently-Effective, Evangelistic-Disciplemaking* sports outreach ministry. It defines the efforts to infuse SR&F outreach ministers with new motivations and inspirations for reaching those far from Jesus and His Church. It also has to do with developing ongoing, personal, mentoring, relationships that enables SR&F outreach ministers to become fully equipped for successful Great Commission endeavors.

Repetitive-Redemptive-Relational

Repetitive-Redemptive-Relational is found at one end of the fourth of the *7- Continuums of Sports Outreach*. It describes one expression of *The Sports Outreach Movement's Evangelistic-Disciplemaking, Philosophical-Principles*. This model uses repetitive and ongoing SR&F leagues, classes or activities to attract those far from Christ and His Church; and also to create interpersonal, relational *Evangelistic-Environments* for the Gospel to be experienced over a multiple-year, time frame. Based on Peterson's "Proclamation-Affirmation" concept; *Repetitive-Redemptive-Relational* verbal "affirmation" of the Gospel follows long periods of lived out "proclamation." Contrasted to a *Mega-Event* philosophy of gathering a large group of people to large scale event, *Repetitive-Redemptive-Relational* focuses on empowering and enabling, long-term, one-on-one or small group *Evangelistic-Disciplemaking* endeavors.

Rejection

One of four classical responses and reactions embraced by sport-related individuals who encounter the dilemma of integrating faith and their sport. It describes those who choose to leave sport because they cannot reconcile the demands of both. *Rejection* often means totally leaving sport but it can also describe a person who continues to engage in sport but rejects a specific aspect of it such as refusing to cheat; follow the instruction of a coach to purposely injure a fellow competitor or take harmful and illegal performance-enhancing substances.

Re-sourcing

Re-sourcing is the first part of the *3-I Continuum* for fully equipping SR&F outreach ministers for the purpose of empowering them to envision, plan for, organize, administrate and evaluate a truly *Strategically-Relevant* & *Efficiently-Effective, Evangelistic-Disciplemaking* sports outreach ministry. It has to do with the creation, production and distribution of *Re-sources* that are: Christo-centric *Level #1 Theological-Truths*; Biblically-Based *Level #2 Philosophical-Principles*; and *Level #3 Methodological-Models*.

Re-training

Re-training is the second part of the *3-I Continuum* for fully equipping SR&F outreach ministers for the purpose of empowering them to envision, plan for, organize, administrate and evaluate a truly *Strategically-Relevant* & *Efficiently-Effective, Evangelistic-Disciplemaking* sports outreach ministry. It has to do with *Instructing* SR&F outreach ministers in how to most effectively utilize and employ the *Re-sources* that have been created, produced and distributed.

Singular-Commitment-Cost

The phrase *Singular-Commitment-Cost* is used in reference to ministries engaging in *Evangelistic-Disciplemaking* outreaches that emphasize there is a cost to becoming a disciple of Jesus. In comparison to Bonhoeffer's concept of "Cheap Grace," churches, ministries and evangelists are encouraged to call people far from Jesus to become life-long, *Dedicated-Disciples*. Rather than simply asking people to "convert" *(Counting-Conversions)* by making a *Day's-Decision,* it is recommended all outreaches clearly communicate becoming a disciple of Jesus costs something! It includes not only receiving Jesus as Savior, but more so, making Him Lord of every area of their life. The *Singular-Commitment-Cost* describes the commitment churches and ministries need to make in "Changing-From" ministry models that strive to be winsome at the expense of proclaiming the whole Gospel; to "Changing-To" outreaches that present the Gospel in its entirety. It also describes the commitment a person needs to consider in making a decision to become a disciple.

Sportsmanship

Sportsmanship (not italicized because it is not original with CSRM) is one of three philosophical approaches to competition and sport. It describes an ethic based on the humanistic-relativism of playing fair; being a good teammate; and obeying the rules of the game. As compared with gamesmanship; a philosophy which highest value is to win, regardless of how; and *Christmanship* that espouses engaging in sport for the glory of God and in ways that honors all co-competitors; sportsmanship values ethics that are based in humanistic-relativism and therefore change according to a shifting societal culture.

Sports Outreach Community

The phrase that generically describes the unique group within the Church of Jesus Christ that uses SR&F outreach ministry to reach all who are far from Christ and His Church. It has four distinct expressions within local churches: a) congregational-based outreaches; b) sports-related, para-ministries; c) fitness/wellness/wholeness based outreaches; and d) recreational/camping experiences and outreaches. This community also includes various sports-related, para-ministry models. The phrase *Sports Outreach Community* is preferred over *Sports Outreach Movement* because the former better communicates this group expresses itself within the Church, whereas *Sports Outreach Movement* connotes the efforts and activities occur as a separate movement from The Church.

Sports Outreach Movement

The phrase that describes the growing community within the Church of Jesus Christ using SR&F methodologies to reach all who are far from Christ and His

Church. It has four distinct expressions: a) congregational-based outreaches; b) sports-related, para-ministries; c) fitness/wellness/wholeness based outreaches; and d) recreational/camping experiences and outreaches. (See the definition of *Sports Outreach Community* which provides a distinction between the words *Sports Outreach Community* and *Sports Outreach Movement* and the rationale for preferring Community

Sports-related, para-ministry
Based on the *Level #1 Ology* of ecclesiology (the theology of The Church), the terminology para-ministry is preferred over para-church. It may seem a distinction without a difference and yet this seemingly subtle distinction can have significant and long-lasting negative implications. The word para means beside, and thus outside of. When used in relationship to The Church it communicates being outside of and thus, not part of the universal Church of Jesus. Conversely, para-ministry indicates a ministry that is organizationally outside of a congregation but still in The Church. There are congregational (often called local church) ministries and there are also ministries not based in congregations.

Sportianity
Sportianity (not italicized because it was not original with CSRM) is used to describe the thoughts, emotions and commitments of people who embrace one end of the Sportianity-Christianity Continuum. In essence its context describes people who make sport their highest priority and thus their commitment to, and their involvement in, sport becomes a type of religion.

Strategically-Relevant
Paired with *Efficiently-Effective*, it is the first half of the *4-Fold Evaluative Rubric*. *Strategically-Relevant* suggests the guideline congregations can use to help assess and determine whether or not a local church SR&F outreach ministry is actually accomplishing its goal of engaging those whom are far from Christ and His Church. It is designed to aid local congregations to define and describe the most strategic and relevant sports, recreational activities and fitness initiatives within specific regions, countries and cultures of the world.

Success-Statistics
Success-Statistics is a phrase that describes how individual evangelists, churches, ministries and missions determine their effectiveness. Some count the number of people who make a *Day's-Decision* as indicated by the raising of their hand, praying a prayer or filling out a card (*Counting-Conversions*) to determine if their outreach was successful. Others see such *Days-Decisions* as but the first

step in becoming life-long, *Dedicated-Disciples* and thus their effectiveness is only assessed by the number of people they have labored to "make disciples" of.

The Movement / The Sports Outreach Movement/The Local Church SR&F Movement

To move is to change location and position. A movement then has to do with change, repositioning and going somewhere—hopefully towards a destination. In this series of books there are two terms that are used interchangeably (*The Sports Outreach Movement / The Movement*) and a third that is very similar (*The Local Church SR&F Movement*). They can all be used to generally describe the activities of a like-minded group of people who are engaged in Christo-centric ministry that is based in sport, recreation, fitness/wholeness/wellness and camping/outdoor pursuits. This *Movement* is generally agreed to have started in the 1940's when a number of activities occurred, beginning with the Venture for Victory initiating its international short-term sports mission trips and ministries such as the Billy Graham Associates began to use elite athletes and coaches as spokespersons at their crusades and events. It has morphed and expanded both in breadth and depth over the last decades. The phrase *The Movement* or *The Sports Outreach Movement* is used to describe and include all four quadrants, whereas The Local Church *SR&F Movement* is used to distinguish such activities within the confines of congregational outreach.

Volatility Scale

The *Volatility Scale* is an instrument that has been designed to chart and predict a competitor's experience. By combining the *EMIC, IMIC* and the *PIL's* it produces a measureable evaluative tool that analyzes what athletes, coaches and others will experience in a particular competitive event. The *Volatility Scale* contains four separate quadrants: Enjoyment; Encounter; Explosion; Exasperation.

Why; When-Where-With Whom; What

These are all tied to the *3-Tier Paradigm* and are specifically tied to one of the three levels of the paradigm:

- *Why*—is connected with the Christo-Centric *Level #1 Theological-Truths* which provide the basic rationale, ethical foundations for, *The Sports Outreach Community*
- *When-Where-With Whom*—are connected to the Biblically-based *Level #2 Philosophical-Principles* which provide the organizational structure for *The Sports Outreach Community*
- *What*—is connected with the *Strategically-Relevant* and *Efficiently-Effective Level #3 Methodological-Models* and describes the specific activities of *The Sports Outreach Community*

Without Reach We Have No Revenue and Without Revenue We Have No Reach
This phrase coined by Greg English communicates the local church SR&F outreach minister must balance "counting beans with counting souls." Both the ministry/outreach and the financing of the ministry are important. The financing empowers and enables the ministry and yet the ministry inspires the giving of the finances. The SR&F outreach ministers responsibility is to ensure both occur.

Addendum #2

EXPLANATORY NOTES FOR THE:
"INSTITUTES OF THE SPORTS OUTREACH COMMUNITY BOOK SERIES"

DISTINCTIVES OF THIS BOOK SERIES

This is the fifth in the "Institutes of Sports Outreach" series of books which will eventually consist of at least 12 distinct works. While each book could stand alone; the entire series is based on, and united through, the overarching organizational structure of the *3-Tier Paradigm* (see chapter 3 in the second book: *Sports Outreach Fundamentals*). Each book either builds upon, and/or refers to others in the series. A quick review of the previous books include…

- The first book (*Christmanship: A Theology of Competition and Sport*) introduced basic theological and ethical foundations, which serve as the basic apologetic for sports outreach.
- The second book (*Sports Outreach Fundamentals*) outlined the *Level #2 Philosophical-Principles* that serve as the biblically-based, organizational structure for ensuring a *Strategically-Relevant* and *Efficiently-Effective* SR&F outreach.
- Book #3 (*Putting The Church Back In The Game: The Soteriology of Sports Outreach*) was the first entry into *Level #1 Theological-Truths* and established ecclesiology as a fundamental theological foundation for sports outreach ministry.
- Book #4 (*The Saving of Sports Ministry: The Soteriology of Sports Outreach*) was the second *Ology* book that serves to undergird *The Sports Outreach Community* with foundational *Level #1 Theological-Truths*. This book was designed to establish a solid theology of soteriology (theology of salvation) that will empower all SR&F outreach ministry to engage in "making disciples.

The series will continue with at least one more *Level #1 Theological-Truth* book starting with the next book: Christology. These theological books will work together to inform and guide the transferable concepts based in *Level #2 Philosophical-Principles* from which *Level #3 Methodological-Models* will emerge.

The oversight for this series of books includes maintaining: a) a consistent editorial board (made up of a strong group of practitioners, academics and editors); b) a general editor; c) book editors; d) book section editors; and e) book and chapter authors (experienced veterans of *The Sports Outreach Community*).

What follows in this and subsequent books is the fulfillment of the plan that emerged from an overall vision, and the distinctive perspective, from which the "Institutes of Sports Outreach" book series was conceived. This all contributes to giving this series of books a unique and catalytic place in propelling sports outreach into its 2nd century.

Further distinctions and core values of The Institutes of Sports Outreach include: I. Vision; II. Orthodoxy and Orthopraxy; III. History & Theology; IV. Citations; V. Use of Italics; VI. Thoughts on *The Movement;* VII. Thoughts on the Words Church, Local Church and Congregation; VIII. Capitalization; IX. Co-Authors; X. Creating the language; and XI. Reasoning Together.

I. Vision—This series of books has been envisioned to communicate the *Information* of *The Sports Outreach Community* for the purpose of resourcing, training, connecting and equipping local church sports, recreation & fitness (SR&F) outreach ministers for the end goal of them being able to mobilize, enable and empower their congregations to fulfill the Great Commission. While it is hoped that this series will also prove to be relevant and beneficial for all sports outreach endeavors, it is written by and for local church SR&F practitioners.

II. Orthodoxy and Orthopraxy—one of the key distinctions of this series of books has to do with the intentional target of the material presented. This series is designed to be a complementary blend of Orthodoxy and Orthopraxy.

Orthodoxy is a word that is somewhat familiar to most within *The Sports Outreach Community*, as it is a much used term within Christianity that describes true-to-the-Bible theology and philosophy. However, not everyone would be able to accurately define it, let alone understand its importance and relevance to SR&F outreach ministry. If such confusion exists about the word orthodoxy, then how much more true would it be about the term orthopraxy, of which most Christians are unfamiliar. Further explanations are helpful.

Orthodoxy and orthopraxy derive from a common Greek root: "ortho" – which means straight, right, or correct. Thus the straightening concept found in both words communicates such straightening will bring about righteousness and correctness. However, the two words each have differing suffixes which sends this correcting righteousness in two different directions.

The suffix "doxy" stems from another Greek word which means doctrine or belief. Its Greek etymological root word is *dexomai*. *Dexomai* connotes a receiving of someone or something, and thus when put together, orthodoxy means to receive and believe a straight, right and correct word from God. "*Doxy*" pertains to thinking and thus, orthodoxy has to do with right and correct doctrinal and theological thinking.

The suffix for the second word "praxis" stems from yet a third Greek word which means to practice. "Praxis" has to do with action and activity. Thus, orthopraxy has to do with the essence of acting in straight, right, correct and/or strategically practical ways. Thus, whereas orthodoxy deals with correct doctrine and theology, orthopraxy pertains to right and correct action based on solid orthodoxy.

The relevance to sports outreach, and to this book, is that any good orthopraxy (*Level #3 Methodological Models*) is based upon solid orthodoxy (*Level #1 Theological-Truths* and *Level #2 Philosophical-Principles*); as explained in many other books in this series. The entire series of books is based upon this *3-Tier Paradigm* which envisions solid theological and theoretical thinking from which *Strategically-Relevant* and *Efficiently-Effective* SR&F Outreach Ministry can emerge.

III. History and Theology—Theology doesn't develop in a historical vacuum. Moreover, theology shapes history. Thus, an undergirding distinction of this series of books is to highlight historical anecdotes of people, ministries, churches, missions and organizations which will be used to either: a) illustrate theology; or b) provide living examples of why theology (or often the lack of it) is important to comprehending and implementing a *Strategically-Relevant* and *Efficiently-Effective* SR&F outreach ministry.

Some of the historical references are ancient, from as early as the 1st Century. However, many will be from the past two centuries; including contributions from current practitioners who share their current experiences as they engage in creating contemporary history—both shaping theology as well as being shaped by theology.

It is envisioned and hoped the linking of the theological and theoretical with the pragmatic and practical will enhance not only the comprehension of the reader, but more importantly, this combination will inspire catalytic new visions for *Strategically-Relevant* and *Efficiently-Effective* SR&F outreach.

These historical vignettes appear throughout the books in the form of special "Time Out" pages that invite the reader to take a "time out" for reflection that would lead to gospel centered action.

IV. Citations—direct quotes are always cited as are more general references that are drawn from specific hardcopy or digital sources; as well as personal conversations. However, some general data is assumed without direct referential citing due to the nature of current day search engine capability. With the wonder of the internet, anyone reading this series of books can have the latest data at their fingertips rather than be saddled with out-of-date statistics available at the time of writing. Readers are encouraged to access current trends and research so as to not be unduly, or even wrongly, persuaded by the outdated data that influenced the narratives found in this series of books; including some that may well be challenged or disproved by future research. This editorial decision is intentionally offered so as to engage readers in seeking truth, rather than falling into the trap of believing the false truth of outdated statistics. Thus, assuming a book to have an existence far beyond a specific period of time of research, the editors have often opted to not always take the space to provide research data that likely becomes out of date within months. However, a quick perusal of the works cited, or any good web-based search would provide any interested reader with the proper references that served to form the basis of an author's assessments and thus be able to make proper assessments of any thesis proposed by authors. Therefore, classic and historic data is always cited but current/fluctuating data is sometimes not cited. A good example of this would be church attendance or growth data. Whereas the current data may suggest a current trend, future readers are encouraged to uncover the data at the time of reading and then decide whether what is proposed is in this book series remains valid.

A unique category of citation is the various "side bars/word boxes." All such side bars are original to the authors of the various books, sections or chapters, unless noted otherwise. There are four major categories of side bars: a) Graphs; b) Charts; c) "Scoreboards," and d) "Time Outs." All four have been designed to help the reader contemplate, visualize and implement the content of the narrative. Examples of all four can be found throughout this series of books with the following distinctions.

Graphs show the results of surveys or anything that can be counted and compared. **Charts** are used to pictorially illustrate the concepts being written about. The third category entitled: **"Scoreboards"** is used to highlight and/or further emphasize a major phrase or concept found within the narrative, with the thought being the reader is being reminded to "keep score" of the various points being made and/or to score points by applying the data to their own ministry setting. **"Time Outs"** allow the reader to take a short break from the narrative, to reflect upon an ancient or contemporary historical model or example of what the narrative is describing.

V. Use of Italics—Italics are used wherever words or terms have been repurposed, created or coined by the authors. Italics are also used whenever unique CSRM language is used. This is done for three main reasons. First, italics are used to emphasize the fact that *The Sports Outreach Community* is in need of creating its own language to accurately define, describe and communicate its unique ethos, culture, structure and mission. Therefore, these unique words and phrases are repeatedly italicized. Second, the goal is to not only familiarize the readers with the important transferable concepts put forth in this book series but more to drill the terms and transferable concepts deep into the psyche of the reader; thus the repetitive use of italics. The third reason is to communicate the unique repurposing of words and/or phrases that otherwise might be understood in ways that are different than for which they are utilized in *The Community* and this book. Italics are also used for all foreign language words.

VI. Thoughts on *The Movement*

The phrase that SR&F outreach ministries are often referred to is: *The Sports Outreach Movement,* or simply *The Movement.* At the time of writing, this is the term used by most SR&F leaders. Overwhelming Victory Press has however, become increasingly less comfortable with the phrase. This discomfort has to do with the subtle communication that what is done in SR&F outreach ministry takes place outside of the traditional body of Christ (The Church), and becomes an entity unto itself (thus a movement) superseding, and existing outside of The Church. In reality this so-called *Movement* is simply one expression of how The Church reaches and incorporates those far from Christ and His Church.

Thus, *The Sports Outreach Movement* terminology that has been used throughout the first books of this series has been changed in this and future editions to the phrase: *Sports Outreach Community.* This is a more theologically correct way to refer to the community of SR&F outreach ministers who are members, ministers and leaders of a local assembly of the worldwide Church.

VII. Thoughts on the Words: The Church, Local Church and Congregation

The words "The Church" will be used whenever the universal body of Christ is intended, and both words (The and Church) will be capitalized to so designate it and differentiate it from a local congregation. Whenever a local assembly of The Church is referenced, it will be done so in lower case (church). Thus, terms such as: local church, congregation, and assembly will not be capitalized. To further aid the communication of this distinction, the word congregation will be used most often when referencing a local assembly of The Church.

VIII. Capitalization

All words relating to, describing or referencing God will be capitalized. This editorial decision serves to communicate and emphasize the Overwhelming Victory Press (OVP) belief that the triune-God is truly worthy of receiving any and all honor possible. Thus the more commonly capitalized words such as God, Lord, Jesus, Holy Spirit will be joined with any pronouns used to refer to God such as Him, He, His and even at times words that reference God such as Who.

Another special use of capitalization is in reference to the Bible. The word Bible and phrases such as Word of God will be capitalized for two reasons. The first is to clearly express OVP's commitment to communicate its belief that the

Bible is sacred literature; above and beyond all other writings and deserves a place of honor. In a day and age in which the Bible is being attacked, criticized and marginalized, even within much of Christian scholarship. The second reason has to do with communicating OVP's belief and commitment that the Bible is the inerrant, infallible and fully trustworthy Word of God; and that it is fully authoritative for The Church. Capitalization of these words should not however be understood that OVP believes the Bible to be God, but rather His Word.

IX. Co-Authors

Another distinction and core value of Overwhelming Victory Press has to do with the recognition that The Church is made up of a myriad of individual disciples of Jesus. This recognition is exemplified in this book series by each book being co-authored by a number of different people. The way these co-authors integrate their contributions is best described through the metaphor of a sports broadcast.

Most sports broadcasts have at least 3 distinct roles that are needed to fully communicate the events of the game, match or race. The first role is that of the "play-by-play" announcer who gives a running narrative, describing each specific play. The second role is often called the "color analyst" and seeks to enhance the running narrative by elaborating on, and further explaining, the "play-by-play." The "color" man/woman provides additional information by explaining the why, the when and the who involved in a specific play or strategy that worked; or in some cases, why it didn't work. The third role in a broadcast team is usually an on the field reporter who conducts interviews and provides up close and personal insights.

The "broadcast team" assembled for the Institutes of Sport Outreach book series is currently made up of four regular contributing authors and individual cameos by other veterans in the field. The "play-by-play" role is filled by Dr. Greg Linville who provides the basic content and oversees the flow of that content. The "color" and "on the field" roles are filled by three others.

Greg English contributes in many of the chapters a piece entitled: A Practitioner's-Perspective. His role is to take the theory of the "play-by-play" and make it relevant to local church SR&F outreach ministers.

P. F. Myers role is to bring an international perspective to the narrative so as to make the data relevant to the *SR&F Outreach Community* throughout the world, and also to enable stateside SR&F outreach ministers to benefit and learn from practitioners in other countries and cultures. Myers' insights can be found throughout the books under the title of: International Insights.

Dr. Vickie Byler joined the broadcast team for the first time in the fourth book of the book series. As a long time Professor and University department chair, her role is to add academic insights coming from research and also by providing information concerning citations. Byler's contributions are found under the title of: Research Reflections.

In addition to these regular contributing authors, there is a lengthy list of SR&F veterans (guest authors) who contribute invaluable, one-off insights. These essays are most often found in side bars entitled: Time Out.

X. Creating the Language – One of the objectives of the Institutes of Sports Outreach book series is to create a common language for the entire *Sports Outreach Community*. It started with coining the word *Christmanship* and has continued throughout the decades with more recent words like *Sports Ministry Pyramid, Missional Sports Communities* and *Locating the Lost*. Each of the words and phrases communicate a specific and unique concept or thought. The new language is made of up of four major distinctions: a) coined original words; b) coined original phrases; c) coined compound words; and d) common words repurposed for specific use within the *Sports Outreach Community*.

Coined original words such as: *Christmanship; Dysconnect; and Ology* have been created to name and describe a new, or unique and specific concept, thought or idea. All coined, original words will not only be italicized but also capitalized for the purpose of further clarity.

Coined original phrases such as: *3-Tier Paradigm; 4-Fold Evaluative Rubric; 5-B's of Sports Outreach; Building With Leaders; Sports Outreach Community; Missional Sports Communities; Sports Ministry Pyramid; Feeding The Flock;* and *Locating The Lost* have also been created to utilize common words in unique combinations to communicate a unique and specific concept, thought or idea. All words in these original phrases will be capitalized for the purpose of bringing further clarity to which words are included in such phrases.

Coined compound words such as: *Evangelistic-Disciplemaking, Day's-Decisions, Counting-Converts; Success-Statistics;* and *Dedicated-Disciples* are common words that have been combined to create a completely new meaning, concept, thought or idea and are thus hyphenated. Both words of the compound words will also be capitalized for the purpose of further clarity.

Repurposed words such as: the four words found in the classical responses to the integration of faith and sport (*Rejection, Redemption, Accommodation & Capitulation)*; the *3-Tier Paradigm* "W" words (*Why, When, Where, With Whom, What)*; or the *5-B's of Sports Outreach* (*Belong, Believe, Baptize, Behave, Become*) are italicized for the purpose of signifying a specific meaning, concept, thought or idea relevant to the *Sports Outreach Community*.

XI. Reasoning Together—a hallmark of the Quaker Church has been the practice of "reasoning together" (Isaiah 1.18) whenever difficult and controversial topics arise. The undergirding premise of belief for this practice has been the realization that due to the fallen nature of humankind, individual Christians often err in maintaining a truly orthodox faith in all areas of doctrine and theology. It is further believed doctrinal heresies are best understood and overcome by "reasoning together."

"Reasoning together" requires three things: A) appealing to the Word of God as a final and supreme authority; B) keeping one's heart warm and one's mind open to the guiding inspiration of the Holy Spirit which is encapsulated by the Quaker concept called the "Inner Light;" and C) engaging in "civil conversations" with spiritual brethren based on the Holy Spirit's empowerment and enlightenment of the holy scripture.

A. Appealing to the Word of God as a Final and Supreme Authority

The Quakers join all Protestant traditions who have historically agreed that the Bible is the source and final authority from which all theological doctrines and ethical mandates are based. More to the point, unless the Word of God is given its proper place as the final authority in all faith and practice matters, arriving at an agreed upon, God-inspired, theological consensus is impossible. Thus, all "reasoning together" is based on determining a correct interpretation of the Bible which becomes the foundation for all Christo-centric, *Theological-Truths* and those truths then inform the formation of biblically-based, *Philosophical-Principles* which are to be applied to everyday life. This may all sound well and good, but even a cursory survey of Church history reveals acrimonious, heated and even violent theological debates have raged throughout the last two millennia. This is where the second pre-requisite of keeping hearts warm and minds open becomes so relevant and necessary.

B. Keeping Hearts Warm and Minds Open

I contend the major reason theological dialogues turn ugly has to do with the heart and minds of those involved. A most important clarifying question has to do with what motivates those in the dialogue: "Do I desire to understand and be convinced of God's theology; or do I want to convince others of my theology?!"

Assuming that all involved in theological dialogues seek God's truth, not political propaganda or ecclesiastical agenda, it behooves all involved to keep their hearts warm to both the Holy Spirit's guidance and their minds open to the "reasonings" of their spiritual brethren. It stands to "reason" that no human possesses a perfect theology. Thus logically, we need one another to come to a Spirit led consensus on what a proper theology is. Furthermore, we only hurt ourselves if we are unwilling to open our hearts and minds to the Holy Spirit speaking to us through the hearts and minds of our brothers and sisters in the Lord. This can only happen by engaging in civil conversations.

C. Engaging Spiritual Brethren in Civil Conversation

This third pre-requisite for "reasoning together" is often the most difficult to achieve; in fact it is nearly impossible to arrive at any consensus about a proper theology if hearts are cold and minds are closed. Furthermore, civil conversations cannot occur unless all conversants honor, love and respect those whom they are engaged with in such conversations—even those with whom they vehemently disagree with because they are so deeply repulsed by the other's views.

Nonetheless, through the centuries, when the three pre-requisites are met that enable such open, honest, direct and deliberate discourses, followers of Jesus have experienced "God's theology" and achieved consensus.

It is in that spirit that the civil conversations about the *Ologies* of *The Sports Outreach Community* are engaged in throughout this book series. If what is proposed in the various books is theologically sound, then it is hoped it would convince others who prior to this "reasoning together" may have believed otherwise. Of course, if what is proposed here is in error, then it is OVP's prayer that the hearts of those making such proposals would remain warm to Jesus and their minds would be open to clearer thinking…with the end goal of not insisting on any one person's theology, but rather *The Sports Ministry Community* would collectively and collaboratively come to consensus and thus attain Jesus' theology.

A Final Word

To revisit and restate the vision of this series: the laser-focus of this series of books is to enhance and expand the gospel-centric, *Evangelistic-Disciplemaking* efforts of individual members and congregations of The Church. This series of books is written by, and for all within, *The Sports Outreach Community* but especially for local church SR&F outreach ministers. It is produced by the publishing arm of the Association of Church Sports & Recreation Ministers (CSRM)—Overwhelming Victory Press (OVP)—for all who are called to this most strategic and catalytic outreach of The Church. The hopes and prayers of the CSRM staff, Board of Trustees and supporters are that the Lord of the universe will use this series to supernaturally empower all who read this series.

— Dr. Greg Linville – Director of Resource Development - CSRM
General Editor for The Institutes of Sports Outreach
From the shores of Lake Erie at Lakeside Chautauqua - 2018

Addendum #3

EXPLANATORY NOTES FOR:

SENT: Missiology for the Sports Outreach Community

The first book of this Institute of Sports Outreach Book Series (*Christmanship*) established the basic apologetic for sports outreach and initiated the process of how sports outreach leaders could think theologically, organize philosophically and compete ethically. It explained the difference between competition, sport and recreation and proposed a Christian Ethic for the integration of faith and sport.

Book two (*Sports Outreach Fundamentals*) outlined how sports, recreation and fitness (SR&F) outreach ministers could envision, plan for and implement a *Strategically-Relevant* and *Efficiently-Effective, Evangelistic-Disciplemaking* outreach ministry. That book rests upon this and other *Level #1 Theological-Truth* books of this series.

The third book (*Putting The Church Back in the Game*) was the first book focused on foundational theological foundations of sports outreach. It explored the vital connection between the theology of The Church and SR&F outreach ministry and concluded all such ministry should be based in and through a local congregation of the universal Church. Furthermore, all SR&F endeavors should either plant a new congregation or enhance or expand existing assemblies.

The fourth book (*The Saving of Sports Ministry*) took another step in establishing the foundational Christo-centric, *Level #1 Theological-Truths* concerning the soteriology (theology of salvation) of The Church as it relates to sports outreach. In other words, it sought to define and articulate a clear and understandable theology of salvation (what is called soteriology in academic circles). It also identified the implications of soteriology for determining the organizational structure for, and pragmatic implementations of, *The Sports Outreach Community*.

This, the fifth book, adds yet another vital theological foundation: Missiology. Missiology, in general, establishes the *Level #1 Theological-Truth* of what is entailed in taking the gospel to the world. In specific, this book focuses on missiological concepts as it relates to *The Sports Outreach Community's* gospel-centric, *Evangelistic-Disciplemaking* endeavors.

As general editor of this book series and author of this book, I make two pledges. The first is of primary importance to all of us who have served as SR&F practitioners: I pledge to make every attempt at making what could become a most high-brow and tedious book, relevant and readable. Yet, even with this said, I hope to challenge SR&F practitioners to grow in their theological comprehension and knowledge; in their ministry ability; and most of all in their relationship with Jesus and His Word. If this book doesn't cause and encourage theological, ministerial and spiritual growth, then I have failed. I want to meet SR&F outreach ministers where they are, but also motivate them to grow in their knowledge, wisdom and ministry. My hope is that we will "meet at the train depot," and agree to travel together. My prayer is that we will be courageous enough to get on the train and allow it to take us to the next stops… and that our final destination will be where God wants to grow us.

The second pledge is to the academy. While I realize this book (and in fact the entire series is not written like, nor does it approximate the kind of academic treatise, article or book that meets typical academic genre, my hope is that true academicians will appreciate the theological and philosophical bedrock upon which the methodology builds. My prayer is that my academic peers will be supportive of my attempts to build a bridge where academia and ministry can meet, and where orthodoxy shapes orthopraxy and orthopraxy stretches orthodoxy.

My fear is that I will fall short of this goal and please no one. I further fear academics will deem what I present as theology light and practitioners will be turned off by weighty language or the occasional complex theory.

This book, *The Mission of Sports Ministry,* is the fifth book in a series projected to include 12 or more total books. This book's specific content is comprised of one sub-set of the *Level #1 Theological Truths* that sports outreach is founded on. It has been preceded by, and will be followed by other *Level #1 Theological Truth* books that will collectively outline and discuss how *The Sports Outreach Community* (including local churches) conceptualize, plan for and implement Sports, Recreation and Fitness (SR&F) outreach ministry. Such ministries when properly understood and organized in and through *Level #1 Theological-Truths* will not only be relevant and strategic but perhaps even more important, will employ models that effectively reach those far from Christ, and do so with the most efficient utilization of all resources. In fact, when properly conceptualized, (from solid theological foundations), SR&F outreach ministries provide The Church in general, and local congregations in specific with the most powerful methodology The Church has for successful gospel-centric, *Evangelistic-Disciplemaking.*

Sadly however, the landscape is strewn with unsuccessful sport and rec programs which have failed because the *Level #3 Methodological Models* were not informed by, conceptualized, planned or implemented in light of the *Level #1 Theological-Truths* which are found in this book and this book series.

Explanatory Notes For This Book

The word theology itself comes from two Greek words: *Theos* – God; and *logos* – (where the English word logic comes from); and when put together it actually means a logic (or study) of God. Thus, theology is a logical study of God. Only when God is fully comprehended can people understand who they are; who they were created to be; and how local congregations are to conceive of, and implement, their gospel-centric, *Evangelistic-Disciplemaking* efforts. What follows in this book is the continuation of a number of introspective looks into the major *Level #1 Theological-Truths* that prove most consistently relevant for envisioning a local church SR&F outreach ministry. I refer to them as the *"Ologies"* of *The Sports Outreach Movement*.

DISTINCTIVES OF THIS BOOK

Transferable concepts – All of the transferable concepts outlined in a previous book of this series (*Sports Outreach Fundamentals*) were based upon, and emerge out of what I have termed: *The Ologies of Sports Outreach*, which are the subject of this and subsequent books in this series. I coined the word *"Ologies"* for this series of books to serve as a catch-phrase for foundational *Level #1 Theological-Truths* that undergird and inform the *Level #2 Philosophical-Principles* from which *Level #3 Methodological-Models* emerge. This book and others in this series are what all the transferable concepts found in the previous book (*Sports Outreach Fundamentals*) are based on, formed by and informed by.

Thus, there may be readers of this book that will question the strategic relevance of this book because it consists of more theory and less pragmatics. To those, I would urge holding this book in one hand and the *Fundamentals* book in the other. These theological foundations are vital to comprehending any effective pragmatic ministry.

Some may then question the order of books. The best way I can explain the order would be to reference Lewis' Narnia series. The story line of the first book of the series (*The Lion, the Witch and the Wardrobe*), was not chronologically the first part of Lewis's mythical history of Narnia. A later book in the series— *The Magician's Nephew*—predated the history of *The Lion, the Witch and the Wardrobe,* and once read, helped make the story line clearer as it connected so many dots. It also had the effect of moving the readers to reread all the previous books in the series; and in doing so, brought an even more significant understanding to the overall message of the author. While I cannot hope to be compared with Lewis's literary skills, it is my hope that this book *The Mission of Sports Ministry* will enable readers to better understand the transferable concepts found in *Sports Outreach Fundamentals*, and thus better be able to envision, plan for and implement a *Strategically-Relevant* and *Efficiently-Effective* SR&F outreach ministry.

History and Theology (Mostly Contemporary)—as articulated in the general introduction to this Institute of Sports Outreach Book Series: "Theology doesn't happen in a historical vacuum; and theology shapes history." Thus, this book continues that tradition in highlighting historical anecdotes of people, ministries, churches, missions and organizations which are used to either illustrate theology or provide living examples of why theology (or often the lack of it) is important to comprehending and implementing a *Strategically-Relevant* and *Efficiently-Effective* SR&F outreach ministry.

The distinction of this book lies in its historical anecdotes being almost exclusively written by contemporary history makers as they reveal history in the making. These vignettes are found in the various 1-2 page "Time Outs" appearing as highlighted word boxes found throughout the book. One unique feature of this book is the "Surrounded by Witnesses" historical vignettes that feature Muscular Christian Pioneers. A different pioneer's quotes and insights are included in most chapters. The hope is that by connecting contemporary sports ministry pioneers to historical models a new model can be envisioned.

I continue to be much indebted to friends and colleagues who were willing to submit their written contributions for this project. This book has been greatly enhanced by these early 21st century models. This pairing of narrative and contemporary history is probably best understood as a sports broadcast. While the narrative I write is the more mundane "play-by-play" the modern history vignettes written by local church practitioners, are the "color commentators" of the broadcast.

My hope is that the transferable concepts of the previous book will be undergirded by this book in such a way as to create newly proposed working models for the expansion and enhancement of *The Sports Outreach Community's* ultimate goal of world-wide *Evangelistic-Disciplemaking*. It is further hoped the relevance of these transferable concepts will maximize the effectiveness and efficiency of thousands of SR&F outreach ministers throughout the world who daily attempt to "go and make disciples."

The *Ologies* found in this and other books in this series are of my own creation stemming from years of directed Bible study and contemplative reflection on my own SR&F experiences. While the general missiological concepts are over a hundred years old, I believe the application to *The Sports Outreach Community* to be seminal, not only in their conception, but also in how they are defined, explained and expressed. Yet, while I state they have been revealed to or discovered by me, I am quick to indicate that they are truly the product of our *Sports Outreach Community* and I am indebted to many, many people who have journeyed with me through this time of revelation and discovery.

Citations

There is one general difference in the citations of this book than for previous books in this series: Citations concerning the Great Commission.

The Great Commission—Due to the nature and topic of this particular book, the Great Commission passage of Matthew 28.19, 20 will not be officially cited with a footnote each time it is referenced. This decision is based on the best stewardship of time, space and effort on the part of authors, editors, graphic artists, printers and of course readers. It will be cited in the actual narrative throughout the manuscript by actually spelling out the words "Great Commission" or by simply incorporating any of the following: "go;" "going;" "go into all the world;" "go to make disciples;" "disciplemaking" etc. Citing the Great Commission in this way actually serves to give Jesus' command to go into all the world and make disciples its well-deserved pre-eminence as the one major reference for the entire book. For official citation purposes, The Great Commission passage is offered just below…

"Go therefore and make disciples of all nations, baptizing them in the name of the Father and of the Son and of the Holy Spirit, teaching them to observe all that I have commanded you. And behold, I am with you always, to the end of the age." Matthew 28.19, 20

Final Words

May this book be used of the Lord to *Inform, Instruct and Inspire* all within *The Sports Outreach Community* to engage, equip and empower their church to envision, plan for, organize, administrate and implement effective missions that will reach and disciple those who are far from Jesus and His Church.

— Dr. Greg Linville – Director of Resource Development CSRM
Author and General Editor for The Institutes of Sports Outreach
From the shores of Lake Erie at Lakeside Chautauqua - 2020

Addendum #4

ACKNOWLEDGMENTS

General Acknowledgments

How can you ever adequately acknowledge all those who have impacted you? I very much see this book, and this entire series of books as being made possible because of the myriad of people who have influenced and inspired me. While I find it difficult to always identify exactly when and where one idea or person inspired another, and similarly, it is often hard to know who inspired whom. What's easier to say is I know I owe much, to many! To that end, I acknowledge that this book is a true synthesis of many influences on my life. Thus, to all who are cited here, to those cited in previous books, and many others, I say again thank you for your part in making this book and this book series a reality!

As always, though much credit should go to others for all that is true and positive in this work; I remain completely responsible for any flaws or shortcomings presented; and in no way wish to suggest any of my errors in reasoning, remembering, or hermeneutics, are the fault of any of my colleagues. In addition, if I have not given adequate or appropriate credit to anyone for their influence, I would humbly ask to bring this oversight to my attention so I can apologize and give proper acknowledgement in future editions.

It should also be noted that much of the content of this book can be found in various articles, chapters, blogs, videos, lectures presentations and treatises I have produced over the years. Nonetheless what appears here originated with me except where noted. One specific example of this was revealed when our editorial board used a digital checker on my previous work and found that some 17% of what I had written had come from other sources! They were relieved to find that over 90% of that 17% of sources not cited were of my own previous writings.

Specific Acknowledgments

Thanks to all Co-Authors
Guest Authors – those who contributed one specific Time Out essay
Mike Molony has been a trusted colleague and friend for many years. Mike has run one of the most significant and influential local church sports ministries in the entire country and has been a champion for non-competitive versions of sport for certain ages and situations. Not only is Mike one of my tallest friends, he may well have the biggest heart of any sports minister I've ever known.
David Waddell is an accomplished author of four of his own books and is another trusted colleague and friend. Little did we know when we first met some 20 years ago that God would bring about an ever deepening weaving of our partnership and collective ministry. I have come to deeply appreciate David and cherish our friendship. Currently the executive director of CSRM, David remains one of the most insightful leaders of *The Sports Outreach Community* and is just plain fun to be around.

Contributing Authors
This entire book series would not be nearly as significant without three ongoing, regular contributing authors; all whom are credited at length in the Explanatory Note Backpiece Addendum of this book. I would be remiss however if I didn't thank each of them here by name: Dr. Vickie Byler; Greg English; and P.F Myers. Thanks to each of you.

Thanks to the Overwhelming Victory Team
Thanks to OVP's Editorial Board who took the time to read through the manuscript; affirming where warranted; and critiquing where needed. This editorial team includes: Dr. Vickie Byler; Greg English; John Garner; Dr. Jimmy Smith; Dr. Stan Terhune; David Waddell, Dr. Steven Waller and Stuart Weir; ... all whom provided great critique and much needed editing.

Thanks to those who take the manuscript and work their magic.
This team includes:
   Wendy Satterwhite, our graphic designer and artist who creates all book covers and continues to take all the rough draft manuscripts and turn them into an amazing final draft suitable for going to print.
   Gordon Theissen, who is the official printer (Cross Training Publishing) for Overwhelming Victory Press and produces such wonderful print versions of each book.

Stan Terhune who is our grammatical editor and is greatly responsible for making sure every "t" is crossed, every punctuation point is in place and every citation is correctly aligned.

Concluding Acknowledgments

Acknowledging Those Previously Cited I want to communicate to all who have been cited more fully in my previous books that you have also impacted this book either through your original influence that helped set the course for this entire series of books or through your continuing insights and support. Although I won't take the space to once again outline your catalytic role in my life, thinking and mission, I will state once more that this book and the entire series would not exist without your unique contribution to my thinking, my experiences and my life in general. Although not specifically cited by name here...I remain indebted to each person acknowledged in previous books: thank you!

A number of additional special people also bear special mention...

My family: I continue to thank God for my Grandparents and parents who prayed for and counseled me throughout life. On a rather sad note, I lost both of my parents this year. The heartache of losing them within a month of each other, is somewhat healed in the fact that an endowment has been established in their name of which Overwhelming Victory Press is the beneficiary. It is fitting that their memorial fund supports a publishing house because both of my parents highly valued books and read to me all during my childhood. I am deeply appreciative and humbled by the fact that their influence on my life continues with their memorial fund that helps to fund the publishing house that I serve as an author and Executive Editor.

In addition my wife, children and their spouses who continue to support and encourage me, and without whom, none of these books would ever be written. Also to my grandchildren who are a constant joy, and who now are participating in local church sports leagues and camps. I write with a hope that this book will help to ensure you and your generation a sporting future through a local church that will be a catalyst in bringing salvation to each of you.

CSRM: This book also would not have come to print without the ever growing and expanding CSRM family. Each current and former Board and staff member played a role in this book being published. A special thanks to Kat Linhart who is amazing in all she does to handle all order taking, shipping and processing of all book orders.

First Friends Church: Not only is this book greatly dependent upon what has been collectively learned through the SR&F Outreach Ministry at First Friends Church, but the ongoing support of the First Friends family continues to be expressed in dedicated prayer and financial assistance towards the publication of this book. Even as this book was being written the church blessed me with the opportunity to continue as a leader in the sports ministry in both the adult men's open basketball league and the basketball clinic that my five and six year old grandsons participated in!

Jay Martin: As cited in Chapter 6, Jay greatly influenced my comprehension of some of the foundational philosophies that undergird this book. In addition, Jay has continued to be an inspiration to me as we have served The Lord, The Church and *The Sports Outreach Community* over this last decade or two. His commitment to Jesus; his wife/marriage; children; church family and ministry partners is not only exemplary, but extremely rare. This book, in fact this entire book series would be greatly lacking without Jay's influence. Thank you my friend.

Final Words

To each of you who have had an impact or an influence on my life and thinking, I say thank you. I recognize this to be much more God's work than mine; a true Church-wide effort. I have felt a weight of responsibility to undertake the exhausting effort to bring it all together in an attempt to further expand and enhance His Church; rather than my personal portfolio. It is to His glory and for the purpose of redeeming the people of sport as well as redeeming the world of sport that I write.

Addendum #5

International Proposals for Local Church & Para-ministry Integration

Sports mission strategies of partnership between local churches and para-ministries

Please note that this is not an exhaustive list. You might even have other things to add.

Sports Personalities

Engaging sports personalities (coaches/managers/athletes etc.) as participants in various leagues, clinics, classes and activities has a proven track record. Sports personalities can be well known professionals or ordinary amateurs who might attract others because they look different, sound different and come from a different country and culture. They continue to be the heroes of many cultures and for this reason, can be beacons of light in many ways. They can extend a helping hand to those who have less opportunity and/or are less fortunate and their testimonies can powerfully encourage people to consider asking Jesus to be their Lord and Savior. Of course it is imperative that their lives be biblical including their commitment to a local church, but huge dividends occur when these cultural icons actively participate in sports-related outreaches.

The combination of sports personalities with sports projects include, but are not limited to, what follows.

Sport Projects

Sports projects are a second strategy that provides an avenue to utilize sports as a stratagem that can uniquely fit in different cultural environments and communities. The use of the term project is used loosely and relates to any focused, intentional, initiative that uses the SR&F strategy to engage a community with the gospel for the purpose of *Evangelistic-Disciplemaking*. Time, length, and activity widely varies according the opportunity, culture, and target group.

The following are recommended models for sports projects local churches can engage in to reach those far from Jesus and His Church or sports-related, para-ministries can use to plant new churches.

- **Top Sport Tours/Clinics** – Para-ministries and churches sponsor national and international teams to come to their area for outreach endeavors.[1] Athletes and coaches become equipped in how to minister

---

[1] It is recommended that para-ministries empower local congregations to engage in the strategy of maximizing the platforms of sports teams and players wherever there is a local church but they are encouraged to use this strategy to plant a church where none exist.

through their sport as they are trained to do ministry, as well as have excellent opportunities to play their sport. Competing locally and internationally, sports teams combine a passion for God and athletic excellence into one unique effort. They can be used to either play competitive games and/or conduct clinics in the midst of using their platform to share about their faith in Christ. One particular example took place in East Asia where participants lived on a sports university campus and built relationships with athletic influencers for a month.

- **Recreational Sport Tours/Clinics** – Para-ministries and churches field recreational multi-sport teams to various countries every year.[2] These teams combine sport with drama, games, and other fun activities to serve a church and reach a community. Athletes and supporters become equipped and trained to do ministry, as they excel in opportunities to play their sport. Recreational sports teams combine a passion for God and athletic excellence into one unique effort. They can also be used to either play competitive games and/or conduct clinics in the midst of using their platform to share about their faith in Christ. In Europe recreational sports teams served local churches as they encouraged and assisted with community outreaches. This strategy has worked many times to open the doors and hearts of a community for the local church and/or other sports-related, para-ministries.

- **Sports Equipment Aid** is a vehicle for mobilizing and delivering aid to local congregations and ministries in less fortunate countries world-wide. It is a unique combination of sport, with its natural capacity to energize people and develop goodwill, and the desire to serve and assist countries torn by war, famine, and poverty. Here's how:
    - The sports mission team partners with businesses, sports organizations/leagues, congregations, denominations and charities to collect sports equipment
    - This equipment is transported to a foreign country with a sports mission team
    - The donated equipment is almost guaranteed to arrive at its destination safely and cheaply because it can be checked as luggage with each individual team member, often within the baggage limit of each person[3]
    - Local indigenous churches organize the distribution of the

---

2   Para-ministries are encouraged to empower local churches in these endeavors, or go it alone to plant a church.
3   Even if an extra fee is charged, it will most certainly be less than exorbitant international shipping costs.

aid through their relief efforts and sports ministry as a part of their *Evangelistic-Disciplemaking* endeavors[4]
- **Global Events** can be used to mobilize congregations to reach their communities with the gospel. People around the world follow events such as the Olympics, World Cups, or World Championships of various sports so using their knowledge of and interest in these events can become a springboard for building relationships. The desire is to accomplish the following:
  - Encourage Christian athletes in their walk with Christ and help them find ways to maximize their platforms to verbally affirm their faith in Christ in a practically relevant way in their own church and community
  - Make church leaders aware of the potential for sharing the gospel through the platform of sports and train them in the SR&F outreach mission vision
  - Assist in organizing sports ministry outreaches around the theme of global events and use these outreaches as a catalyst for churches to develop on-going sports missions
- **Extreme Adventure/Survival Camps**
  Adventure camps vary in length. Some last a day, others for a week. They are organized by various para-ministries and congregations to challenge participants mentally, physically, and spiritually. Some are for competitive athletes and others are for recreational athletes who are looking to be stretched in their faith and character. During the camp participants hear directly from God's Word, glean biblical perspective on such topics as motivation, attitude, persevering through tough times, and winning and losing, as well as develop leadership qualities that will be of value in both life and competitive play. These camps have been used in Australia, New Zealand, Nigeria, South Africa, Zimbabwe, Russia and throughout Europe as well as in the USA to spiritually impact the athletes in these countries. Congregations in these areas can encourage their sports people to attend these camps as a part of their discipleship process.

---

4 Assisting congregations in this way in countries that may not have the expertise or financial resources to set up sports ministries can be a tremendous blessing when done sensitively and in an organized manner. The churches may also choose to donate some equipment to local sport clubs as a way to build and foster good relationships in their community. Be forewarned about one specific problem to be avoided. This has to do with creating a dependency on American/Western aid that perpetuates an "Americans are saviors" mentality instead of empowering local partners and encouraging their independence.

Sports Media

Production of sports media pieces (videos of sports personalities' testimonies; Bible studies; websites; movies; books; pamphlets; tracts etc.) can expose millions of men, women and children annually to the gospel of Jesus Christ through the following ways:

- Serving The Church, ministries, and other organizations by providing media resources which communicate the Gospel message through sports and athletics
- Facilitating and assisting athletes and coaches to give testimony to the person of Jesus Christ and their personal faith
- Being culturally relevant and prioritizing communication in the native tongue

When done in partnership with the local indigenous church, there is lasting fruit as local believers interact and follow-up with those who come to know Christ to start *Missional Sports Communities*. The teams are able to demonstrate Sports Ministry and encourage, challenge, motivate, and train the church leaders and youth to develop their own ongoing ministry through sports as they participate with the teams and see sports ministry demonstrated before their eyes.

Addendum #6

Sports Challenge Event

(Adapted by P. F. Myers from Rodger Oswald and Church Sports International)

As a local church attempts to launch or grow a SR&F mission, significant effort will be required to recruit, mobilize, and stimulate people to consider how they might be involved. A Sport Challenge Event (SCE) is designed to stimulate and energize a congregation and its leadership to either launch a sports ministry or develop and expand an existing ministry.

What is a SCE? SCE is a fast-paced, high energy evening of low-key competition using a sports theme. This event involves competitions between tables (of four to ten) in a variety of events. These competitive events can include the wearing of uniforms once worn by those who attend (points can be awarded based on the age of the uniform, and the fact that the athlete can still "get into" the uniform). Wearing the colors of one's favorite team can create a similar competitive environment. Competition between tables includes coming up with a team name and cheer (factoring for originality, enthusiasm, and volume when asked to stand and shout out their name and cheer), a sports trivia contest, and various "adapted" sports skill events such as mini Olympic events (such as a shot-put competition using cotton balls, a javelin competition using toothpicks). In addition to the competition, the evening should include a dessert of some sort.

While the fun of the competition and the dessert provides a warm an enjoyable atmosphere, everyone is there to accomplish some goals relative to starting or developing the SR&F mission. In order to do this, these elements can also be included:

1. A stimulating slide show or video that depicts sports ministry in action
2. A short presentation by the pastor or key congregational leader about how SR&F fits into the vision, mission and overall schedule of the congregation
3. A brochure about SR&F missions that can be given to those in attendance
4. A SPORTS SURVEY CARD – This card allows each individual in attendance to list their skills (athletic; officiating; organizing), their sport(s) and also provides an opportunity to volunteer and serve (see below).

Other features for the event could be music, prizes for the winning table, or having a high-profile athlete or coach as a speaker who shares his testimony. Keep in mind each congregation and location has specific needs and thus, each SCE should be designed to fit the local church's specific situation.

Possible Program Schedule

19.05	Introduction & prayer
19.10	Explanation of competitions
19.15	Competitions begin (five to six mini-competitions is a good number)
19.45	Dessert is served
19.55	Testimony from someone who came to Jesus through an SR&F outreach
20.05	Video or slide show
20.15	Challenge for the future (pastor/key church leader)
20.30	Explanation of SPORTS SURVEY CARDS/prayer/fill out cards
20.40	Competitions concluded
20.55	Announce table contest winners
21.00	Closing prayer

sample

SPORTS & RECREATION SURVEY

First Name _____
Last Name _____
City _____ Zip Code_____
Cell Phone _____ Work Phone_____
Email _____

Please check the activities in which you would like to participate. Double check those you would be willing to lead, coach, or offer any assistance.

___ **PRAYER TEAM**
___ **SPORTS MINISTRY LEADERSHIP TEAM**
___ **ACTIVITY LEADERSHIP TEAM**

___ Youth Football	___ Cycling	___ Tennis
___ Adult Football	___ Adult Basketball	___ Youth Basketball
___ Running	___ Aerobics	___ Youth Volleyball
___ Adult Volleyball	___ Camping	___ Skating
___ Ice Skating	___ Badminton	___ Hiking/Backpacking
___ Sailing	___ Fishing	___ Squash
___ Swimming	___ Skateboarding	___ In-Line Skating
___ Referee	___ Umpire	___ Official
___ Other _____		
___ Other _____		
___ Other _____		

Addendum #7

Conversation

The Gospel, Still the Bottom Line
The Gospel still must be the bottom line for all SR&F missions. Consider the following email exchange I had with a friend.

FRIEND: "Aren't there enough ethnic and religious divisions in South Asia already, without you trying to inject your brand of Christianity into the mix. I have always thought that the idea of using sports as a pretext for evangelism is rather devious. If you give a starving man food only if he will listen to your message, he will certainly listen to your message. But, it is the food he wants, not your message. There are many hundreds of brands of religion in this world. The "unreached," as you put it, are not unreached at all. Their local religion, whatever it might be, has been there all along for them. You, a total outsider, want to take that away from them. Someday, when you are back at home in the United States, I hope a Tibetan will knock on your door and ask you to join them for a meal, a friendly game of basketball, and some talk about why you should give up Christianity and accept Buddhism as a way of life."

MY RESPONSE: "I appreciate your perspective, but honestly it demonstrates a lack of understand for the work that I am doing. For one thing it's not, as you call it, just my brand of Christianity but rather a faith that is shared by many others. In fact, I have been invited to work with local indigenous people who are also followers of Christianity and fellow-believers in Jesus. Moreover, whenever I am here I follow their lead. In addition, I also don't believe there is nothing devious or coercive about what we do. It's not about religion but rather, it's about entering into and developing relationships that come naturally as we play sports together. If at some point a discussion about faith arises, I will listen to anything my new friends want to share about their religion and I'm always happy to share about Jesus. By the way followers of Jesus know its about a relationship with Him; not about a religion. We believe that He can be the Savior for anyone, regardless of what religion you grow up with or are taught. Jesus died for all people of all countries and cultures, and we believe He is the key to understanding this earthly life as well as the eternal life that comes at the end of this one. Your email would seem to indicate that you may have been misinformed about Jesus and thus you probably don't fully understand who He truly can be for you. As to your hope about a Tibetan Buddhist becoming my friend, well, I would gladly welcome that Tibetan into my home, not only for a game of basketball and a meal, but also to learn about Buddhism!

FRIEND: The problem with your argument is that you insist on thinking that Christianity is the only legitimate religion. Many thoughtful Christians realize that the literal acceptance of Jesus as the "only" way for being "saved" (whatever that means) is a bit much to believe, as is the notion that there is another life after this one. I suppose you want to reach the "unreached" because otherwise, they will burn in Hell? This is not a logical expectation for many thoughtful Christians, who have a clearer mind about what is and what is not possible in our real world. Thoughtful Christians may not say it, but in their mind, they realize that Lazarus was not actually raised from the dead, and that a few fish did not actually feed thousands.

By the way, I go to church nearly every Sunday, and try to live a decent life based on good Christian principles. However, I do not swallow whole the words of the Gospels. And yes, I meet Jesus every time I care for someone in need. Why not try going to south Asia and try learning about their predominant religions and why they practice them; not why they should practice yours."

MY RESPONSE: I would love for you to meet my indigenous friends in South Asia. They would be glad to tell you about THEIR Jesus who, in many cases, has done miraculous physical healings in their own lives and in the lives of their family members. I will not meet the Lazarus of the Bible until heaven of course, but I have met many others who have experienced the healing power of Jesus themselves. Beyond those special miracles Jesus has also brought hope, joy, peace, meaning and fulfillment to literally millions throughout South East Asia and beyond. I say all of this to say it's not only about a future eternity in heaven or hell, but also is very much about the present life here on earth.

I'm also glad to know that you attend church regularly and try to live by good Christian principles. That is certainly admirable. Your use of the word "try" is interesting because that, in and of itself, tells me that you sometimes fail... like all of us do. (I am sad to say that I fail quite often) That is exactly why we need a Savior/Jesus, because we can never be good enough for God on our own...no matter how good we think we are. He alone is holy and perfect, and of course all humans are not, but I thank God that though Jesus was without sin, He paid the price for our sin and made it possible for us to become perfect in God's eyes. Jesus himself claimed to be "the Way, the Truth, and the Life." It is Jesus who made the exclusive claim to be the "only" Way. Still Jesus is for all people regardless of their religion... so the inclusivity you are seeking actually depends on us, not him, because it involves our individual choice and our stubbornness to accept him because we think we know a better way... but I am sure you know all this and have thought about these things already. Ultimately it comes down to faith, and that is what makes it difficult to accept.

So I challenge you to read the Gospels again, a little every day for the next 30 days. Take a fresh look, no matter what conclusions you have come to in the past. This time don't just use your brain but also ask God to open your spiritual eyes to show you Jesus for who He really is.

Is he just a good moral teacher, a liar, a lunatic, or could he actually be the Messiah (God in the flesh who came to save the world)?? I believe God will show you. In my own journey I have found Jesus to be the Messiah and the Answer to life. I think you will too. I am sure nothing I write here would ever convince you anyway. You are on your own spiritual journey just as I am, and you have to decide for yourself what to believe. I appreciate this discussion. Thanks again for being in touch."

Addendum #8

SCOREBOARD

Incorporating a Laborers-List (Matthew 9.37, 38)

1. Create a *Laborers-List* for each league, camp, clinic, activity, class and event.
2. The list includes a space for the number of leaders needed, i.e.: if you need 10 coaches and 10 assistant coaches for a youth basketball league the *Laborers-List* for that league should have 20 spots for you to fill in names of potential coaches.
3. It is recommended to add a few extra spots on your list in recognition that God may have "ordained" others.
4. The next step is to begin to pray over the list—that God will move in their hearts and prepare them for your "recording" of His call on their lives to become a local missionary as a coach, league director or event leader.
5. While there is no absolute biblical method to the prayer, there are a number of biblical references to prayer and it would seem biblical to recommend praying for 40 days before officially recruiting those on the *Laborers-List*.

Laborers-List Check List

Name of Person	Date of Original Prayer	Invitation Letter Sent	Personal Follow Up	Response	Training Meeting Letter	Attended Training Meeting	Other

Addendum #9

SCOREBOARD

Financing SR&F Ministry

Budget Planning Sheet For: _____

Ministry Expenses - General

Publicity / Advertising

Promotional Materials _____

Social Media _____

Other Media _____

Total _____

Staffing

League Directors _____

Coaches _____

Officials

    Games x 2/3 _____

Scorekeepers

    Games x 2/3 _____

Assigner Fee _____

Total General Expenses _____

Total Number of Participants _____

    Cost per Participant _____

SCOREBOARD

Ministry Expenses – Per Participant

Year End Awards

    Participation gifts   _____

        Champ gifts   _____

    Year End Banquet

        Food   _____

        Supplies   _____

        Speaker   _____

        Equipment   _____

    Uniform

        Players x 8-12   _____

        Coaches x 1-3   _____

    Devotional packets

        Players/Coaches x 15   _____

        Total   _____

Equipment

    Permanent $1 per player   _____

    Seasonal $2 per player   _____

Ministry Support

    Gift to CSRM

        $1 per player   _____

Sub-total Participant Expense   _____

Total Participant Fee   _____

Addendum #10

Sources Consulted For This Book

Barrett, David B. and Todd M. Johnson. *World Christian Trends, AD 30-AD 2200: Interpreting the Annual Christian Megacensus.* Pasadena, CA: William Carey Library, 2001.

Camp, Steve. "Living Dangerously in the Hands of God" (song), in *Justice* (album). Chatsworth, CA: Sparrow Records, 1988.

Doggett, Lawrence Locke. *The Life of Robert R. McBurney.* Cleveland: F.M. Barton, 1902.

Duff, Alexander. *India and Indian Missions: Including Sketches of the Gigantic System of Hinduism, Both in Theory and Practice; Also Notices of Some of the Principal Agencies Employed in Conducting the Process of Indian Evangelization.* Edinbugh: J. Johnston, 1839.

_____. *Missions, the Chief End of the Church.* Edinburgh: J. Johnston, 1839.

"Eric Liddell, 1902-1945."
<www.ccminternational.org/English/who_said_that/eric.liddell. htm#.X4gxM9BKiM9> (used in chapter 9)

"Finishing the Task" <https://www.finishingthetask.com> (used in chapter 3).

"Geloven in Sport" [Believe in Sports] (Nxtmove Organization) www.Nxtmove.nl (used in chapter 3).

Global Frontier Missions <https://globalfrontiermissions.org/> (used in chapter 3 for Byler, Vicky. "Research Reflections: Unreached People Groups" sidebar).

Harbin, E. O. and Bob Sessoms. *The New Fun Encyclopedia Set: A Guide to Using Sports and Games in the Life of the Church.* Nashville: Abingdon Press, 1976.

Higgs, Robert. *God in the Stadium: Sports and Religion in America.* Lexington, KY: University Press of Kentucky, 1995.

Johnson, Todd M. and Kenneth R. Ross. *Atlas of Global Christianity: 1910-2010.* Edinburgh: Edinburgh University Press, 2009.

Johnson, Todd M. and Gina A. Zurlo, eds. *World Christian Database.* Liden/Boston:Brill, 2015. <worldchristiandatabase.org>

The Joshua Project. "Lists: All Progress Levels." <https://www.joshuaproject.net/global/progress> (used in chapter 3)

Lewis, R. W. "Clarifying the Remaining Frontier Mission Task." *International Journal of Frontier Missions,* vol.35, no. 4, Winter 2018, p. 164.

Linville, Greg. *The Christ of Sports Ministry: The Christology of Sports Outreach.* Canton, OH: Overwhelming Victory Press (forthcoming).

_____, *Putting the Church Back in the Game: The Ecclesiology of Sports Outreach.* Canton, OH: Overwhelming Victory Press, 2019. (AGON Institute of Sports Ministry Series, v. 3)

_____. *The Saving of Sports Ministry: The Soteriology of Sports Outreach.* Canton, OH: Overwhelming Victory Press, 2020. (AGON Institute of Sports Ministry Series, v. 4)

_____. *Sports Ministry Pioneers: 19th Century Models for 21st Century Sports Outreach.* (unpublished book)

_____. *Sports Outreach Fundamentals: Biblically-Based, Philosophical Principles for Strategically-Relevant & Efficiently-Efficient Disciplemaking.* Canton, OH: Overwhelming Victory Press, 2018. (AGON Institute of Sports Ministry Series, v. 2)

MacDonald, George and Michael R. Phillips. *The Musician's Quest.* Minneapolis: Bethany House Publishers, 1984. Originally published under the title: *Robert Falconer.* London: Hurst and Blackett, 1868.

Maston, R. B. and Baptist Training Union. *A Handbook for Church Recreation Leaders*. Nashville: Sunday School Board of the Southern Baptist Convention, 1937.

Mathews, Basil Joseph. *John R. Mott: World Citizen*. London: Student Christian Movement Press, 1934.

Mott, John R, (John Raleigh). "The Beginnings of the Student Volunteer Movement." Student Volunteer Movement for Foreign Missions. *Addresses Given at the Twenty-Fifth Anniversary of the Origin of the Student Volunteer Movement for Foreign Missions at Mount Hermon, Massachusetts, Sunday, September 10, 1911*. New York: Student Volunteer Movement, 1911. Pp. ?

_____. *Confronting Young Men with the Living Christ*. New York: Association Press, 1923.

_____. *Evangelization of the World in This Generation*. New York: Student Volunteer Movement for Foreign Missions, 1900.

_____. *Strategic Points in the World's Conquest The Universities and Colleges Related to the ... Progress of Christianity*. New York: Revell Co., 1897.

Moulton, Harold K., ed. *The Analytical Greek Lexicon Revised*. Grand Rapids, MI: Zondervan, 1982.

Myers, P. F. (Paul F.) *Church Based Sports Ministry Training Manual*. Canton, OH: Association of Church Sports & Recreation Ministries (CSRM), 2015.

_____. *Church Based Sports Ministry Workbook*. Canton, OH: Association of Church Sports & Recreation Ministries (CSRM), 2015.

_____. *The Life of the Shoe: Sports Outreach for the World*. Canton, OH: Overwhelming Victory Press, 2020. (AGON Institute of Sports Ministry Series; v. 8)

National Council of the Young Men's Christian Associations of the United States of America. Browne Historical Library. *Archives of YMCA Connection [with John R. Mott]*, New York, N.Y.

Paton, William. *Alexander Duff: Pioneer Missionary of Education*. New York: George H. Doran, 1923.

Petersen, Jim. *Church Without Walls*. Colorado Springs, CO: NAVPress, 1999.

_____. *Living Proof*. Grand Rapids, MI: Zondervan, 1997.

Richardson, Don. *Peace Child: An Unforgettable Story of Primitive Jungle Treachery in the 20th Century*. Bloomington, MN: Bethany House Publishers, 2005.

Ripkin, Nik and Gregg Lewis. *The Insanity of God: A True Story of Faith Resurrected*. Nashville: B & H Publishing Group, 2013.

Sessoms, Bob and Carolyn Sessoms. *52 Complete Recreation Programs for Senior Adults*. Nashville: Convention Press, 1979.

Sessoms, Bob. *The Volunteer Coach*. Nashville: Convention Press, 1978.

Shedd, Clarence Prouty. *Two Centuries of Student Christian Movements*. New York: Association Press, 1934.

Smith, George. The Life of Alexander Duff. New York: A.C. Armstrong, 1879.

_____. *Twelve Pioneer Missionaries*. London: Thomas Nelson and Sons, 1900. Includes a chapter on Alexander Duff.

Smith, Thomas. *Alexander Duff, D.D., L.L.D.* London: Hodder and Stoughton, 1883.

Swindoll, Charles R. *Growing Strong in the Seasons of Life*. Grand Rapids, MI: Zondervan Publishers, 1994.

The Traveling Team. "Missionaries and Workers." <www.thetravelingteam.org/missionaries-and-workers> (used in chapter 3)

Uttermost Sports. <www.uttermostsports.org> (used in chapter 9)

Vermilye, Elizabeth B. *The Life of Alexander Duff*. New York: Revell, 1890.

Waddell, David. *Worship Wars: The Kings Lead the Battle to Spirit and Truth.* Bloomington, IN: Westbow Press, 2018.

Walls, Andrew. "Duff, Alexander." *Biographical Dictionary of Christian Missions*, edited by Gerald H. Anderson, New York: Macmillan Reference USA, 1998, pp. 187-188.

Walsh, W. Pakenham. *Modern Heroes of the Mission Field.* New York: Revell, 1915.

Wilder, Robert P. *The Great Commission: The Missionary Response in North America and Europe.* London: Oliphants Ltd., 1936.

Williams, J. E. Hodder. *The Life of Sir George Williams.* London: Hodder & Stoughton, 1906.

Yale University. Divinity School. Library. *WSCF: The world Student Christian Federation and John R. Mott Collections.*

Addendum #11

Sources Consulted For This Book Series

Personal letters and correspondence
Decades of listening to Renewing Your Mind by Ligonier and Truth for Life broadcasts

Akabusi, Kriss and Stuart Weir. *Wisdom for the Race of Life.* Oxford: Bible Reading Fellowship, 1999.

Aldrich, Joseph C. *Life-Style Evangelism: Learning to Open Your Life to Those Around You.* Portland, OR: Multnomah Press, 1993.

Anderson, J. Kerby. *Christian Ethics in Plain Language.* Nashville, TN: Thomas Nelson, 2005.

Atcheson, Wayne. *Impact for Christ: How FCA Has Influenced the Sports World.* Grand Island, NE: Cross Training Publ., 1994. About the Fellowship of Christian Athletes.

Babb, K. "Where College Football is a Religion and Religion Shapes College Football," *Washington Post*, 29 Aug. 2014. Available at <http://www.washingtonpost.com/sports/colleges/where-college-football-is-a-religion-and-religion-shapes-college-football/2014/08/29/8d03de32-2dfa-11e4-bb9b-997ae96fad33_story.html?wpmk=MK0000200>.

Baker, William J. *Playing with God: Religion and Modern Sport.* Cambridge, MA: Harvard University Press, 2007.

Barton, Bruce. *The Man Nobody Knows.* New York: Collier Books, 1987, c1925.

Bateman, Charles T. *The Life of General Booth.* New York: Association Press, 1912.

Begg, Alastair. *Pathway to Freedom.* Sound recording (12 CDs). Cleveland, OH: Truth for Life, 2003. ID 20501. Series of sermons on Exodus 20, the Ten Commandments.

Beisser, Arnold R. *Madness in Sports.* New York: Appleton-Century Crofts, 1977. Quoted in The Plain Dealer, section G, Jan. 18, 1987, p. 3.

Belcher, Richard and Richard P. Belcher, Jr. *A Layman's Guide to the Sabbath Question.* Southbridge, MA: Crowne Publications, 1991.

Benge, Janet and Geoff Benge. *Eric Liddell: Something Greater Than Gold.* Seattle, WA: YWAM Publishers, 1998.

Bonhoeffer, Dietrich. *The Cost of Discipleship.* Revised [2nd] and unabridged ed., containing material not previously translated. New York: Macmillan, 1963, c1959.

Boyers, John. *Beyond the Final Whistle: A Life of Football and Faith.* London: Hodder and Stoughton, 2000.

Boyers, John. "Manchester United FC." *Being a Chaplain*, edited by Miranda Threlfall-Holmes and Mark Newitt. London: SPCK, 2011, pp. 81-84.

Braisted, Ruth Evelyn Wilder. *In This Generation: The Story of Robert P. Wilder.* New York: Published for the Student Volunteer Movement by Friendship Press, 1941.

Brewster, Paul. *Andrew Fuller: Model Pastor-Theologian.* Nashville, TN; B&H Publishing Group, 2010.

Broneer, Oscar. *The Odeum.* Cambridge, MA: Published for the American School of Classical Studies at Athens by Harvard University Press, 1932. (American School of Classical Studies at Athens. Corinth; v. 10)

_____. *The South Stoa and Its Roman Successors.* Princeton, NJ: American School of Classical Studies at Athens, 1954. (Corinth; v. 1, pt. 4)

_____. *Temple of Poseidon.* Princeton, NJ: American School of Classical Studies at Athens, 1971. (Isthmia; v. 1)

Browne, Leonard. *Sport and Recreation, and Evangelism in the Local Church.* Bramcote, Nottingham, Eng.: Grove Books, 1991.

Buchanan, Mark. *The Rest of God: Restoring Your Soul by Restoring the Sabbath.* Nashville, TN: Thomas Nelson, 2006.

Byl, John. *Intramural Recreation: A Step-By-Step Guide to Creating an Effective Program*. Champaign, IL: Human Kinetics, 2002.

_____. *Organizing Successful Tournaments*. Champaign, IL: Human Kinetics, 1999.

Byl, John and Tom Visker. *Physical Education, Sports and Wellness: Looking to God As We Look at Ourselves*. Sioux City, IA: Dordt Press, 1999.

Chan, Francis. *Letters To The Church*. Colorado Springs, CO: David C. Cook, 2018.

Chariots of Fire (Videorecording) / Warner Bros. Pictures; a Warner Bros. and Ladd Company release; presented by Allied Stars; an Enigma production; original screenplay by Colin Welland; produced by David Puttnam; directed by Hugh Hudson. Burbank, CA: Warner Home Video, 2003. DVD. Originally produced as a British motion picture in 1981.

Chawner, D. "A Reflection on the Practice of Sports Chaplaincy." *Urban Theology*, vol. 3, no. 1, 2009, pp. 75–80. Available at <http://www.urbantheology.org/journals/journal-3-1/a-reflection-on-the-practice-of-sports-chaplaincy>.

Church Sports International (a ministry partner under Share the Savior organization (website): www.sharethesavior.org

Clowney, Edmund, P. *The Church*. Downers Grove, IL: Inter Varsity Press, 1995.

Coakley, Jay J. *Sports in Society: Issues and Controversies*. 9th ed. Boston: McGraw Hill Higher Education, 2007.

Conner, Ray. *The Ministry of Recreation*. Nashville, TN: Convention Press, 1992.

Connor, Steve. *A Sporting Guide to Eternity: A Devotional for Competitive People*. Fearn, Eng.: Christian Focus, 2002.

_____. *Sports Outreach: Principles + Practice for Successful Sports Ministry*. Ross-shire, Scotland: Christian Focus Publications, 2003.

Conrad, Tim. *Game Plan*. Florissant, CO: Thistle Productions, 2009. (Sapphire Lake series)

_____. *Go the Distance*. Florissant, CO: Thistle Productions, 2010. (Sapphire Lake series)

Couey, Richard B. *Building God's Temple*. Minneapolis: Burgess Pub. Co., 1982.

CSRM: *The Association of Church Sports and Ministers* (website): www.csrm.org

Dahl, Gordon. *Work, Play and Worship: In a Leisure-Oriented Society*. Minneapolis: Augsburg Pub. House, 1972.

Daniels, Graham and Stuart Weir. *Born to Play!* Bicester, Eng.: Frampton House, 2004.

_____. *The Sports Stadium: How to Share Your Faith in the World of Sport*. Bicester, Eng.: Frampton House Publications, 2005.

Darden, Robert. *Into the End Zone*. Nashville, TN: Thomas Nelson, 1989.

Davis, John Jefferson. *Evangelical Ethics: Issues Facing the Church Today*. 3rd ed., rev. and expanded. Phillipsburg, NJ: P&R Pub., 2004.

Deford, F. "Religion in Sport." *Sports Illustrated*, vol. 44, no. 16, 1976, pp. 88–100.

Dickson, John. *The Best Kept Secret of Christian Mission: Promoting the Gospel with More Than Our Lips*. Grand Rapids, MI: Zondervan, 2010.

Digby, Andrew Wingfield and Stuart Weir. *Winning is Not Enough: Sports Stars Who Are Going for Gold and For God*. London: Marshall Pickering, 1991.

Doggett, Lawrence Locke. *The Life of Robert R. McBurney*. Cleveland: F.M. Barton, 1902.

Dorsett, Lyle W. *A Passion for Souls: The Life of D.L. Moody*. Chicago: Moody Press, 1997.

Driscoll, Mark. *The Radical Reformission: Reaching Out without Selling Out.* Grand Rapids, MI: Zondervan, 2004.

Ehrmann, Joe. *Inside Out Coaching: How Sports Can Transform Lives.* New York: Simon & Schuster, 2011.

Eisenman, Tom. *Every Day Evangelism: Making the Most of Life's Common Moments.* Downers Grove, IL: InterVarsity Press, 1987.

The English Standard Version Bible: Containing the Old and New Testaments with Apocrypha. New York: Oxford University Press, 2009.

Esar, Evan, editor. *The Treasury of Humorous Quotations.* English edition edited by Nicolas Bentley. London: Phoenix House, 1951.

Evans, Tony, Jonathan Evans and Dillon Burroughs. *Get in the Game.* Chicago: Moody Publishers, 2006.

Finney, Charles G. *How to Promote a Revival.* Antrim, Ireland: Revival Pub. Co., 1948.

Gamble, Richard, Andrew Parker, and Denise M. Hill. "Football, Sports Chaplaincy and Sport Psychology: Connections and Possibilities." *Sports Chaplaincy: Trends, Issues and Debates,* edited by Andrew Parker, Nick J Watson, John B White. London: Routledge, 2016, pp. 182-194.

Gardiner, E. Norman. *Athletics of the Ancient World.* Oxford, Eng.: Clarendon Press, 1930.

Garner, John, ed. *Recreation and Sports Ministry: Impacting the Postmodern Culture.* 2nd ed. Lynchburg, VA: Liberty University Press, 2017.

Gough, Russell Wayne. *Character is Everything: Promoting Ethical Excellence in Sport.* Fort Worth, TX: Harcourt Brace College Publishers, 1997.

Green, Michael. *Evangelism Through the Local Church.* Nashville, TN: Oliver-Nelson, 1992.

Grubb, Norman P. *C.T. Studd, Athlete and Pioneer.* Atlantic City, NJ: World-Wide Revival Prayer Movement, 1947.

Guttman, Allen. *Sport Spectators*. New York: Columbia University Press, 1986.

Hamilton, Duncan. *For The Glory: The Untold and Inspiring Story of Eric Liddell, Hero of Chariots of Fire*. New York, NY: Penguin Press, 2016.

Harris, Harold Arthur. *Greek Athletes and Athletics*. Bloomington: Indiana University Press, 1966, c1964.

_____. *Sport in Greece and Rome*. Ithaca, NY: Cornell University Press, 1989. Originally published 1972.

Heschel, Abraham Joshua. *The Sabbath: Its Meaning for Modern Man*. New York: Farrar, Straus & Giroux, 2005, c1951.

Heskins, Jeffery and Matt Baker, editors. *Footballing Lives: As Seen by Chaplains in the Beautiful Game*. Norwich [Eng.]: Canterbury Press, 2006.

Higgs, Robert. *God in the Stadium: Sports and Religion in America*. Lexington, KY: University Press of Kentucky, 1995.

Hodder-Williams, J. E. *The Life of Sir George Williams: Founder of the Young Men's Christian Association*. New York: A.C. Armstrong, 1906.

Hoffman, Shirl James. *Good Game: Christianity and the Culture of Sports*. Waco, TX: Baylor University Press, 2010.

Hoffman, Shirl James, ed. *Sport and Religion*. Champaign, IL: Human Kinetics Books, 1992.

Holm, N. "Toward a Theology of the Ministry of Presence in Chaplaincy," *Journal of Christian Education*, vol. 52, no. 1, 2009, pp. 7–22. Available at <http://www.academia.edu/1256854/Toward_a_Theology_of_the_Ministry_of_Presence_in_Chaplaincy>.

Holy Bible, Containing the Old and New Testaments: Authorized King James Version, With a New System of Connected References ... New York: Oxford University Press, 1945. Originally published 1611, the most published English Bible, available in countless editions.

The Holy Bible: New Century Version, Containing the Old and New Testaments. Dallas, TX: Word Bibles, c1991.

The Holy Bible: New International Version, Containing the Old Testament and the New Testament. Grand Rapids, MI: Zondervan Bible Publishers, c1978.

Hopkins, Charles Howard. *History of the Y.M.C.A. in North America.* New York: Association Press, 1951.

Hughes, Thomas, 1822-1896. *The Manliness of Christ.* Philadelphia: H. Altemus, 1896.

_____. *Tom Brown at Oxford.* First published: Cambridge, Eng.: Macmillan, 1861. Many modern editions are available.

_____. *Tom Brown's School Days.* First published: Cambridge, Eng.: Macmillan, 1857.
Many modern editions are available.

Hunter, George G. *How to Reach Secular People.* Nashville, TN: Abingdon Press, 1992.

Johnson, Elliot. *Focus on the Finish Line: Hurdles Female Athletes Face in the Race of Life.* Grand Island, NE: Cross Training Pub., 1997.

_____. *Heroes of the Faith: Advice from God's Athletes.* Grand Island, NE: Cross Training Pub., 1995.

_____. *The Point After: Advice from God's Athletes.* Grand Rapids, MI: Zondervan, 1987.

_____. *Strong to the Finish.* Grand Island, NE: Cross Training Pub., 1998.

Johnson, Elliot and Al Schierbaum. *Up Close with The Savior.* Grand Island, NE: Cross Training Pub., 1994.

Keddie, John W. and Sebastian Coe. *Running the Race: Eric Liddell, Olympic Champion.* New York: Evangelical Press, 2007.

Kluck, Ted. *The Reason for Sport: A Christian Fanifesto*. Chicago: Moody Press, 2009.

Kohn, Alfie. *No Contest: The Case Against Competition*. Boston: Houghton Mifflin, 1986.

Krattenmaker, Tom. *Onward Christian Athletes: Turning Ballparks into Pulpits and Players into Preachers*. Lanham, MD: Rowman & Littlefield, 2010.

Ladd, Tony and James A. Mattheson. *Muscular Christianity: Evangelical Protestants and the Development of American Sport*. Grand Rapids, MI: Baker Books, 1999.

Larson, Knute. *The Great Human Race: How to Endure in the Marathon of Life*. Akron, OH: The Chapel Press, 2002.

Linville, Greg. *A Contemporary Christian Ethic of Competition*. Canton, OH: First Friends Church, [1990s?]

_____. *Christmanship: A Theology of Competition and Sport*. Canton, OH: Oliver House Publishing Inc., 2014.

_____. *Does Sport Ministry Aid Local Church Evangelism?* Ashland, OH: Ashland Theological Seminary, 2007. Thesis (D. Min.)—Ashland Theological Seminary.

_____. *Executive Director's Blog*. www.csrm.org/blog.html Accessed 8 April 2013.
This blog contains many of Greg Linville's writings.

_____. *Overwhelming Victory: A Coaching Manual*. Ashland, OH: Ashland Theological Seminary, 1987. Project (M.A.)—Ashland Theological Seminary.

_____. *Putting the Church Back in the Game: The Ecclesiology of Sports Outreach*. Canton, OH: Overwhelming Victory Press, 2019

_____. *Sports Outreach Fundamentals: Biblically-Based, Philosophical-Principles for Strategically-Relevant & Efficiently-Effective Disciplemaking*. Canton, OH: Overwhelming Victory Press, 2018.

———. "Sports Chaplaincy and North American Society: Strategies for Winning in the Club House." In Parker, Andrew, Nick J. Watson, John B. White, editors. *Sports Chaplaincy: Trends, Issues, and Debates*. London: Routledge, 2016.

———. *Surrounded by Witnesses*. Canton, OH: Association Press, 2005.

———. *Theology of Competition*. Canton, OH: Overwhelming Victory Ministries, [1990s]

———. *The Saving of Sports Ministry: The Soteriology of Sports Outreach*. Canton, OH: Overwhelming Victory Press, 2020.

Lloyd-Jones, David Martyn. *Darkness and Light: An Exposition of Ephesians 4:17-5:17*. Grand Rapid, MI: Baker Book House, 1982.

Magnusson, Sally. *The Flying Scotsman*. New York: Quartet Books, 1981. Biography of Eric Liddell.

Malony, Newton and Southard, Samuel, eds. *Handbook of Religious Conversion*. Birmingham, AL: Religious Education Press, 1992

Martens, Rainier. *Joy and Sadness in Children's Sports*. Champaign, IL: Human Kinetics Press, 1978.

Mason, Bryan. *Beyond the Gold: What Every Church Needs to Know About Sports Ministry*. Milton Keynes, Eng.: Authentic Media Ltd., 2011.

———. *Into the Stadium: An Active Guide to Sport and Recreation Ministry in the Local Church*. Milton Keynes, Eng.: Authentic Media Ltd., 2003.

———. *Maintaining Pace*. Canton, OH: Overwhelming Victory Press, 2020.

Mattingly, Don. *Recreation for Youth*. Nashville, TN: Convention Press, 1986.

McCasland, David. *Eric Liddell: Pure Gold: A New Biography of the Olympic Champion Who Inspired Chariots of Fire*. Grand Rapids, MI: Discovery House, 2001.

McCown, Lowrie and Valirie J. Gin. *Focus on Sport in Ministry*. Marietta, GA: 360° Sports, 2003.

McDowell, Josh. *Evidence That Demands a Verdict: Historical Evidence for the Christian Scriptures*. 2nd ed. San Bernardino CA: Here's Life Publishers, 1981.

_____. *More Evidence That Demands a Verdict: Historical Evidences for Christian Scriptures*. Rev. ed. San Bernardino, CA: Here's Life Publishers, 1981.

McLemore, Clinton W. *Street Smart Ethics: Succeeding in Business Without Selling Your Soul*. Louisville, KY: Westminster John Know Press, 2003.

Michener, James A. *Sports in America*. New York: Random House, 1976.

Moore, R. Laurence (Robert Laurence). *Touchdown Jesus: The Mixing of Sacred and Secular in American History*. Louisville, KY: Westminster John Knox Press, 2003.

Morrow, Greg and Steve Morrow. *Recreation: Reaching Out, Reaching In, Reaching Up*. Nashville, TN: Convention Press, 1986.

Morse, Richard Cary, 1841-1926. *History of the North American Young Men's Christian Associations*. New York: Association Press, 1913.

_____. *My Life with Young Men: Fifty Years in the Young Men's Christian Association*. New York: Association Press, 1918.

Murray, Andrew. *Absolute Surrender*. Chicago: Fleming H. Revell, 1897.

Murray, Iain H. *A Scottish Christian Heritage*. Edinburgh: The Banner of Truth Trust, 2006.

Neal, Wes. *The Handbook on Athletic Perfection*. 3rd ed. Grand Island, NE: Cross Training Publishing, 1981.

Neal, Wes. *The Handbook on Coaching Perfection*. 2nd ed. Milford, MI: Mott Media, 1981.

Newman, Wendell T. *Organizing for Recreation Ministry*. Nashville, TN: Convention Press, 1990.

Nix, Stan. *Sports Stories and the Bible*. Carlsbad, CA: Magnus Press, 2003.

Olivova, Vera. *Sport and Games in the Ancient World*. New York: St. Martin's Press, 1985.

Oswald, Rodger. *Sports Ministry and the Church: A Philosophy of Ministry*. Campbell, CA: Church Sports International, 1990s.

_____. *A Theology of Sports Ministry*. Campbell, CA: Church Sports International, 1993.

Parker, Andrew, Watson, Nick J. and White John B., eds. *Sports Chaplaincy: Trends, Issues and Debates*. New York, NY: Routledge, 2016.

Parrott, Mike. *Team Huddles: Sports Devotionals*. Grand Island, NE: Cross Training Pub., 2000.

Peterson, Jim. *Church Without Walls*. Colorado Springs, CO: Nav Press, 1991.

_____. *Living Proof*. Grand Rapids, MI: Zondervan, 1997.

Piggin, Stuart and John Roxborough. *The St. Andrew Seven: The Finest Flowering of Missionary Zeal in Scottish History*. Edinburgh; Carlisle, PA: Banner of Truth Trust, 1985.

Pollock, John Charles. *The Cambridge Seven: A Call to Christian Service*. London: Inter-Varsity Press, 1969, c1955.

Prebish, Charles S. *Religion and Sport: The Meeting of Sacred and Profane*. Westport, CN: Greenwood Press, 1993.

Prime, Derek. *Active Evangelism: Putting the Evangelism of Acts into Practice*. Ross-shire, Scotland: Christian Focus, 2003.

Putney, Clifford. *Muscular Christianity, Manhood and Sports in Protestant America, 1880-1920*. Cambridge, MA: Harvard University Press, 2001.

Rader, Benjamin G. *American Sports: From the Age of Folk Games to the Age of Televised Sports*. Englewood Cliffs, NJ: Prentice Hall, 1990.

Rainer, Thom S. and Lewis A. Drummond, eds. *Evangelism in the Twenty-First Century: The Critical Issues.* Wheaton, IL: Harold Shaw Pub., 1989.

Rainer, Thom S. and Eric Geiger. *Simple Church: Returning to God's Process for Making Disciples.* Nashville: B&H Publishing Group, 2011.

Ray, Bruce A. *Celebrating the Sabbath: Finding Rest in a Restless World.* Phillipsburg, NJ: P&R Pub., 2000.

Reich, Frank. "Competition and Creation." *IIIM Magazine Online*, v. 4, no. 6 (Feb. 11- 17, 2002), pp. 1-9. http://thirdmill.org/magazine/issues.asp/volume/4/number/6 Accessed 8 Apr. 2013.

Roques, Mark and Jim Ticknor. *Fields of God: Football and the Kingdom of God.* Carlisle, PA: Authentic Lifestyles, 2003.

Rushworth-Smith, David. *Off the Ball: a Sports Chaplain at Work.* Basingstoke [Eng.]: Marshalls, 1985.

Sauer, Erich. *In the Arena of Faith: A Call to a Consecrated Life.* Grand Rapids, MI: Eerdmans, 1955.

Sjogren, Steven, Dave Ping, Doug Pollock. *Irresistible Evangelism.* Loveland, CO: Group, 2004.

Smith, Jimmy and English, Greg, eds. *Sports Ministry That Wins: How to Initiate, Build, and Manage a Sports Ministry Program.* Canton, OH: Overwhelming Victory Press. 2017.

Spalding, Greg. *Run the Greatest Race: Be a Disciple Who Makes a Difference.* Pittsburgh, PA: City of Champions Pub. Co., 1996.

Sport: An Educational and Pastoral Challenge: Seminar of Study on the Theme of Sport Chaplains, Vatican, 7-8 September 2007 / Catholic Church. Pontificium Consilium pro Laicis. Citta del Vaticano: Libreria Editrice Vaticana, 2008.

Sports Ambassadors (Website): www.onechallenge.org/go/sports-ambassadors/

Stanley, Andy. *Louder than Words.* Sisters, OR: Multnomah Press, 2004.

Stetzer, Ed. *Christians in the Age of Outrage: How to Bring Our Best When the World Is at Its Worst*. Carol Stream, IL: Tyndale House Publishers, 2018. ISBN 978-1-4964-3362-6

Stoll, Sharon Kay and Jennifer M. Beller. *Who Says This is Cheating? : Anybody's Sports Ethics Book*. Dubuque, IA: Kendall Hunt Publishing, 1993.

Strobel, Lee. *Inside the Mind of Unchurched Harry and Mary: How to Reach Friends and Family Who Avoid God and the Church*. Grand Rapids, MI: Zondervan , 1993.

Takamizama, Eiko. "Religious Commitment Theory: A Model of Japanese Christians." *Torch Trinity Journal*.

Thiessen, Gordon. *Cross Training Manual: Playbook for Christian Athletes*. Grand Island, NE: Cross Training Pub., 1991.

Tinley, Josh. *Kneeling in the End Zone: Spiritual Lessons from the World of Sports*. Cleveland, OH: Pilgrim Press, 2009.

Threlfall-Holms, Miranda and Mark Newitt. *Being a Chaplain*. London: SPCK, 2011. (SPCK Library of Ministry).

Verhey, Allen. *The Great Reversal: Ethics and the New Testament*. Grand Rapids, MI: Eerdmans, 1984.

Walker, Dan. *Sport and Sundays : Christian TV Presenter Dan Walker Tells His Story*. Rev. and Updated Ed. Leominster, Eng.: Day One Publications, 2010, c2009.

Walker, Jon. *Costly Grace 90-Day Devotional: a Contemporary View of Bonhoeffer's The Cost of Discipleship*. Abilene, TX: Leafwood Publishers, 2010.

Warner, Gary. *Competition*. Elgin, IL: David Cook, 1979.

Webb, Bernice Larson. *The Basketball Man: James Naismith*. Lawrence: University Press of Kansas, 1973.

Wier, Stuart. *Kriss*. London: Marshall Pickering, 1996.

_____. *More Than Champions: A Sport Stars' Secrets of Success.* London: Harper Collins, 1993.

_____. *The Ultimate Prize: Great Christian Olympians.* London: Hodder Christian, 2004.

_____. *What the Book Says About Sport.* Oxford, Eng.: Bible Reading Fellowship, 2000.

Wood, Stuart. *Keeping Faith in the Team: The Chaplain's Story.* London: Longman Dartman and Todd, 2011.

Young, David C. *A Brief History of the Olympic Games.* Malden, MA: Blackwell Pub., 2004.

Addendum #12

Epilogue

Communicating the Gospel...or Not?!

What Harold didn't anticipate… and what the pastoral staff that was mentoring him didn't understand was, Harold's playing baseball every Sunday morning did not communicate what was intended! By playing with "the guys" he was attempting to communicate his love for them and he had high hopes that opportunities would occur for being able to "speak the gospel" to his unbelieving friends. This was all a well-intentioned motivation. However, what he didn't understand was that "his actions spoke louder than his words." What his participation each Lord's Day signaled and communicated was that playing baseball was more important than participating in his congregation's activities and furthermore, you could be a Christian without participating in any ongoing connection to, or participation in, a church.

Harold's hope to find opportunities to have "evangelistic" conversations was realized. His teammates did indeed hear Harold's verbal proclamations of the gospel, but they more deeply sensed that playing sports trumped any church participation. His verbal proclamations were not wrong in and of themselves, but must be evaluated by what was communicated overall. The overall message was faith in Jesus and religion are okay, but sports are more important. Harold's teammates witnessing Harold's prioritizing of sports over church meant church attendance was inconsequential in terms of being a growing disciple of Jesus.

At best, Harold's teammates respected his claims to be a Christian but at the end of the day, they saw no compelling reason to become a Christian.